M000289482

Reading THE Rails

Reading the rails: *By hunkering down and putting your hand on a rail that's still warm from a train's passage, you can sometimes divine something about the train that just passed, or about a specific person on it, or about the places the rails eventually lead to...*

—HOBO SLANG

Reading THE Rails

by Matthew Stevenson

Odysseus Books

READING THE RAILS
Copyright © 2016 by Matthew Mills Stevenson

ISBN 978-0-9709133-1-9 (hardcover)
ISBN 978-0-9709133-2-6 (e-book)

Manufactured in the United States.
This book was printed on acid-free paper in the United States.
This paper meets the requirements of ANSI/NISO Z39.48-1992

Fulfillment: Odysseus Books c/o Pathway Book Service, 4 White Brook Road,
Gilsum, New Hampshire 03448. 1-800-345-6665.
Fax: 1-603-357-2073. E-mail: pbs@pathwaybook.com
Other inquiries: Odysseus Books. Attention: David Wogahn, publisher
publish@partnerpress.org
Please visit the book's Web site: www.odysseusbooks.com
To contact the author on any matter, such as to arrange a speaking engagement,
please use: matthewstevenson@sunrise.ch

Edited by Michael Martin, Robert Juran, Martin Daly and Zina Klapper.
Jacket and book design by Nanette Stevenson.

Library of Congress Cataloging-in-Publication Data
Stevenson, Matthew Mills, 1954- author.
Reading the Rails / by Matthew Stevenson.
p. cm. (Odysseus Books)
ISBN-13: 978-0-9709133-1-9 (cloth: alk. paper)
1. Stevenson, Matthew Mills, 1954—Travel. 2. Voyages and travels. I.Title.

10 9 8 7 6 5 4 3 2 1
First edition

Contents

RAILROAD MAN   3

IRON CURTAINS   25

Peace in Our Time: Prague to Berlin   27

Balkan Ramble   32

Berlin Diary   65

Polish Corridors   69

Across Romania to Transnistria   97

OUTBOUND FROM THE FINLAND STATION   131

The Trans-Siberian to Mongolia   133

China in the Shadow of War   180

Night Trains Around Malaysia   234

Crusading Across Syria   245

AMTRAKS ACROSS AMERICA   283

Private Car to Pittsburgh   285

Amtrak Runs Off the Rails   290

New England Ramble   295

Enjoying the Journey   300

Boondoggle Express   305

In Praise of Slow Rail   310

PLAYING WITH TRAINS   315

Acknowledgements   325

Reading THE Rails

Good night, America, how are you?
Don't you know me I'm your native son,
I'm the train they call The City of New Orleans,
I'll be gone five hundred miles when the day is done.

—STEVE GOODMAN, "CITY OF NEW ORLEANS"

Railroad Man

The Pennsylvania Station in New York
Is like some vast basilica of old
That towers above the terrors of the dark
As bulwark and protection to the soul.

—Langston Hughes,
"Pennsylvania Station"

ALTHOUGH MODEL TRAINS were left under my early Christmas trees and I now spend part of the year in a house that sits alongside railroad tracks in the Swiss Alps, I have never thought of myself as either a railroad buff or a trainspotter. I do not have greasy notebooks marked with engine numbers. Nor do I collect conductor pins from such defunct lines as the Wabash or the Rock Island. I do have a few coffee mugs with railroad insignias and posters of Art Deco steam engines departing European stations. For me, the pleasure of the rails is to ride them, and as I write of train journeys past, my mind is already running forward to rail trips I would love to make: The *Lhasa Express* to Tibet; the *Empire Builder* from Chicago to Seattle, which sweeps across the Great Plains and northern Rockies; some segments of the Berlin-to-Baghdad line. I once bought a book simply for the title—*A Short Wait Between Trains*—thinking that perhaps it described that part of my life spent on railroad platforms, metaphorically or otherwise, with my head craned down the tracks to catch the first glimpse of the engine's headlight.

Because I grew up on New York's Long Island, all of my child-hood rail journeys began first on the commuter line of the same name and then under the soaring vaults and imperial eagles of Pennsylvania Station. In the early 1960s, the Long Island Rail Road served the suburbs with double-decker steel cars and heavy seats that could be flipped to the direction the train was headed. From the age of seven, I would ride into Manhattan on my own. My mother would take me to the station in Manhasset, where we lived, purchase a half-fare ticket, and then inform the conductor I was traveling on my own. Selecting a seat just behind where the engineer stood, I would spend the forty-five-minute trip into New York City staring up the tracks through the engineer's compartment window. In Pennsylvania Station, my father, having come from his office, would be waiting with his suitcase on the platform. Thread-ing our way through the dank underworld connecting the Long Island to the Mount Olympus of crack express trains and Pullman sleepers, we would vanish together into the American heartland.

I was ten years old when the first wrecker's ball hit the façade of Pennsylvania Station. I had no appreciation of architectural preservation and, given my love of sports, I probably thought it would be cool that a new Madison Square Garden would be so accessible to the trains I rode regularly. But I am sure another side of my boyhood imagination sensed the loss of civility in its destruc-tion. My father commuted daily through its great portals, chroni-cling its dismemberment at the dinner table as if the Visigoths had recaptured Rome and were carrying off the Forum in pieces. The books in his library evoked the romance of the trains he had rid-den since the 1920s. *Steel Rails to Sunrise* was one history he had about the Long Island Rail Road. Later I noticed that many titles closely tracked the decline and fall of American passenger service. As the rubble of Pennsylvania Station was carted off to the New

Jersey Meadowlands, my father returned home one evening with a book entitled *To Hell in a Day Coach*.

I should remember more than I do about the physical layout of Pennsylvania Station. Parts of the main waiting room were filled with girders and glass, much like early pictures of London's Covent Garden. One entered the station along Seventh Avenue through a long line of columns and under the phalanx of stone eagles. In my mind, the interior of the station was dirty and cold, and to get from one side to the other we were always taking back stairs or brushing against an underground Nedick's, then a popular lunch counter that specialized in orange drinks. Nor has it helped my memories that in the forty years after Pennsylvania Station was torn down, the so-called "new" Penn Station has been forever a work-in-progress—a job site with horrible waiting areas, no air conditioning, and the sense that the glory of railroading had been traded in for a cheap suburban strip mall. Even today, on my trips to New York and almost daily passage through Penn Station, I can't suffer through its many indignities without silently cursing the Pennsylvania Railroad executives who thought that imploding the columns might somehow make their product more appealing.

Pennsylvania Station died in 1964, perhaps so that many other landmark buildings in the New York City could survive. The only happy consequence of its destruction was the birth of the city's preservation movement, which clearly saved Grand Central Terminal either from a similar fate or from the presence of a skyscraper leaping out of the station's extraterrestrial ceiling. Even in the 1960s I found Grand Central to be the warmer of the two stations. I loved the silhouette of the famous waiting-room clock, and how the New York Central rolled out a red carpet to the *Twentieth Century Limited*.

MY FIRST RAIL TRIP, at age six, was to the coalfields of Pennsylvania. My father and I rode the Reading Railroad from Philadelphia to Tamaqua, not far from the town of Jim Thorpe, then called Mauch Chunk. Two years later, in summer 1962, we left Pennsylvania Station hopscotching our way westward through Cincinnati and St. Louis until we headed north toward Chicago. We were traveling in August and staying in what were then called "commercial hotels," few of which had air conditioning. I remember the buckets of ice, a fixture of each hotel room, more than the uncomfortable heat. I watched baseball in St. Louis and toured the stockyards in Kansas City, and then spent several pleasant days along Lake Michigan just outside Chicago. While working, my father left me with family friends, who took me to the beach, toured me around Chicago's Loop, and treated me to ice cream in the late afternoon, until it was time to board the night train back to New York.

A few years later we again passed through Chicago, only this time it was our first stop—not the last—as we were headed west to visit national parks. Sadly, it is impossible now to tour the West by train and see much of the national park system, which seemingly has become a ramp off the Interstate system. In several instances, Amtrak comes close to some of the famed parks, notably Glacier and a few in Colorado, but little travel infrastructure now connects railroad stations to the national parks. In 1967, despite the gloom that had settled over the passenger rail network, it was still possible to see much of the West from dome and sleeping cars. From Chicago, my father and I went overnight to Omaha, and then caught another train to Wyoming, where we went by minivan to Grand Teton. We must have been away ten days to two weeks. In my mind anyway, nearly every other night we were on a sleeper crossing the Great Plains, where after dinner I would sit in the dome car reading my books and watch lightning storms roll across the cornfields.

It was on one of these family train trips to the West that I sensed that the end might be near for my childhood on rails. My father and I were in Chicago and had wanted to come home on the famed *Broadway Limited*. For some reason it wasn't running. We were put aboard another Chicago-to-New York sleeper, *The General*, which got stuck in western Pennsylvania and arrived in the East hours behind schedule. As we sat for hours near Altoona or somewhere, I could sense from the adult conversation in the parlor car that no one on board thought passenger service had much of a future. Planes were too fast, and trains were too slow. In the America of the late 1960s, to ride the train from New York to St. Louis or Kansas City implied that you were lacking the ambition then required to move up the corporate ladder.

What sealed the fate of passenger train service in America was the merger, and then the bankruptcy, of the Pennsylvania Railroad and the New York Central. The deal had first been announced in 1962, when both companies were mainstays of railroading and corporate America. Although still a Little Leaguer, I saw myself as a "New York Central man," both because of my affection for Grand Central Terminal and because I associated the Pennsylvania with Philadelphia and Pittsburgh and their rival sports franchises. At first the idea of bringing together the Central and the Pennsylvania seemed breathtaking, even to a boy. The merger spoke of conglomeration, railroad trusts, the ascendancy of the robber-baron Morgans and Vanderbilts, and a coming era in which only a handful of mammoth railroads would survive. Then it took six years for the Interstate Commerce Commission to approve the combination. By February 1, 1968, even I could sense that railroads were dead men rolling. On that date, the merged companies had only $13 million in cash on hand. Within three years the Penn Central had dissolved into the largest bankruptcy in U.S. corporate history.

I have long had an interest in understanding why the Penn Central collapsed. An early book on the subject, *The Wreck of the Penn Central*, went into and out of print faster than I could get my hands on a copy. In his primer about economic folly, *Bad Money*, my friend L.J. Davis wrote, "It was the largest merger in American corporate history. It survived—if that is the word for it—for 872 days." His point is that both railroads were broke when they came together, not unlike the Erie and Lackawanna, of which he says: "It was more a death watch than a merger." In the case of the Pennsylvania and the New York Central, he concludes: [given that] "the roads were paying massive taxes that their competitors in the airline and trucking industries were entirely free of, it is easy to see how the golden goose was led to the slaughter."

More recently I found another wonderfully written account of the Penn Central collapse. *The Men Who Loved Trains* by Rush Loving Jr. starts with the failed merger but takes the story to its conclusion, when the Consolidated Rail Corporation or Conrail, the remnant of Penn Central, was sold to CSX and the Norfolk & Southern railway for more than $10 billion. His conclusion is that thirty years after it folded, the logic of the Penn Central merger was finally realized for its shareholders.

THROUGHOUT THIS ERA of corporate intrigue, I continued to ride the rails as if it were still the golden age of railroading. In winter 1974, as a sophomore at Bucknell University, I enrolled in a course on Canadian economics, largely because it was to be taught on transcontinental trains running between Montreal and Vancouver. The rolling seminar met on New Year's Day in Montreal. For the next thirty days our group of about eight students followed Professor Peter Kresl on and off trains in Ottawa, Winnipeg, and Edmonton. In those days Canada still had competing transcon-

tinental service. The Canadian National had the northern route
to Vancouver, while the Canadian Pacific ran more to the south
through Calgary, Banff, and Lake Louise. A one-way ticket to
Vancouver cost fifty dollars. As we were traveling in January, snow
and sub-zero temperatures were constant companions. Alas, fifty
dollars did not buy us berths in the sleeping cars, so we spent the
days in day coaches, reading and looking out the window, and then
the nights in the bar car, debating the merits of various Canadian
beers.

Off the trains, Professor Kresl convened classes in various
boardrooms and corporate offices, where he lectured on the economics of the Athabasca tar sands or explained marginal price
theory in the context of western timberlands. Had the course been
the only one offered during my college years, I would have thought
the experience worth the price, as the trip fixed the ideal conditions
in which I prefer to learn: a combination of books, conversation,
professorial leadership, and long train rides to absorb the material. (In all the arguments about Amtrak's future, why has no one
suggested turning it into a university?)

My undergraduate course in European railroads came the following year, when I spent my junior year abroad at universities in
London and Vienna. In between the semesters, I bought an Inter-
Rail pass (valid in numerous countries, good for a month) with the
idea of learning something about Europe. Alas, about all that I
learned is that January is a bad month to do anything in Europe,
including riding the rails. I went north to Germany and Norway,
east toward Hungary (where I was turned back at the Iron Curtain
border) and south toward Italy. European trains in those days had
a certain Continental elegance. Passengers rode in compartments
of six seats, some of which had their own doors to the platform.
The corridors were smoky and dirty. I hated arriving in a dark and
cold city, and wandering the side streets near the station searching

for either a youth hostel or a cheap hotel. The real problem of that month—leaving aside that I got sick halfway through and hung up my rail pass—was that I was a man in motion without any firm destination. I blamed myself for having no definite purpose. All I was doing was walking around slushy cities and taking refuge in museums that didn't really interest me. For a while I tried to track down some of the locales mentioned in the works of Ernest Hemingway and George Orwell. But I didn't need to get my feet wet in Paris or London to figure out that I was down and out. Never again would I set off without a clear destination—even on a train.

My first taste of Asian trains came during the summer of 1983. Emotionally, that was a year of discontent, as I had been laid off from my job and was having trouble finding a new one. In June, the magazine of Pan American Airways, *Clipper*, asked me to write an article on the upcoming South Korean Olympic games. I agreed, asking only that I be given a round-the-world ticket. At that time, Pan Am had a gap in its international service between Hong Kong and Karachi, Pakistan. I decided to fill it by taking the train whenever I could on my passage from the Korean peninsula to Pakistan.

I loved everything about both Korean and Japanese trains. When I finished writing the article in Seoul, I took the train south to Taegu and Pusan. South Korea is not a large country. The trains felt like rural English day coaches. They were spotlessly clean, the staff was pleasant, and the train left me near where a boat sailed overnight to the Japanese port of Shimonoseki. At the docks I remember being unsure, when asked, if I wanted a "Western" or "Japanese" stateroom. I chose Japanese, and opened the door on a cabin that for accommodation had only a stack of blankets on a carpeted floor. Half the blankets I used for a mattress, and the other half I used for warmth. The next morning in Japan, I caught the train for Hiroshima, which is on the main line to Osaka and Tokyo.

In the 1980s the high-speed Japanese bullet trains were still a novelty. For a week I rode them all over Japan. Although I was traveling in summer, I never found the cars crowded. Nor did any platform guards, with white gloves, ever push throngs into one of my cars. At times I found the speeds a little too high for me to enjoy the terraced landscape; it felt as if I were traveling around Japan in a horizontal elevator. But Japan taught the world—a lesson still lost on American railways—that high-speed corridor trains need their own segregated high-speed track to justify the billions of dollars needed for such rapid service.

As trains did not run east to west through Indochina, I flew from Hong Kong to Calcutta, where at Howrah Station I tried to catch an air-conditioned train to Bombay. That July the monsoon season was imminent, and "the city of dreadful night," as Kipling called it, was hot and steamy. It took me hours just to buy the ticket. In between I visited the clinic of Mother Teresa and explored the city in a rickshaw. Most of what I know about Indian bureaucracy I know from my rounds to buy a train ticket in Calcutta. In separate railway offices, I had to buy a ticket, a reservation, and then a berth in a sleeping car. I found myself in all sorts of paper-strewn offices—drinking milky tea, explaining to various officials the date and time that I wished to cross India to Bombay. Inevitably I was told that I had to visit yet another office, at which point the agent would call for a secretary to escort me to the grand Victorian station offices, where I would repeat the ceremony in yet another office piled high with railroad dispatches. After three days, I had my tickets.

The air-conditioned train was scheduled to leave in the early evening from Howrah Station, where thousands of pavement dwellers arrive late in the day to spend the night on the platform. I had read about such a congregation (Kipling calls them "the railways people"), but I only believed it when, in search of my platform,

I had to high-step my way across what looked like a rock-concert campground. Oddly, I could find no trace of my air-conditioned train to Bombay. I remember walking frantically around the slumbering humanity, not sure if I was reading the departure board correctly. Finally, a conductor on another train told me: "Oh, that one is canceled. But you can come with me." He had his whistle in his mouth, and was close to dropping his signal to move the train along. I hustled into a compartment and soon discovered that instead of taking a two-day express across the Indian subcontinent, I was on a three-night ordinary train, which for ventilation had bars across open windows.

My compartment on the *Bombay Mail* had four bunks. The last passenger aboard, I was given a lower berth without any bedding. For a long time, in the terrible summer humidity, the train ran slowly through the industrial slums outside Calcutta. I felt sentenced to purgatory and could feel my traveling companions eyeing me suspiciously, especially when it became clear that I was traveling without food or bedding. The bunk was hardwood covered with a sheet of plastic. I slept with a rolled-up shirt as my pillow. When I woke up early the next morning, hot and sweaty, the train was creeping along the Ganges outside the city of Benares (now called Varanasi), where I looked enviously at pilgrims washing themselves in the murky holy waters. For food, I discovered that the choice was to rush madly around station platforms when the train stopped or to buy a tray of greasy chicken that vendors would slide between the bars of the train window. Neither held much appeal. Nor did the open tap of water that overflowed on most platforms. In that era before bottled water, I subsisted largely on the Indian version of Pepsi-Cola, sold under the trade name Thumbs Up, which gave ordering a certain simplicity.

After my first unsettled night on my rock-hard berth, I grew to enjoy my fellow travelers. We took turns food-shopping on the platforms. They shared with me Indian travel sweets, which tasted like pressed sawdust. Some of the men, like me, were in their late twenties. For some reason several of them decided that I owned a restaurant or a hotel in New York. For the last two days of the journey, they politely badgered me to hire them as waiters or busboys. Nothing I could say would persuade them that I did not own restaurant, and after a while I found it easier to adopt the persona of an aloof hotelier than to argue in the Indian heat. Outside Bombay, the monsoon struck with a vengeance, washing out the tracks. The last fifty miles of the journey ended in a swarm of taxis that confusingly descended on the landlocked train. Some of the restaurant staff came with me in Bombay, and spent the ride polishing their resumés.

I did manage to ride one air-conditioned train in India that summer. I took one on the line between Bombay and Delhi, and had looked forward to a good night's sleep in my upper berth. Then a ruckus erupted under my bunk. The Indian railways (I was familiar with their arcane booking practices) had sold tickets to a honeymooning couple, but had put the bride and groom in separate compartments. The bride was ticketed to be in with me. I told the conductor that I would be happy to change places with the groom so that the honeymoon could continue. The conductor would have nothing to do with such gallantry. He insisted that everyone keep his or her assigned places. It was starting to feel like a Bollywood comedy until I took the conductor aside and appealed to his sense of reason, not to mention greed. He paced and shouted that it was "his train" but finally consented to ten dollars' worth of reason, and the couple, who became friends, named their first son Matthew.

My last train ride in summer 1983 was between Delhi and the Pakistani cities of Lahore and Rawalpindi, across the otherwise closed border between India and Pakistan. The first leg of the journey ended in Amritsar, where Sikh militants had once tried to kill Indira Gandhi and where British troops in 1919 had massacred rebellious Indians, including women and children, who had gathered to protest of against colonial rule. In Delhi, I had obtained a visa for Pakistan, but initially thought the train would run across the border, as it does at most international frontiers. During the violent partition of the two countries in 1947, so-called death trains had rolled in both directions, filled with massacred civilians fleeing toward ethnic and religious cohorts. Sometimes even the train engineers were killed, and the trains rolled aimlessly until they ran out of steam.

In my case, I had to walk across the border at Wagah with a porter carrying my bag on his head. I cleared Indian customs, whose officials were unhappy that I was going to Pakistan. Then I walked about 500 yards and came to Pakistan's immigration office, where I met similar reservations, but about India. I was only one of a handful of travelers making the crossing that day. Still, it took a long time, as if I had crossed an abyss or a labyrinth, not simply a border. When the questions ended, I took a taxi into Lahore, a city of graceful tranquility, where I later caught an express north to Rawalpindi, the terminus for my summer on the Asian rails.

IN 1991, I MOVED TO SWITZERLAND, which has 34,000 miles of superb track. Swiss trains operate with the precision of the locally made watches. Along with a network of intercity express trains, the country has a web of privately owned mountain railways, which haul elegant coaches and dining cars to isolated peaks and forgotten villages. The most spectacular train is the *Glacier Express*, which connects the demimondes of Zermatt and St. Moritz. My favorite mountain railroad is the Montreux-Oberland-Bernois (affectionately called the MOB), which links Montreux and Lake Geneva with the tableland valleys around Gstaad and the Pays d'Enhaut. In 2000, my family and I used the railway to hike around the region—trekking from one station to another, and then returning each night to our hotel, a youth hostel in Sanaan. A few months later, perhaps succumbing to the thin air, we bought an ancient if dilapidated chalet just along the railway tracks. The house, dating to the 17th century, had sat vacant for several years. Clearly, no other buyers liked the proximity of the tracks. But for me they were a buying point, as I would rather live abreast scenic trains than noisy cars.

One reason I like living in Switzerland is that the country still takes railroading seriously. A train or a bus connects every Swiss town or village, and children travel free until the age of sixteen. For $150 a year I can buy a pass that lets me travel for half fare anywhere in the country. Only once in sixteen years can I recall a train being late. In recent years the system has refurbished its dining cars, which serve simple yet elegant meals, even on remote stretches of track. My only regret is that the country is too small to have sleeping cars, but in Germany and across Eastern Europe there are still a number of night trains to places such as Bucharest and Warsaw.

As MUCH AS I ENJOY and admire European railroads, they have not replaced the affection I hold for long-distance American trains. For me the pleasure of overnight train travel is to eat a meal in the diner or to spend much of the day reading or looking out the window. My ideal train journey is from New York to Chicago (leave in the late afternoon, arrive not too early the following morning) or Chicago to New Orleans (roughly twenty hours down the Mississippi, arriving late afternoon in the Crescent City). I also love the sleeper from New York's Pennsylvania Station to southern Florida. For childhood vacations, we would often ride the Seaboard Coast Line or the *Silver Meteor*, leaving New York in the gloom of winter to wake up amidst the red clay and scrub pines of southern Georgia.

For me, Amtrak has taken most of the pleasure out of American trains. The food is dreadful, and the service indifferent. It recently took me seven hours to travel 225 miles from Austin to Dallas. Not long ago, on a business trip to Florida, remembering the night trains of childhood, I priced a sleeper ticket from Jacksonville to New York. When I heard the one-way fare was $565, I flew instead. Indeed, for much of the last thirty-seven years I have had a love-hate relationship with Amtrak. I appreciate that it represents the vestiges of the rail passenger business, but I hate how the company is run.

In the 1970s, most of my train trips were up and down the East Coast, in what were called "Amfleet" coaches. The seats were adequate, as was the leg room, but the carpeting on the train walls, the small windows, and the food service gave train travel the feel of low-flying airplanes. Since then I have ridden Acela, Metroliners, and the new double-decker trains of the West. Some of these new trains are elegant, if by now slightly tired. Nor is Amtrak to be blamed for the dilapidated state of American track, which accounts for the dilatory schedule (from Austin to Dallas the train, on its good days, averages 39 miles per hour). Whenever I board an Amtrak train, I think about the windows and diners on European trains, if not the observation cars of my childhood.

Despite my Amtrak resentments, I have been a steady customer in the many years of its mediocre existence. In summer 1974, while traveling on the *Empire Builder* across Montana, I met another railroad man, Ian MacClaren Cipperly, who had spent his life on the rails, mostly for the Pennsylvania Railroad. In that year, I was twenty and he was seventy-five. We spent a happy two days in the top of a dome car, crossing the Great Plains and talking about the history of railroading. He epitomized all that is admirable in railroad men: he was courteous, direct, humorous, clever, and had a superb sense of American railroad geography. He knew where freight trains could "make up time" and where was the best place "to put the varnish [elegant passenger trains] in the hole [on a siding]." Rush Loving does not mention him in *The Men Who Loved Trains,* but Ian's spirit fills many of its pages. I last saw Ian in Cleveland, when he was in his eighties and had come off the rails. I felt as if I were visiting a sailor now living far from the sea. We had lunch and he gave me, as a parting gift, a history of the Pennsylvania Railroad, with an inscription that I still treasure:

> *May the "rails" always rise to meet you.*
> *May you "engineer" your "breaks" in such a*
> *fashion that you will "conduct" yourself in*
> *un-"flagging" pursuit of your admirable*
> *hobby "railroading"*
>
> *Many pleasant miles and no "detours"*
>   *Your friend,*
>   *Ian*

To me, Ian MacClaren Cipperly was the mythical railroad figure of E.M. Frimbo come alive. On one of my trips across country I had stumbled across the memoirs of America's "greatest railroad buff." ("In the first place, he looked a lot like a conductor on a crack express. He had the same pink face…He did not produce a pocket watch, but we knew he had one.") The co-authors of the delightful book *All Aboard with E.M. Frimbo* are Rogers E.M. Whitaker and Tony Hiss. They met through the *New Yorker* magazine, where Whitaker was an editor and Hiss was a contributing writer.

Much of Frimbo's persona is lifted from the life of Whitaker, who logged some 2.7 million miles on passenger trains and who, during World War II, enlisted in the Army to help map troop movements across the United States. Early in the book Frimbo confesses: "My ambition has been to ride over every single foot of passenger trackage in the United States." Sometimes he travels with the dashing Contessa, a woman of charm and wealth, and sometimes with his Persian cats. ("It wasn't long before the cats were allowed to prowl up and down the parlor car.") In style and temperament, Frimbo has the imperturbable air of Phileas Fogg consulting his Bradshaw on the best trains to take across India. He does not like the Prado museum in Spain, because it has no paintings of trains. The serious side of Frimbo was his devotion to passenger rail service as a sensible, cost-efficient, and romantic way to move people around a country. At one point he sniffs: "Cars and airplanes, sir, are the natural enemy of railroads. What is a car? It is a rolling sneeze."

BEFORE HE DIED IN 1981, Rogers E.M. Whitaker wrote an essay for the *New York Times*, "Amtrak, the Caboose," in which he summarizes why Amtrak is a failure. For almost thirty years I have kept the clipping pressed into his book, as if it were a rose that once sat on a linen-covered dining-car table. Whitaker writes:

> Amtrak, which has—surprisingly—attained the age of eight, is an institution unique among the multitudinous enterprises established by our federal government: It was deliberately designed by its proponents to be not self-perpetuating but self-destructing.
>
> The perfect model for Amtrak would have been the original United States Post Office. It had the power to order railways to carry mail on whatever trains it wanted, to set the price it would pay, and to levy fines for dilatory performance. Amtrak

was given no such regulatory powers. In return for relieving the railways of the cost of running passenger service, it was rewarded with slower trains, delays because of poor track and freight-train wrecks, and arbitrary changes (or no notice at all) of route. The costs of all this were assessed against Amtrak. None of the Amtrak services were of Amtrak's choosing; for some years the law specified that the [U.S.] Department of Transportation would design the network of routes, and some of its choices served vastly underpopulated territory.

A more modern critique of Amtrak comes from Joseph Vranich, a former spokesman for the company who has written two books about its failings: *Derailed* and *End of the Line*. His argument is that since its inception in 1971, Amtrak has been the recipient of almost $30 billion in federal and state subsidies, and for all that money, the country still does not have an efficient passenger rail network. He complains that the Amtrak route structure is hopelessly mired in costs and that long-distance trains cannot compete with more cost-efficient airlines. He favors spinning off passenger rail service to private companies, much like what was done in England, and granting franchises for key service to companies more competitive than Amtrak, a state monopoly.

Critics of Vranich, including his former colleagues at Amtrak, believe he is shilling for those who would pull the plug on all American passenger trains. Vranich, however, quotes with approval the sentiments of a former Amtrak senior officer, who said: "I think there's two questions: [The first is] 'What's the future of passenger rail in America?' There is a completely separate question, which is, 'What's the future of Amtrak?' You can imagine a brilliant future with passenger rail with Amtrak gone."

Amtrak is two companies. It has its corridor service between Boston and Washington, and a similar schedule between Los

Angeles and San Diego. That business hauls more than half of all Amtrak passengers, and makes money. The other railroad is the one operating the long-haul trains between places such as Los Angeles and Chicago. In one much-circulated study, it was estimated that the *Sunset Limited* cost Amtrak, and thus the government, $347 for every passenger who boarded that transcontinental train. Despite the notoriety of this statistic, there are even worse figures about Amtrak's performance.

In 1910, nearly all intercity trips were taken by rail. By 1920, one of railroading's high-water marks, 20,000 daily trains crisscrossed the country. By 1969, only 500 passenger trains remained, and many of those were the subjects of "discontinuous hearings" before the Interstate Commerce Commission. By the time Amtrak took over, only 384 trains were left. Of those the new railroad monopoly kept 184, most of which ran up and down the Northeast Corridor. In the great liquidation of American passenger service, Amtrak inherited only 730 miles of track. Its greatest assets are the tracks between Boston and Washington and the tunnels under New York's East River and the Hudson. (By owning the tunnels, Amtrak can threaten to disrupt commuter service around New York whenever its subsidies come up for renewal.)

Today, trains account for 0.1 % of all intercity passenger miles, although Amtrak accounts for 25 million passengers annually (planes fly 712 million people annually in the U.S). Amtrak, however, is on the hook for $3.3 billion in federally guaranteed debt, and it requires between $1 billion and $2 billion in annual subsidies to keep passenger trains on the rails. It spent some $3.2 billion to introduce Acela ("accelerate" plus "excellence"), only to be delivered cars with imperfect specifications, which make the run to Washington only slightly faster than the crack trains of the 1940s. Little wonder that Vranich describes the corporation as another bloated federal bureaucracy, there to garnish subsidies and the reputation of politicians who happen to represent districts served by a train. He quotes one of its founders, now disillusioned: "Amtrak does not have a commitment to excellence…its overriding concern is to assure its institutional survival."

Half of Amtrak's costs go to labor. Reading Vranich, I sense that what keeps Amtrak cars rolling is not men in Congress who love trains so much as constituents on their payroll. What else explains what Vranich calls a "weak, politically inspired route system"? Rush Loving recounts how it was one of his heroes, Jim McClellan, who, nevertheless, designed the problematic Amtrak system. He writes: "By early 1971, guided by McClellan's vision of which routes and trains were the best, they all had the new system laid out, and the board of incorporators gave its approval. Amtrak's route structure has not undergone any major changes since then."

As much as I personally enjoy riding trains across the vast and beautiful American interior, I cannot imagine how in the last forty years Amtrak has failed to develop practical corridor service throughout the United States. What prevents it from offering fast, frequent service between such cities as Washington and Raleigh, Chicago and Minneapolis, Dallas and Houston, or Miami and Tampa—to name but a few logical corridor connections? Amtrak could also develop markets for auto trains, if people need their cars at the other end, or it could compensate for slow track with comfortable seats, rolling business centers, good food, and wireless Internet connections. Instead, Amtrak seeks to compete with service and food as abysmal as that served on the airlines, but then charges a lot more for the inconvenience. Vranich writes: "Loyalty to trains is more intense than loyalty to Amtrak."

To Vranich "the sensible solution is to separate the future of passenger rail from the future of Amtrak and focus on maximizing public investments through a franchising and development process."

He writes persuasively about England, which gave up on BritRail in 1993 and awarded franchises to a host of transportation companies, including Richard Branson's Virgin Trains. As someone who is often on British trains, I can confirm that the service is vastly improved. Recently in London I went from King's Cross station to Cambridge in forty-five minutes, a trip that in the 1970s often could take ninety minutes. English rail cars are now modern and clean. Now the British government must address the problem of upgrading signals and track, whose poor conditions have led to several deadly wrecks. But England has a stronger passenger rail culture than that in the U.S.

The British still live in towns and cities, while the U.S. is becoming an endless, Walmarted suburb connected by interstate highways. Switzerland deals with a decentralized population by putting time-shared cars and bicycle rentals at nearly all railway stations. Would the U.S. be fighting oil wars that cost $6 billion a month if cars were needed only for the last three miles of every journey? Why isn't the Iraq war seen as a subsidy to the auto industry? The government may pay $347 each to subsidize passengers on the *Sunset Limited*, but think of the energy that could be saved if it rebuilt American railroads instead of Anbar Province in Iraq.

I also like Vranich's suggestion that the long-distance passenger service should first be landmarked, as if part of the national parks, and then spun off to the cruise-ship industry. In the U.S. and Canada, tourist trains are areas of growth and efficiency. As most long-haul passengers are on board for a vacation, they might as well enjoy some cruising elegance. As they do now in western Canada, American trains could stop near historic towns or offer themed trips related to bicycling, jazz, Native American culture, or baseball—to name a few excursions that would provoke my interest. Who wouldn't want to sign up for a train cruise that visited a number of minor league ballparks or made stops at the important Civil War battlefields?

I DO NOT EXPECT AMTRAK to adopt my railroad schemes. Since I was a young boy, I have watched passenger service in the U.S. plunge down a steep grade to irrelevance, and no amount of my wishing will bring back the crack express trains or High Plains sleepers of my childhood.

The utopian railroad conversations that find a receptive audience are those that I still have with my father, now 93, but who until recently commuted by train to an office in Manhattan. In recent years, when I would stay with my parents in New Jersey, he and I would ride into the city together, catching a New Jersey Transit train from Princeton Junction into Penn Station. Though he walked with a cane and did not see very well, my father would still bull rush the train doors, as if he were boarding the last train to Shanghai, not simply a morning commuter into New York. On the mornings when we would ride in together, the conversation would inevitably turn to railroading. We would talk about new tunnels that could be dug under the Hudson, how to get Amtrak trains into lower Manhattan, or my ideas to link American cities with corridor service, auto trains, and Amtrak University.

When growing up, my sisters and I often went with him on business trips, and that meant taking the trains. In March 1965, my older sister and I went with him from New York to Mexico. Except for a few gaps in the line, we did it all by rail. We went from New York to Atlanta, and then to Mobile and New Orleans, before taking an overnight train to Harlingen, Texas. After we crossed into Mexico from Brownsville, we discovered that many older American Pullmans ended up south of the border, but still provided memorable service. We ended our rail odyssey in Oaxaca, south of Mexico City, and then flew in a DC-3 to Acapulco for a day of swimming.

Believe it or not, I think it is still possible for an American father and his children to ride the train from New York to Acapulco. In my house, the *Thomas Cook Overseas Timetable* arrives in regular intervals. I spend many Sundays drawing my finger along its printed tracks. To get to Acapulco, you would take the *Crescent* from Penn Station to New Orleans, enjoy a few days in the French Quarter, and then connect on the *Sunset Limited* (enjoy that $347 subsidy while you can) to El Paso. Now comes the tricky part. After crossing the border on foot and arriving at the Ciudad Juarez train station, see if you can find a train from there to Zacatecas. The Cook timetable is blank on service there from Ciudad Juarez, but once you get to Zacatecas, I sense that a cruise train, *Expresso de la Independencia*, leaves every Wednesday for Mexico City—at the delightful hour of 5 a.m.

In Mexico City, the Ferrocarriles Nacionales de Mexico does show a connection (in theory) to Oaxaca, but again no times are listed. You might inquire at Buenavista Station, where just before our night train departed, in March 1965, my father vanished in the platform maelstrom to buy a grilled chicken so we would have something to eat on board. He cut the departure fairly closely, and as a ten-year-old I assumed that I would become an orphan of the rails. Maybe that is what happened.

IRON CURTAINS

"It recalled a certain Hungarian saying: 'One should never voluntarily enter a room or a country the door of which cannot be opened from the inside.'"

—ALAN FURST, *KINGDOM OF SHADOWS*

Peace in Our Time:
Prague to Berlin

I FIRST SAW BERLIN in the winter of 1990, when the Wall was coming down in fragments and being sold to tourists in small plastic bags. The two Germanys had yet to unify, and Berlin still felt like a Cold War cul-de-sac, with a barbed wire scar slashed across its magnificent boulevards.

In 1990 West Berlin was memorable for Bauhaus apartment buildings and cabaret lights. East Berlin—while drab on the edges with vast tracks of worker housing—had many of classical Berlin's most famous landmarks: the Brandenburg Gate, Museum Island, various opera houses and numerous palaces, many of which had been converted to house such organizations as the People's Solidarity Friendship Committee. At least East German socialism and poverty spared numerous historic buildings from the wrecker's ball or conversion to a discotheque.

Twenty years later, Berlin is at the center of a unified Europe. The line between East and West has vanished, save for the ceremonial bricks that weave through the city streets. The site of Hitler's bunker is a playground and parking lot. Elsewhere, the city neither celebrates nor obscures its dark history, which is that of Central Europe: memories of the struggles of fading empires.

Recently, to get to Berlin, if not to wallow in history and to read several books, I took the train from Prague and included a stop in Dresden. The journey took all day and cost $150, including a three-course meal in the dining car. I have taken college courses that covered less ground in three months than my daylong ride across several imperial divides.

Prague remains incomparable. I have a guidebook that includes it on lists of the "best" and "worst" of Europe. In winter the cobblestones glimmer under snow and ice. The Charles Bridge feels like a footpath between classical Rome and the kings of Bohemia, who lived in Hradčany Castle—a soaring presence over Prague, much like the works of Franz Kafka, who wrote in its shadows.

To guide me around Prague, I had *Too Strong for Fantasy*, the memoirs of the American writer Marcia Davenport. The daughter of legendary operatic soprano Alma Gluck, Davenport wrote novels for Scribner's editor Maxwell Perkins in the 1930s and later fell in love with Czech Foreign Minister Jan Masaryk, whose death by defenestration marked the end of the Czechoslovak Republic in 1948.

Before Stalin crushed the Czech democracy, Davenport lived in the neighborhood near the castle on what she calls "the most beautiful street in Europe." I found the house on Lorentanká that she renovated and the window in the ministry from which Masaryk fell to his death—bookends of hope and tragedy.

The Soviets asserted that Masaryk's plunge was suicide. His friends, including Davenport, suspect that he was pushed. Before his fall, Masaryk had been summoned to Russia. Davenport writes: "He went to Moscow as the Foreign Minister of a sovereign state and returned as a lackey of the Soviet Government." His execution is testament to the well-worn quote that "the master of Bohemia is the master of Europe."

Between Prague and Germany, the train crossed the Sudetenland, the borderlands that were part of Czechoslovakia in 1938
but which, in Munich, British Prime Minister Neville Chamberlain gave to Hitler in exchange for "peace in our time." Jan
Masaryk confronted Chamberlain and British Foreign Minister
Lord Halifax when they returned from Munich to London. Davenport recalls: "He said to them, 'If you have sacrificed my nation
to preserve the peace of the world, I will be the first applaud you.
But if not, gentlemen, God help your souls.'"

The Sudetenland reminded me of the Berkshires in western
Massachusetts, a land of rolling hills and low mountains that give
way to villages and valleys of farmland. I had lunch as the train
snaked its way along the River Labe and Děčín, a town mentioned
in Alan Furst's *Kingdom of Shadows*, a haunting novel that describes
what the Allies lost when they conceded Czechoslovakia without
a fight.

Furst is the poet laureate of European night trains and the
World War II politics of central Europe. (A typical sentence reads:
"One should never voluntarily enter a room or a country the door of
which cannot be opened from the inside.") Read him for history, a
sense of 1939, and for pleasure. One of Furst's characters asks at the
time of Munich: "Will the Czechs fight?" He is given the answer:
"They have thirty-five divisions, can mobilize up to one million
men, and have a defensive line of forts that runs along the Sudetenland border. Said to be good—as good as the Maginot Line.
And, of course, Bohemia and Moravia are bordered by mountains,
the Shumava. For the German tanks, the passes, especially if they
are defended, will be difficult."

Chamberlain surrendered the Sudetenland and its mountain
fortresses. Military historians, including William Manchester,
have written that had the Allies chosen to make a stand in Czechoslovakia, the German army would have overthrown Hitler in a

coup. Winston Churchill's remark to Chamberlain, also quoted by Furst, was: "You were given the choice between war and dishonor. You chose dishonor, and you will have war."

After I had dessert (itself worth the journey) and coffee in the dining car, the train arrived in Dresden, as beautiful as a fragment of classical sculpture. Even now much of the downtown is vacant. Where city planners have rebuilt the cathedral, the opera hall, and the baroque esplanade along the River Elbe, Dresden recalls the grandeur lost to American fire bombers.

A city of no military significance, Dresden was destroyed on February 13, 1945. Then a prisoner of war, the American novelist Kurt Vonnegut was a witness to the destruction, which he later described in *Slaughterhouse Five*. (The name is the English translation of the address of Vonnegut's prison.) He estimated that 130,000 civilians were killed in the raids. Later calculations put the deaths at 25,000. Vonnegut's narrator, Billy Pilgrim, describes Dresden after the bombing as looking like "the surface of the moon."

Dresden is a village when compared to Berlin, which sprawls over a hundred square miles. In between clumps of office buildings and government squares, Berlin has rivers, bike paths, cafés, the rebuilt Reichstag, and such esoteric museums as one devoted to "Checkpoint Charlie" (the crossing between East and West). In all, the city has some 250 museums and galleries.

When I was in Berlin, the subway and buses were on strike. It meant I had to walk everywhere, which was no hardship in a city of such elegant sidewalks. Along Unter den Linden, Berlin's Park Avenue, there are universities, cathedrals, concert halls, embassies, hotels, and even a President John F. Kennedy Museum, which recalls his famous 1961 oration, which ended with the words "Ich bin ein Berliner" (which unfortunately translates into something resembling "I am a pastry"). I walked along the Wilhelmstrasse and wandered around Prenzlauer Berg, which used to be a worker's paradise but is now the domain of latte-swigging urbanites, for whom the Stasi, the former East German secret police, is probably a dance step.

Balkan Ramble

FOR YEARS I HAVE STUDIED the arrival and departure boards at the Geneva airport, not far from where I live. Always my eye wanders to the flights to and from Pristina, the main city of Kosovo. Invariably, especially during the foggy winter months, those flights are delayed or canceled. Around the airport, I see clusters of men in thick leather jackets, huddled around cups of black coffee and clutching cardboard boxes, waiting for news of their flight to Kosovo. On several of my own trips to Belgrade, I thought of flying through Pristina to avoid plane changes around Europe. Each time, however, I was told that it was difficult, if not impossible, to travel overland between the two cities, even though Kosovo is a Serbian province. More recently, when I was searching for a cheap one-way ticket to Athens, I thought again of the connection through Pristina, figuring I could then ride the train across Macedonia to Greece.

Because the website of Air Prishtina was fickle, I went to the airline's office in Geneva. In otherwise affluent Switzerland, it felt like I had stepped into a Balkan travel agency. On the walls were uninspiring tourist posters of Kosova, the name of independent Kosovo. The air was thick with cigarette smoke. While explaining how to buy a ticket, the agent never got off the telephone. Instead of handing me a schedule, he wrote the links to several websites on a small slip of paper—the kind spies bring in from the cold—and waved me out the door. Nevertheless, several weeks later I boarded a charter jet that belonged to a company called Edelweiss (Air Prishtina does not own any planes) and flew two hours southeast to one of the cauldrons of modern Europe. If Europe has war any time soon, the chances are it will start in Pristina.

Denied access to Serbian airspace and a direct path to Kosovo, the Air Prishtina flight flew a circuitous route (of political correctness) over Albania, Lake Ohrid, and the Former Yugoslav Republic of (FYRO) Macedonia. The in-flight magazine praised the Pristina airport, rebuilt with United Nations money, as one of the best in Europe. From the outside it looks like a Yugoslav bus station. Inside it is clean, modern and efficient. Although legally they were standing on the borders of Serbia, the immigration officers were Albanian, in the uniforms of the United Nations Mission in Kosovo (UNMIK). Since the 1999 war over Kosovo, the province has been a protectorate of the UN and NATO (the occupying troops on the ground wear KFOR, or Kosovo Force, badges). During 2008, Kosovo declared its independence from Serbia, renaming itself Kosova. It is the seventh country to emerge from the wreckage of Yugoslavia, joining Slovenia, Croatia, Bosnia-Herzegovina, Serbia, Montenegro, and FYRO Macedonia as national creations in what elsewhere is transnational Europe.

Dr. Irid Bicaku met me outside Adem Jashari airport. He is the local coordinator of Foundation Project Health, a Swiss charitable organization that in Kosovo promotes AIDS prevention. An Albanian man in his thirties with sandy hair, an easy smile, and an aura of competence, Dr. Bicaku spoke English with only a trace of an accent. We had exchanged several emails before my arrival. I had thought we might simply drive into the city from the airport and have a coffee at the hotel. Instead, driving toward Pristina, we found that we were like-minded travelers. I had numerous questions about the struggles in Kosovo and listed the places that I wanted to visit. In turn, Irid answered all my questions, and warmed to my traveler's curiosity. In all, we spent two days driving around Pristina and Kosovo, talking about war and independence.

Irid had grown up partly in Serbia, where his father had a job in education. He attended medical school at Prishtina University, the scene of so many confrontations between Serbs and Albanians. (Usually the disputes involved the language of instruction, although one of the worst started over food service.) During the 1999 war he and his family were "evacuated" to Macedonia. Their house in Pristina was damaged but not destroyed. They returned to it three months later. One of his brothers fought with the Kosovo Liberation Army (KLA), but with his several languages and medical training, Irid had worked in the Stenkovec refugee camp and cared for his parents. I admired his intellectual curiosity, his sense of history, his humor, and his ability to navigate not just the small mountain roads of Kosovo, but life in an unsettled land.

Rather than drive directly to the Hotel Luxor, which I had reserved on the Internet, we made a detour through Kosovo Polje— what the newspapers might call a "Serb enclave" near Pristina. In 1389, the Turks defeated the Serbs in battle here on what is called the Field of Blackbirds. Over the years the fighting over Kosovo became a memory as sacred to the Serbs as Troy is to the Greeks or Agincourt to the English—battles that have lived on in ballads, prayers, literature, and art to help shape the psychology of the modern nation. If the Serbs go to war again over the question of Kosovo, it will be in part to safeguard the memories that roll among several hills on the edge of Pristina.

Kosovo: *field of blackbirds*

DRIVING FROM THE AIRPORT to the battlefield, what first struck me was the sight of scattered multi-family houses rising out of the farmland. I recalled similar unfinished houses from my travels in Albania. Irid confirmed that guest-workers in Switzerland and Germany were a main source of earnings for Kosovo. As few families trusted banks—even though the banks in Kosovo are neither Serbian nor Albanian, but Austrian—they put their savings into these four-story houses, which in various phases of construction are dotted around the high valley of Kosovo. In a region as impoverished as Kosovo, I had not expected to find so many €400,000 multi-family houses.

The Pristina suburb of Kosovo Polje has largely been cleansed of its Serbian population. We passed an Orthodox church that appeared to be rotting, if not gutted, behind a chain-link fence. Albanian builders were redeveloping a few of the "evacuated" Serbian structures. Otherwise, the neighborhood reminded me of the South Bronx in New York after some of the blackout riots in the 1970s. Vacant lots were strewn with garbage, and cars were abandoned on the street. Several hundred thousand Serbs were evicted from Kosovo at the end of the 1999 war. President Slobodan Milosevic had first tried to purge the region of its Albanian population. Three months later, when the Albanians returned to Kosovo—thanks to NATO's bombers and intervention—they repaid the Serbs in the same coin of the realm.

At my request, Irid stopped at the Pristina train station, which is located in Kosovo Polje. My 1960s-era guidebook writes: "Kosovo Polje is a small, shabby station, a mere halt of a few buildings. A doss house stands beyond the yard...It might be a wayside scene in *War and Peace*." In the era of Yugoslav prosperity, Marshal Tito had constructed a large station here, no doubt to not just integrate

Kosovo into the Yugoslav rail network but integrate the autonomous region into the socialist federal republic. When we arrived at the once impressive station, it was empty and forlorn. All the platforms were deserted, and no trains appeared to be running. I had wanted to inquire about daily service between Kosovo Polje and Skopje, the capital of FYRO Macedonia. No clerks were around to answer my questions. From the Internet, however, I did know that the United Nations had established, as a joint-stock company, Kosovo Railways, and it operated what is called the "Freedom of Movement Train." This service operated the length of Kosovo, from Lesak (near the Serbian border) to Kosovo Polje and sometimes Skopje. North of Mitrovica, only Serbs rode the train, and south of it, only Albanians.

To get to the medieval battlefield at Kosovo Polje, Irid and I skirted the fringes of Pristina and the local power plant that was spewing exhaust from its towers across the valley. It looked like a Pittsburgh steel mill, and indeed Irid spoke about the mines around Kosovo Polje that, together with agriculture, were important sources of local revenue. He was not sure that either one of us could visit the Field of Blackbirds, as KFOR troops had it surrounded. Indeed, when we drove into the national park entrance all I could see were armored personnel carriers, tanks, and rolls of concertina wire, which, had they been available to the Serbs in 1389, might have turned the tide against the attacking Turks. A solider from Slovakia approached the car, and I showed him my American passport. In turn, he conferred with his commanding officer, and they decided to let both of us climb the panoramic tower and see the battlefield. All the while, we were in the company of a heavily armed soldier, who said he had served for six months in a makeshift barracks near the parking lot. Kosovo is one of the few places on Earth that needs soldiers to guard history.

In many ways, I am surprised that Shakespeare never came to terms with Kosovo, as the battle might well have been a template for some of his stirring tragedies. In 1389, on the Field of Blackbirds, there was courage, Christianity, Islam, defeat, eternal salvation, and no shortage of betrayal. (Othello spoke of *"Pride, pomp, and circumstance of glorious war!"* although by comparison, Kosovo makes the Moor's story seem as mundane as a job interview.) For those who want the complete tale, may I suggest Rebecca West's *Black Lamb and Grey Falcon*, her 1941 travelogue of her extensive travels around Yugoslavia in the late 1930s. I read West's book in 1990, on a long train ride from Montenegro to Belgrade. The book was published after the Germans had shattered Yugoslavia on Palm Sunday, 1941. I have always read the book—which is long and heavy going, but still rewarding—as an attempt to save in print a medieval society that West feared might not survive the intrusions of fascism in Europe. Much of what she sought to preserve was the poetry and ballads that sprang from the struggles at Kosovo Polje. To the modern world, most of that verse is lost in translation, or dismissed as Serbian background noise to excuse ethnic cleansing in Bosnia. But West was prescient when she wrote: "Kosovo speaks only of its defeats."

Together with our Slovakian armed guard, Irid and I stood on the tower of Kosovo Polje and reconstructed events as well as both of us could remember. On their march north to conquer heathen Europe, 70,000 Turks encountered the lines of about half that number of Serbs, strung across the valley of Kosovo. At the height of its transient empire in the 11th and 12th centuries, Serbia had stretched from what is now northern Greece into Kosovo and the southern Balkans. ("Serbias have come and gone, and they have moved about," writes Professor Stevan K. Pavlowitch in *Serbia: The History of an Idea.*) In the initial phases of the battle, the Serbs rushed the Turkish formations. One historian writes: "It looks suspiciously like a case of Slav impulsiveness." What turned the tide against the Serbs, however, was the betrayal of Vuk Brankovic, who (perhaps in collaboration with the hated Turks) retired from the action together with his cavalry of twelve thousand.

The day was saved for the Serbs, at least in national memory, by the visitation of a "grey falcon" to Prince Lazar, the Serb commander. One translation of the epic poem describes it this way:

> *There flew a falcon, a grey bird,*
> *From the holy city, from Jerusalem*
> *And carried in its beak a swallow.*
> *But that was not a grey falcon,*
> *It was the holy man Elijah:*
> *And he does not carry a swallow,*
> *But a letter from the Mother of God…*

Fortunately for Lazar, who had the Turks at his throat, the choice offered in the letter was a "win-win" solution. He could choose defeat on the battlefield but inherit a heavenly paradise, or he could defeat the Turks and be assured "an earthly kingdom." Lazar, and thus the Serb nation, traded victory at Kosovo Polje for eternal salvation. Toward the end of the battle, Murad, the Turkish commander, got his own invitation to immortality when a Serbian soldier, Milosh Obilich, sneaked into the Ottoman's tent and stabbed him in the stomach—which, I sense, is the scene with which Shakespeare would have ended his unwritten play. The battle established Kosovo as one of the fault lines between Christians and Moslems in the Balkans.

Pristina: *a Jackson Pollack painting*

IRID AND I LEFT THE BATTLEFIELD toward dusk and drove into downtown Pristina. In the 1970s, I had seen donkey carts on the main street, which is now called Mother Teresa Boulevard. (Albanian by birth, she was born near Skopje in what is now FYRO Macedonia.) Pristina today, sitting in the trough of low rolling hills, has the feel of a city under occupation. Visible everywhere are the vehicles of the Organization for Security and Cooperation in Europe (OSCE), not to mention KFOR troops and encampments. Elsewhere in Pristina there are nondescript hotels, a soccer stadium, a sprawling university, and office buildings, many of which looked to have been constructed according to a socialist five-year plan. Even the new mosques looked like Tito had designed them, much the way he tried to juggle all the nationality questions in the last incarnation of Yugoslavia.

After the 1389 battle of Kosovo, the Serbian nation drifted north to the plains around Belgrade, where they eventually achieved a form of limited autonomy within the Ottoman Empire. From the gates of Vienna in 1683, the Turks spent the next two centuries retreating toward what is now called Istanbul. The knell for the Turks in Europe was sounded in 1912-13, as a result of the Balkan wars, in which a coalition of South Slavs (Yugo means south) attacked the Turks on numerous southern European fronts. Albania, previously a Turkish *vilayet*, was a stepchild of the Balkan wars, but the borders of the newly founded country did not follow the contours of Albanian nationality. Kosovo, for example, became Serbian in 1913—for the first time since 1389. But in the intervening years it had remained a flashpoint between either Serbs and Turks, or Christians and Moslems.

An ethnic map of the southern Balkans, including Kosovo, has always looked like a Jackson Pollock painting. During the middle years of the nineteenth century, Serbs and Albanians coexisted in the Turkish occupied lands. The 1878 Treaty of Berlin tried to prop up the crumbling Ottoman Empire, but—much as in the 1990s—the attempt to allocate towns and villages to one country or another touched off what today is called ethnic cleansing. The Yugoslav historian Alexander Dragnich writes:

> The 30 years after the Congress of Berlin, 1878 to 1912, were colored by the deliberate persecution and physical extermination of Serbs and their forced migration from Turkey. It was not until this period that the ethnic balance in Old Serbia— that is, Kosovo and Metohija and northwest Macedonia—was finally destroyed. In those 30 years about 400,000 people left this region for Serbia, at least 150,000 of them from the area north of Mt. Sara—Kosovo and Metohija. This pogrom took on tragic proportions after the war in Crete between Turkey and Greece in 1897.

In 1912, it was the Albanians who felt aggrieved because one-third of their nation was left outside the newly constituted state. During World War I, Kosovo was a ferocious battleground between Allied and Axis powers. But Bulgaria, Turkey, and Austria-Hungary were on the losing side, and Kosovo was awarded to the Kingdom of the Serbs, Croats, and Slovenes (later rechristened Yugoslavia) as a spoil of war. As the English writer Edith Durham wrote in 1909, the borders that were drawn in Berlin "floated on blood." She also noted that that "the Kosovo plain is now, by a large majority, Moslem Albanian."

Serbs were moved to Kosovo during the interwar years. Nevertheless, it remained a predominantly Moslem region. In World War II, according to the historian Miranda Vickers, "the Kosovars welcomed the Italian occupation" of Albania in 1939, as it allowed them "to pay off old scores, especially against Serbs resettled there between the wars." Italy used Albania to stage its invasion of Greece, which, when it failed, prompted Germany to support the Italians by attacking the Balkans, beginning with Serbia. In the fighting from 1939 to 1945, ethnic Albanians serving in a German SS division, "Skanderbeg," were among the most ruthless in promoting the Nazi cause. Many Albanians supported the Axis powers, knowing that an Allied victory would award Kosovo to the Serbs, which is what happened in 1945.

Tito hoped that a weak Serbia would mean a strong Yugoslavia. He gerrymandered nationalities within the federal republic to distribute Serbs around Croatia, Bosnia-Herzegovina, and Macedonia while at the same time grafting Albanian Kosovars and Hungarians onto the Serbian republic. Kosovo was never a republic of Yugoslavia, but either a "nationality" or an "autonomous region" of Serbia. At times nationalist aspirations in Kosovo would cause disturbances and demonstrations for additional autonomy—as I witnessed on my visit to Pristina in 1976. Until the collapse of Communist Eastern Europe, wealthy Yugoslavia was more attractive to Albanian Kosovars, by comparison, than Enver Hoxha's cult of personality in Albania. The devolution of both Maoist Albania and Titoist Yugoslavia set in motion the inevitability of Kosovo's independence. In short, when Albanians in Kosovo were one of many nationalities within Yugoslavia, they could tolerate dependence on Belgrade. Once Yugoslavia became Serbia reduced to its 1878 borders, they wanted out of the rump federation.

Gratchanitsa: *a borrowed place on borrowed time*

I ENJOYED THE HOTEL LUXOR. It was clean, reasonably priced, served good food and local beer (Peja), and was quiet during the night. For the next day, however, Irid had my ambitious itinerary to drive around western Kosovo. So we were on the road at 7 a.m., which made us the only Sunday morning sightseers in Pristina.

First we drove to Pristina's central hospital, a dreary complex of buildings past the university. Irid spoke at length about local health care. Professionally he had two jobs: one as a practicing physician, and the second working for Project Hope in the cause of AIDS prevention. Only with two jobs could he make ends meet. The conditions under which he had to treat patients made Kosovo sound like the Third World. Since Yugoslav times after World War II, medical care has been free, as was Irid's medical education. Now there is no money either to pay medical staff, including doctors, or to buy needed drugs or equipment. He described antiquated operating theaters and dirty emergency rooms. While not a huge problem in Kosovo, AIDS is a by-product of the many foreign soldiers serving in KFOR and the underground railways of prostitutes that move stealthily across southern Europe. Only with charitable funds from Switzerland can he carry on his work with AIDS prevention.

Leaving Pristina, we made a detour to Gratchanitsa, perhaps the most celebrated Serbian church in Kosovo. When Serbs speak of resisting Kosovo independence or protecting Serbian medieval monasteries, they often have Gratchanitsa in mind. Delicate frescoes crown the vaults above the candlelit altar, and the prayers being sung in the small chapels link this heavenly paradise to that which was acquired on the nearby Field of Blackbirds. To get into the grounds of the church, I had to show my passport to a Swedish solider and pass through a small gate that was surrounded with sandbags and barbed wire. Walking around the church, Irid and I met one of the nuns, an older woman who wanted to know who I was. When she learned I was American, she recited a litany of denunciations of the U.S.: about the Clinton administration, the 1999 air attacks, and the arrogance of its earthly kingdom. I think she would have spit on me had she had a holy dispensation for such a blessing. After a while I simply drifted away from her and let Irid digest the tirade. The neighborhood around Gratchanitsa is another "Serb enclave," where the few remaining Serbs might well live inside circled wagons. I could sympathize with the nun's anger. The town feels empty and gloomy, reminding me of a quote about Hong Kong, "a borrowed place living on borrowed time."

During our drives around Pristina, Irid and I spent much time talking about the local economy. These discussions were prompted by the presence around the city of huge gas stations, as might be found off freeway ramps in Los Angeles. In a land of two million people with relatively few cars, why all the service stations? Irid could only guess, but spoke about the underground economy, which was always looking to change cash into fixed assets. He also said that when the Deutschmark was changed into the euro, Kosovo was one of the few places around Europe where it was possible to change a suitcase full of cash into something tangible—a house, a car, or, for that matter, a gas station. As best as I could determine, Kosovo survives on guest-worker remittances, foreign aid, Islamic slush funds, soldiers of fortune, some mining and agriculture, and, at its edges, on the trafficking of girls, drugs, and easy money. At least it's easy to find gas.

1999: *the causes of war*

WE DROVE TOWARD PRIZREN over a series of back roads, through towns and villages where the 1999 war was fought between the Kosovo Liberation Army and irregular columns of the Yugoslav army, police, and death squads. By conventional accounts, notably those of the Clinton administration, the cause of the war was Slobodan Milosevic's aggressive attempt to piece together a Greater Serbia. In the rolling hills of western Kosovo—some even covered with fallow vineyards—the fog of war is more evident than theories of Balkan *lebensraum*.

On the trip I was reading Tim Judah's *Kosovo: War and Revenge*, an account of the fighting written by the then London *Times* correspondent in Belgrade. He writes that Milosevic "came to power by exploiting the issue of Kosovo. In this sense the cancer that killed Yugoslavia began in Kosovo." In the 1980s, as a Communist appa-ratchik, Milosevic had championed the cause of Kosovo's Serbs, which by then accounted for only 13 percent of Kosovo's population of 1.7 million. During the 1990s wars of the Yugoslav succession in Croatia and Bosnia-Herzegovina, the aggrieved parties in Kosovo included both Serbs and Albanians. In short, the province had a constitutional structure that suited no one.

As it had lost its autonomous status in the 1970s, Kosovo had little standing within the federal republic of Yugoslavia. It was a dependency within Serbia, but it repeatedly exercised its veto powers over Belgrade, infuriating leaders such as Milosevic. Judah writes that "while Kosovo had a say in the running of Serbia, Serbia had no say in Kosovo and in particular could not safeguard the Serbs there…" As Yugoslavia unraveled, Kosovars found them-selves as the only non-Serb nationality in the truncated federal republic, which now included only Serbia and Montenegro. In her history of Kosovo, *Between Serb and Albanian*, Miranda Vick-ers sums up the conflict: "The Albanian claim to Kosovo is also based on demography since they constitute more than 90 percent of the total population, while the Serbs' claim derives purely from history and emotion."

The American-brokered Dayton Peace Accords of 1995 officially ratified the dismemberment of Yugoslavia, but they also cast the die for war over Kosovo. Dayton put together the artificial construct that is modern Bosnia—a ward of the international community made up of three hostile populations—but it did not address the future of Kosovo and its majority Albanian population. Judah writes: "Just as Dayton and its failure to deal with Kosovo had traumatized Kosovo's Albanians, its Serbs had suffered a similar, shocking real-ization. When the Croatian army stormed back into the Krajina region of Croatia and some 170,000 Serbs fled in three days, it dawned on many of the Kosovo Serbs that they, too, were doomed."

Yugoslavia collapsed throughout the 1990s; so did Albania, adding further fuel to the smoldering nationalist fires in Kosovo. In the post-Communist era, Albania went through a series of failed governments, some of which ran the economy as if it were a pyramid scheme. In 1997 the country came apart as though it were a failed savings bank and the citizens conned depositors. In the informal bankruptcy proceedings—essentially, government property was looted—more than 1 million weapons of the Albanian army were carried off, largely to the borderlands between Albania and the rump states of Yugoslavia, including Kosovo. Previously the Kosovo Liberation Army had been a rabble without arms. Now it could send its armed bands from Albania into Kosovo with the knowledge that the Clinton administration blamed Milosevic for all the problems in the Balkans. Kosovo might well have been a province of a sovereign state, Yugoslavia, but it was one the NATO powers were determined to crush. Its storyboard also suited the prime-time requirements of the modern American presidency. President Clinton (who has a boulevard named after him in Pristina) might well have quoted William Randolph Hearst, who said to an illustrator at the start of the Spanish-American War, "Give me the drawings and I will give you the war."

Milosevic furnished the pictures himself, sending the world photos of a shocking number of massacres from the villages through which Irid and I were now driving. During 1998 and into 1999, the KLA and Serb policemen fought running battles throughout Kosovo. At the conference of Rambouillet, convened to negotiate a solution, U.S. Secretary of State Madeleine Albright said: "We have made it very clear to Milosevic and the Kosovars that we do not support the independence of Kosovo—that we want Serbia out of Kosovo, not Kosovo out of Serbia." Milosevic, however, thought the demands meant otherwise, and answered the NATO *demarche* by sending into Kosovo 40,000 police and soldiers, who set about to rid Kosovo of its Albanian population. Milosevic dared NATO to stop him, which it did, with bombs launched against both civilian and military targets around Yugoslavia.

During the 78-day war, according to author Tim Judah, about 760,000 Kosovo Albanians left the province. Some 445,000 went to Albania, 245,000 to Macedonia, and about 70,000 to Montenegro. After the fighting stopped, 250,000 people (mostly Serbs) left Kosovo. Judah concludes: "Just as the policy makers underestimated the Serb will to expel or encourage the flight of as much of the Kosovar population as possible, they now underestimated the unrelenting thirst for revenge amongst the Albanians returning home." He might well have quoted Edith Durham, who observed in 1909: "Of one thing the populace is determined: that is, that never again shall the land be Serb."

Western Kosovo: *onward to Prizren*

As IT WAS A WARM AUTUMN DAY full of sunshine, it was pleasant to drive with Irid around western Kosovo. We weaved into the hills around Orahovac, which had been largely Serbian before the war. Someday the area may be the Napa Valley of Kosovo, as the fields around the town are covered with vineyards, most of which are jumbles of weeds. Irid spoke about the climate of Kosovo being perfect for grapes. He also drove slowly through Krusha, on the main road between Pec and Prizren, where during the war all the men of the village were rounded up and massacred. We walked gingerly through the ruins and broken glass of a Yugoslav motel that, in the Tito era, had been popular for weddings and Sunday lunches. It struck me as a casualty of neglect more than of war, but nearby was a KLA cemetery, where each of the tombstones had the portrait and unit banner of a dead Albanian warrior. The frontiers are still floating on blood.

The historian Miranda Vickers, whose latest book with James Pettifer is entitled *The Albanian Question*, has described Prizren as the most authentically preserved Ottoman town in the Balkans. Irid and I parked the car along the river that cuts through the center, the Prizenska Bistrica, and wandered through the back streets of the historic quarter, which has the air of the nineteenth century. Mosques and minarets crowd some of the town squares, while on the hillside that looms above Prizren are Orthodox churches and palaces.

Before the Balkan Wars, a popular Serbian song was "Onward, onward to Prizren," which gave the ancient capital of Serbia the lost qualities of Jerusalem. In 1880 a British traveler wrote: "Prizren is, with perhaps the exception of Mecca, the most dangerous spot for a Christian in all Mohammedan countries." Edith Durham in *High Albania* describes her 1908 visit to Prizren, noting presciently that it "is a large town, and highly picturesque...Each nation that designs to pick up the pieces, when Turkey in Europe bursts up, keeps a Consul on the spot....There is something truly pathetic about the way Turkey, everywhere, carefully protects the gentlemen whose only *raison d'être* is to hasten the dismemberment of the land." Serbia recaptured Prizren from the Turks in 1913, but through the 20th century no town, by my reckoning, has seen so many overlords come and go through its narrow lanes.

Irid and I, together with a professor friend of his, stopped for coffee at one of the many outdoor cafés. Gazing around the square, I tried to calculate which countries had ruled Prizren in the last hundred years, and came up with a list that included Turkey, Serbia, Austria-Hungary, the World War I Allies; the Kingdom of Serbs, Croats and Slovenes; Yugoslavia, Italy, Nazi Germany, Tito's Partisans, Yugoslavia, NATO, UNMIK, and soon Kosovo.

The professor had a relation to Irid's family, and I enjoyed his company and commentary as he walked me around Prizren. A man in his seventies, with thinning gray hair and a lean frame, he wore an old gray suit and a narrow tie. Generally he had a coffee or a cigarette in his hand, and his academic passion was to prove that Albanians (Illyrians, not Slavs) had a claim to large tracts of the Balkans. Together we walked to the League of Prizren Museum, which is brand new. In March 1999, at the outbreak of the Kosovo war, the Serbs had burned the old museum to the ground.

The League of Prizren was formed in 1878 with the goal of unifying into one country the entire Albanian nation. Inside the museum there is a large map showing all the villages of Greater Albania. Dated 1877-1881, the claim stretches in the south from the Greek port of Preveza to Podgorica (the current capital of Montenegro) in the north and then east to include large sections of Macedonia and Greece. The rump state of Albania came into being only in 1913, in part because Austria-Hungary wanted to deny Serbia access to the sea. Vickers writes: "The Florence Line that decided the frontiers of the new Albanian state satisfied neither the Albanians nor their Balkan neighbors." The Austrian historian Frederic Morton is more scathing, writing: "The nationhood of that nation did not exist. But Vienna guaranteed the integrity of the phantom. After all, Austria was the illusionist among the great powers." When Kosovo unites with Albania, as will surely happen, the phantom nation will be that much closer to realizing the dreams of the League—provided the Serbs, Greeks or Macedonians are not yet again humming the tune to "Onward, onward to Prizren."

Looking back at Kosovo: *lost, dead, gone*

IN THE GRAND PLAN for the weekend, Irid and I had hoped to drive over the mountains from Prizren to Tetovo, an Albanian town in western FYRO Macedonia. Some of my road maps, admittedly dating to 1976, showed a road cutting across the remote frontier. Irid wisely did not want to chance it that such a road was still open. During the 1999 war, in fleeing to Macedonia, he had spent almost a week in a traffic jam on the Macedonian border, and here he preferred the safer crossing, on the main road between Pristina and Skopje. To get there we drove along a winding mountainous road past Serbian monasteries and through the Serb enclave at Strpce, guarded by KFOR troops. The countryside reminded me of autumn in Vermont, except that all the villages we passed had either new or rebuilt mosques, many of which had shiny tin domes. It cast Kosovo as a subdivision of prefabricated Islam.

The professor had come with us when we left Prizren. Leaning toward the back seat, I asked him what would happen to the Serbian monuments once Kosovo was independent. He said most of the sites were a product of the "occupation," meaning the period of Serb and Yugoslav rule after 1912. In that case, he did not see much interest in protecting the monuments indefinitely with KFOR troops once Kosovo was free from Serbia. I sensed that the monasteries would be burned, and that no one locally would miss them, except for the Serbs, like the fiery Gratchanitsa nun.

Since 1999, many Serbian buildings have gone up in flames. On March 17, 2004, for example, what might be described as a pogrom was launched against Serbs in Kosovo. Twenty-two people were killed and several hundred wounded. A priest at the Decani monastery, one of the most enduring in Serbian culture, said: "It was a real Kristallnacht." Later a newsletter for a Norwegian organization that defends religious freedom, *Forum 18*, reported: "In the southern town of Prizren all the Serbian Orthodox sanctuaries were set on fire. The diocesan house, the theological faculty, the fourteenth century church of the Ljeviska Holy Mother, the monastery of the Holy Archangels, and the church of St. Saviour, which is on the hills just outside the town, were all set on fire and destroyed." In conclusion it was noted that neither KFOR nor UNMIK had made any arrests in the attacks, which many felt were launched with central planning.

Much as I did, Edith Durham left Kosovo believing it to be a hopeless cause, at least for the Serbs. She wrote: "I felt that so far as Prizren and its neighborhood were concerned, the cause was lost, dead and gone—as lost as is Calais to England and the English claim to Normandy." Driving through mountain ranges of southern Kosovo, I was of the same opinion. Judah comes to a similar position when he quotes an Orthodox priest, who says: "Kosovo has the same destiny as Asia Minor, once full of wonderful Christian sites and now all ruins and ash, or Constantinople [Istanbul] now a Muslim city, or Palestine which once had flourishing Christian communities." It would be nice to think that under an independent Kosovo, the remnants of Serbian culture could be preserved, especially given that all the countries of the region will someday have to co-exist within the European Union. In that, they will have a good chance to prosper. In the meantime, nation-building in the Balkans may continue toasting independence with Molotov cocktails.

The Train Across FYRO Macedonia: *the gardeners of Salonika*

I SAID GOODBYE TO IRID at the Skopje railway station. In many ways the Macedonian capital remains the most Titoist of former Yugoslav cities. An earthquake devastated Skopje in1965, at the height of Tito's prosperity and central planning, and the city that survives today has wide boulevards, monuments to the workers' paradise, and a central station of vast socialist sensibility.

My plan was to take the overnight train to Athens, to be there in time for professional meetings the next morning. Before leaving Switzerland, I had tried on several occasions to buy the Macedonia rail ticket to Athens. Each time I went to the Geneva station, the agent told me that the Macedonian and Greek computers were "down," and thus I could buy a ticket on the sleeper only when I arrived in Skopje. That made me nervous, and my unsettled feelings were confirmed when all I could buy in Skopje was a coach ticket to Thessalonika. Only in the Greek city—I was told at the forlorn Macedonian office—could I buy the overnight ticket. In the meantime I waited in hot sunshine for the *Olympus*, an express that, according to the schedule, connected the capitals of Slovenia, Croatia and Serbia with Thessalonika. The train that arrived thirty minutes late had only four second-class coaches, and none of the restaurant cars mentioned in the timetable. I scrambled to find a seat in a crowded but comfortable compartment, and spent the next five hours reading and looking out the window.

Otto von Bismarck said the power controlling the Vardar Valley controlled the Balkans. Based on my train observations, the power is now in the hands of small farming villages and wagons piled high with hay. Rumbling south across Macedonia in the second-class day coach, I recalled spending several pleasant days in Thessalonika, reading about the forgotten World War I campaign in the Vardar Valley. As the Western Allies were bogged down in the trenches, the British and French tried to launch a new envelopment strategy into central Europe by attacking north from Salonika (now Thessalonika). In late 1915, Allied troops were transferred from Gallipoli and Egypt, and landed on the Macedonian coastline.

Alan Palmer's *The Gardeners of Salonika* makes the point that "had an inter-Allied force landed in the Balkans in February 1915 rather than in October, the outcome of the war would have been drastically altered." Instead Allied forces took their time coming ashore at what Palmer describes as "a second-rate Port Said with Alexandrine undertones, neither in Europe nor in Asia but of both." There were disagreements with the Greek government, which was more interested in attacking Turkey than liberating Skopje. So bogged down did the invasion force become in Balkan trenches that French prime minister Georges Clemenceau nicknamed them "the gardeners of Salonika." Not until 1918 were the Allies able to push north through the Vardar Valley and break the combined Austrian-Bulgarian front. Neither from Gallipoli nor Salonika could the Allies exploit Europe's allegedly soft underbelly. In reality, it proved rock-hard.

Some of the heaviest fighting took place around Idomeni, now a Greek border town with FYRO Macedonia. Greece dislikes both the name and the political pretensions of the former Yugoslav republic. To Greeks the name Macedonia is associated with Philip and Alexander the Great, not an independent and non-Greek nation. When I was exploring how I might get from Skopje to Athens, I discovered that no direct air service connects the neighboring capitals. Now, in the early evening, the *Olympus* stopped at the border, and immigration officials went through the train and collected everyone's passport. To get them back, we had to get off the train and stand around the frontier office in the station. Nearby a railway café was grilling meat, and more than a few passengers, knowing the delays at the border, sat down at the tables and ordered a full meal. The rest of us milled around the sentry post until one of the officers, by shouting the nationalities of the passengers, returned the passports. I was the only American on board the train. There were many Greeks but no Macedonians.

Night Train to Athens: *qualities reminiscent of dental surgery*

THE MAIN RAILWAY STATION in Thessalonika, at 10 p.m. on a Sunday, was a madhouse. I stood in several lines until I found the window where it might be possible to buy a ticket in a sleeping car. The clerks at the head of the lines kept opening and shutting their windows, and I felt uneasy because the station was so busy at this late hour. Clearly I wasn't the only passenger headed toward Athens for a morning meeting, something that was confirmed when I discovered that not only were there no berths available, but that I could not even buy a seat reservation. Had the meeting not been the following morning in Athens, I would have checked into a hotel, and continued the march in daylight. As the reason I was going to Athens was to see the management of a seaplane company, I decided I had no choice but to buy an unreserved coach ticket and push my way aboard in what would clearly be a crowded train.

Having spent many nights on trains, I can say this journey ranks with the worst in my experience. In theory, this leg was the continuation of the *Olympus*, but that train had been hauled away to the yards. In its place were day coaches. All the lights in the car were phosphorescent, giving the ride qualities reminiscent of dental surgery, although my cramped seat was wedged forward, making me feel like a crash dummy. Had the Hellenic Railways turned off the lights and run the train as an express to Athens, the night might have been bearable. Instead, the train stopped everywhere. Clearly the $10 billion for the 2006 Summer Olympics did not include anything extra for sprucing up the railways.

I need not have rushed. After showering in a hotel near the station, I presented myself at the office of the seaplane company late in the morning. In short, I had been asked to write an article about its services. This was my chance to meet the management, and they had said I could fly back with one of the planes to Corfu, where I was headed from Athens.

Needless to say, the seaplane had never left Corfu. Nor was it flying into Athens to pick me up. I learned all this in the offices of the company, which brought to my mind the phrase "fly by

night." Listening to the spiel about how seaplanes are environmentally friendly, how they can land anywhere, or how they cruise
at one thousand feet, all that raced through my mind was how I
would now get myself to Corfu, off the western coast of Greece, in
the Ionian Sea. I knew that both domestic Greek airlines flew to
Corfu, but I also knew that a last-minute ticket would be expensive, and I dreaded—in my tired railway state—heading out to the
new Athens airport, an hour from the city. In the end I decided
to take the bus to Corfu. Yes, it would be long, but it was easy to
arrange and I could read my book. With any luck it might pass near
Actium, where in 31 B.C. the Roman republic had been buried
in a sea battle between Octavian and Mark Antony. I had long
dreamed of seeing it. At least on the bus I would get closer than I
would on a plane—even one that floated.

Lord Elgin's Marbles: *who killed Homer?*

IT WAS A WARM EVENING in Athens, and the Acropolis glimmered
in the sunset. I sat on the rocks overlooking both the Agora and
the Parthenon. I spend a lot more time than I should thinking
about Lord Elgin. (Did he save the marbles or disfigure them?
I can never make up my mind.) On this evening, I lacked the
enthusiasm to tackle the Acropolis. I was dragging, and had not
long ago climbed the same set of polished marble steps. The best
I could muster was my book and a table at Café Dionysus, one of
my favorite restaurants in the world. It has a perfect view of the
Parthenon, and it's where I read the lines: "How did we grow so
utterly distant from those [meaning the ancient Greeks] to whom
we have devoted our lives?"

The quote comes from Victor Davis Hanson's *Who Killed
Homer?* A professor at California State University (Fresno) and
celebrated commentator on the confluence of Greek and modern

history, he writes a column for *National Review* and has published numerous books on military and classical warfare.[1] *Who Killed Homer?* refers to professors of classical studies, who, according to Hanson and his co-author, John Heath, have sucked the life-blood out of the study of Greece and Rome. When I first bought my copy, I mentioned the title to my friend, also a professor of classics, Peggy Brucia, and she replied: "Yes, and I know some of the murderers." In short, Hanson and Heath argue that the insistence of making Greek history conform to the prerequisites of political correctness has consigned the study of the classics to the fringes of academia. They despair: "If only we who teach the Classical worlds had as many undergraduates—or just interested Americans—as there are professors and graduate students! But then we would need people who think and act like Greeks, not Classicists, to teach us about Greece." The book has made Hanson either loved or hated within the world of classical studies. One of his enraged critics went so far as to denounce him to the Federal Bureau of Investigation as a possible suspect in the then hunt for the Unabomber. His followers—for the most part non-academics, I would imagine—subscribe to the belief that "the Greeks provided a blueprint for an ordered and humane society that could transcend time and space, one whose spirit and core values could evolve, sustain, and drive political reform and social change for ages hence." In my own case, I was riding the bus to Corfu partly

---

1 I first encountered his name when researching an essay about the death on Okinawa of Captain Robert Fowler, a Marine officer and my father's close friend. Fowler had served as an officer with the 1st Marines (C Company, 1st battalion) during the battles of Guadalcanal and Cape Gloucester, in which my father was the company's commander. But then Fowler took command of his own company, Fox, of the 29th Marines. In writing about his death on almost the last day of the battle for Okinawa, I learned from some of the men in his company that the namesake of Victor Davis Hanson had served with the 6th Marine Division on Okinawa and that he had been killed in fighting for Sugar Loaf, one of the low hills along the Shuri Line. According to one of the officers in Fox Company, it was Robert Fowler who devised the strategy that finally captured Sugar Loaf, which, while it was holding out, cost some 3,000 American casualties, including Victor Hanson.

to commune with the ancient Greeks, and Hanson's book made for a diverting seat companion.

In many respects, Hanson's book delivers a broadside against cultural relativism—the academic premise that Greeks should not be held in higher esteem than, say, a remote Papuan tribe. While making the point that the civilizations in Rome and Greece were special, at least for those now living in the Western world, he side-swipes his colleagues in the Academy, including those who later thought him to be as threatening as the Unabomber. For example, he writes: "Instead, like finance and law, the study of Greek in the last twenty years became a profession, a tiny world—but a world of sorts nonetheless—of jets, conferences, publicity, jargon, and perks." Or: "And somehow reaching an elite university, not teaching America about the Greeks, has become the goal of most of our philhellenes in Classics' last hour…In the process we lost both the student and the general reader, Homer's only links to the world outside Classics."

Hanson admires those—amateurs and professionals—who are passionate about passing on their learning of the ancient Greeks, citing his mentor and professor, Colin Edmonson, who advised: "The Classicist must some time visit Greece, dabble in the strange modern lingo, walk the battlefields, try her hand with spade and trowel…" (To hear Hanson tell it, most classical scholars could not calculate the distance between Marathon and Athens.) I skipped over the pages that sounded like the minutes of the world's longest faculty meeting, but I warmed to his reminder that in classical times all generals were elected by open vote, and I heed his darker warning that the United States does not own the copyright to the democratic process:

Americans must not assume that they will continue to think and act like Greeks merely because their Founders—for the most part students of the Classics—two centuries ago re-established on this continent a free economy, constitutional government, an egalitarian idea, and a tradition of liberal dissent modeled after the ethos of the Greeks.

While I read Hanson, the bus skirted the city of Corinth, crossed the gulf of the same name near Patras, and took a succession of smaller roads through Epirus, the mountainous region of northern Greece. Every few hours the driver would stop at a roadside restaurant, and stay long enough for passengers to order a full meal. It turned a four-hour drive into an all-day journey, but one which thrilled me when I figured out that we would drive right not only by Actium but also Missolonghi, where the poet Lord Byron died in 1824 during the Greek civil war.

It is hard to know exactly what killed Byron. During his last days, suffering from what sounds like nervous exhaustion, he refused leeches and to be bled. He had crossed to the mainland town from the island of Cephalonia ("This is a veritable school of disillusion," he wrote while there) and was trying to rally the Greeks to independence from the Turks. It is possible that he suffered from a deadly form of epilepsy, but it is hard to imagine that with modern medicine he would have died at age thirty-six of what now reads like a wasting disorder. The town of Missolonghi, otherwise nondescript—especially when seen from a bus—erected a large statue in his memory and placed it in what they call the Garden of Heroes.

Glimpse of Actium: *Antony and Cleopatra skip town*

THE ROMAN ENCAMPMENT at Actium is at the mouth of the Bay of Ambraccia, at what is now called Preveza. A tunnel goes under the narrow channel, connecting the two spits of land at the mouth of the bay. In 31 B.C. Mark Antony had positioned his republican army on the southern peninsula, in his campaign to dislodge Octavian (later known as Augustus) as the imperial leader of Rome. Antony's army had numerous generals but, effectively, Cleopatra was his second in command at Actium.

As a result of the naval engagement fought just offshore from the mouth of the harbor—to use Hollywood language—Octavian got the empire, and Antony got the girl. Initially the two fleets matched up in long facing lines. Antony commanded the right wing of his fleet and Cleopatra had the reserve. Although the encounter initially went well for Antony, something caused Cleopatra to slice through Octavian's lines and set sail for Egypt. Stricken either as a commander or a lover, Antony broke off the battle to follow Cleopatra, thus leaving Actium, not to mention republican Rome, at the mercy of Octavian.

Shakespeare immortalized the battle, writing, in the words of Canidius, one of Antony's generals:

> She once being loof'd,
> The noble ruin of her magic, Antony,
> Claps on his sea-wing, and, like a doting mallard,
> Leaving the fight in height, flies after her:
> I never saw an action of such shame;
> Experience, manhood, honour, ne'er before
> Did violate so itself.

It is hard to know exactly what happened at Actium. I am not sure I got closer to the truth by traversing it on a bus, much as it pleased me to see it. There was an element of a family blood feud in the battle, as Antony had romanced and married Cleopatra while still married to Octavian's daughter, Octavia. Also, Antony's first wife, Fulvia, schemed against Octavian. The Roman historian Ronald Syme concludes: "The course, character, and duration of the battle itself is all a mystery—and a topic of controversy. There may have been little fighting and comparatively few casualties." He believes that the iconography of Actium mattered more than the actual battle, writing:

> Actium was a shabby affair, the worthy climax to the ignoble propaganda against Cleopatra, to the sworn and sacred union of all Italy. But the young Caesar required the glory of a victory that would surpass the greatest in all history, Roman or Hellenic. In the official version of the victor, Actium took on august dimensions and an intense emotional coloring, being transformed into a great naval battle, with lavish wealth of convincing and artistic detail.

Octavian does not become the sole leader of Rome until he follows both Antony and Cleopatra back to Egypt, where one is killed and the other commits her dramatic suicide. (Elizabeth Taylor certainly enjoyed the role. Remember her line: "*There are never enough hours in the days of a queen, and her nights have too many.*") But the tombstone for the Roman republic is often laid at Actium.

The Greek Island of Corfu: *Ionian republics*

I FELT AT HOME on Corfu even though I had not been there since 1976. That earlier summer, together with my parents and younger sister, I had visited with the family of Stephen Mannessey, who lived on a large estate in the center of the lush island. In memory, I recall that it looked out on the sea through tall pine trees, and that the property had its own chapel. In the early 1930s, Stephen and my father had attended the same summer school in Geneva, at 10, rue St. Léger. His mother, whom I met in the summer of 1976, had been a friend of my grandmother, who spent several summers in the 1930s administering a program in Switzerland for international students. She had taken my father, then twelve, with her, and they had both befriended the Mannessey family from Corfu. On this trip, after I had settled into my hotel, I inquired if anyone knew the Mannesseys, and was told that three brothers, including Stephen, were dead, but that their children still lived on Corfu. I never did reconnect with them on this visit, but I warmed to the family connections on the island.

Corfu town is one of many graceful Venetian legacies along the Adriatic Sea. From the rail of a ferry, it comes into focus as if it were a J.M.W. Turner painting. Turner returned often to the themes of Venice and the Adriatic Sea, especially as the lines in his work broke down from the clarity of neo-classicalism to the blur of pre-Impressionism. In additional to the seafront line of Venetian houses, Corfu has two imposing fortresses—one along the harbor and the other dominating the hill above the main squares. Unfortunately, during my several walks around the town it was wet and windy. Dodging the rain, I sat for a long time in an Orthodox church, listening to a priest chant to a congregation of cruise ship passengers. Under the covered archways of The Liston, originally a barracks for Napoleonic soldiers, I drank espresso and ate little biscuits, looking out on a lawn where the English or their island imitators still play cricket. But without the foul winds, I would not have discovered another family link on the island.

Having at last connected with the seaplane company, I spent my last morning on the island looking for the parliament of the Ionian Republics. The manager of the Hotel Imperial, Spyros Michas, had given me a book, *Corfu: A Journey Through the Ages,* and the night before I had spent a pleasant dinner reading about the island's political history. When we met in his office, his first words were to remind me that Corfu and the nearby islands had never fallen to the

Turks. (Hence Byron's presence on nearby Cephalonia, to use it as a staging area in his war of Greek liberation.) The Byzantine Empire had been present on Corfu from 337 to 1204, after which began two eras of Venetian rule, the latter of which lasted from 1386 to 1797. (The book's author, Giorgios Ch. Sourtzinos, writes: "The Venetian occupation was not tyranny, it was protection.") Venice was unable to protect Corfu from Napoleon, who had his way locally from 1807 to 1814, after which he ceded the island to the British, who in turn tolerated the democratic experiment known as the Ionian Republic. The confederation of the Ionian Islands was modeled on the United States, and I visited its small parliament building—a graceful rotunda similar to Thomas Jefferson's Monticello.

The Serbian Exile: *a fighting retreat*

IT WAS AT THE PARLIAMENT BUILDING that I became aware that I might be able to visit the Museum of Serbs on Corfu 1916-1918. I had read about it in my book, but the desk clerk thought it was closed. Nevertheless, an official in the parliament encouraged me to knock on the museum's front door. After a long wait, a suspicious-looking man opened the door slightly, as if admitting me to a cell meeting. When I explained that I wanted to visit the museum, he opened the door and gestured for me to sign the guest book. There was no charge. Because of the rain and wind outside, the small rooms were dank and gloomy. On the back street of a holiday town, I was surprised to see so many other people making their way around such an obscure museum. I have to assume that they were vacationing Serbs, but their heavy dress and dark expressions made it clear that they were not here for a good time.

The museum tells the story of the Serbian retreat in 1915-1916 from Belgrade to Corfu, where the remnants of the army and government struggled for survival on the island's hospitable shores. In all, several hundred thousand Serbs were killed, taken prisoner, or died of disease on the forced march to the sea, and one of the casualties of the defeat was my father's cousin, Radoje Stanojevič.

Until 1915, the Serbian army had managed to fend off the attacks of the Austro-Hungarian Empire, which had launched the war in 1914 after the murder of Archduke Franz Ferdinand in Sarajevo by a Serb nationalist. An eyewitness account of the retreat, *With Serbia into Exile*, by an American volunteer, Fortier Jones, writes of the stalemate: "...Serbia's whole army numbered about three hundred and fifty thousand—were massed along the Bulgarian border to guard the nation's one hope—the single line of the Orient Railway from Saloniki to Belgrade." That thin line collapsed when Austria-Hungary succeeded in bribing Bulgaria to join the Axis powers, and the joint Austro-Bulgarian forces crashed into Serbia, from two directions, in late 1915. A map on the museum wall shows the path of the Serbian retreat, which went across Kosovo and the Albanian mountains to the coast and Corfu. As best they could, the Serbs attempted what might be called a "fighting retreat." There were few weapons to battle the snow and ice, not to mention Austrian bombers and Albanian guerrilla attacks. Jones writes of the suffering:

> To me the name of Kossovo calls up one of the most terrible spectacles I shall ever see. The plain on the day after we left Mitrovitze epitomized all that is sordid, overwhelming, heart-rending, and intermingled in that strange maze, which is ever the wonder of onlookers at the tragic puzzle of war, all that is noble, beautiful, sublime. Until that day I did not know the burden of the tiny little word "war," but never again shall we who traversed the "Field of Blackbirds" think of war without living again the snow-filled horrors of our march.

The museum cabinets have swords, uniforms, and old photographs of the winter conditions, but nothing as graphic as Jones' prose. He describes the army passing through Pristina:

> Fighting one's way down these lanes of hell, stumbling over carcasses, wading knee-deep in slush and refuse, looking into myriads of wild, suffering eyes set in faces that showed weeks of starvation and hardship, the world of peace and plentiful food seems never to have existed...If ever there was a hell on earth, Prishtina, which from the hilltop yesterday afternoon looked like heaven, is that hell.

My grandfather's family came from a small village near Nish. By 1916, my grandfather, Milivoy Stanoyevich, was living in New York, working as a professor of languages and history. His nephew, Radoje, and my father's cousin made the march and would have encamped on Corfu, where in the early days of the exile some three hundred soldiers and civilians died every day. They were either buried at sea, in what was called the "Blue Graveyard," or in the harbor of Corfu on Vido Island. In all some 10,000 Serbian soldiers were interred in and around Corfu. A correspondent of the *New York Sun* reported: "I went to visit the island where are the sick soldiers. The Greeks call it the island of Vido, but the Serbs call it now the Island of the Devil, or more often, the Island of Death." In the case of my father's cousin, he survived his two years on Corfu, but then died of influenza when he returned home to Serbia—to be buried in the same small village cemetery where my grandfather's ashes joined him in 1976.

It was also on Corfu that Yugoslavia was born. Alan Palmer writes in *The Gardeners of Salonika*: "On July 20, 1917, the leading spokesman for the Yugoslavs in exile, Ante Trumbic, a Croatian from Dalmatia, signed an agreement with Nikola Pasic at Corfu affirming the unity of the Serbs, Croats and Slovenes and declaring that a Yugoslav Kingdom should be established after the war... the 'Corfu Pact' appeared to broaden the basis of Serbian war aims. It removed many of the hesitations which had held back Yugoslav patriots from joining a narrowly Serbian army." Against the backdrop of the Serb suffering during the war—one-fifth of its population perished—and the Allied victory, the new Yugoslav kingdom was awarded Kosovo.

In that time, to quote Abraham Lincoln, it seemed "altogether fitting and proper" that Serbia should govern Kosovo. In our era that gesture seems oppressive and colonial. The *New York Times* wrote in a recent editorial: "Eight years after NATO went to war to stop the ethnic purge in Kosovo, it's time for the international community to recognize the province's independence from Serbia." Kosovo may make its way in the community of nations. Its best chance for success will come if it can protect and embrace the region's rich historical legacy, and make it accessible to Serbs. Jones writes: "To go through what the young boys of Serbia tasted first in full tragedy on Kossovo and in succeeding weeks drank to the dregs of lonely painful death, is a thing that I, for one, cannot grasp." I know, from seeing their own graveyards in places such as Krusha, that Albanians have similar haunting passages in their history. Maybe it is for these reasons that Victor Hanson recalls the counsel of Sophocles that war is "the father of our sorrows."

Berlin Diary

ON A RECENT TRIP, to deal with Berlin's excesses of space and history, I rented a bicycle and decided to ride some of the contours of the city from World War II, beginning at the Cecilienhof Palace, site of the Potsdam Conference, and ending where the Germans had surrendered to the Russians. In between I was curious to know the extent to which modern Berlin lives in the shadows of its past.

Allied bombers and East German city planners laid waste to much of imperial Potsdam, but the hot and cold wars spared the site of the conference, which unfolded over several weeks in July-August 1945, in a building that reminded me of a suburban golf club.

The Big Three—Truman, Stalin and Churchill (until the British voted Churchill from power, replacing him with Clement Attlee)—met in a paneled living room, modeled after a similar salon in Danzig, one suitable for Hanseatic burghers. It is fitting that World War II ended in a room borrowed from the city that was at the center of its origins. As a cause for war, the Free City of Danzig is hard to beat.

The Treaty of Versailles, in 1919, made the German port a ward of the League of Nations, but under Polish sovereignty, and

Hitler wasn't the only German who viewed its loss as a grievance of an unjust peace. (In World War I, Poland had largely sided with the Central Powers, although the peace awarded it large swaths of Germany.)

Truman came to the world stage of Potsdam with Adm. William Leahy and Secretary of State James Byrnes—not to mention good Midwestern intentions—to partition Europe along lines that might prevent further conflict. The Red Army had beaten Truman to Berlin, and Stalin took the view, as had Napoleon, that the country that controls Berlin controls both Germany and Europe. Anthony Beevor tells the story of the Soviet encirclement in *The Fall of Berlin 1945*, and it is a harrowing tale—even if the Soviets were taking down the capital of Nazi Germany. Stalin deceived the Allies by saying that the main objective of his advance was not Berlin—allowing Eisenhower to stop on the Elbe—and then the Russian army raped and looted its way into the capital.

Some two million German women, many in Berlin, were violated, as partial payback for the brutal crimes the German armies had committed after their Russian invasion. It's hard to imagine, for the Soviets and the Germans, that these accounts have ever been settled.

From Potsdam, which echoes Frederick the Great as much as Stalin's peace, I rode along the Brandenburg lakes to Wannsee, where, in January 1942, a conference was held at which it was agreed to push ahead with what was called the Final Solution.

Hitler was not present, but a number of high-ranking Nazis and Gauleiters were there, including Adolf Eichmann, who kept minutes, which codified the systematic destruction of the Jewish nation throughout the Reich and occupied territories. Wannsee is a suburban town and lake, now largely devoted to sailing and yacht clubs, and the conference took place in a villa that earlier was the weekend house of a Prussian industrialist. Even today it is difficult to comprehend genocidal business taking place in such a beautiful setting. But the Nazis treated Berlin and its environs as if it were a baronial castle, one complete with banquet halls and dungeons.

For much of the afternoon at the somber museum, I read the transcript of Eichmann's trial in Jerusalem, where he made the Wannsee Conference sound like a corporate retreat. As drained as I felt when leaving, I remain unconvinced that Wannsee was the only door through which the Final Solution entered the lexicon and history.

By January 1942, the Dachau concentration camp had been in business for almost 10 years, gas was being used on prisoners at Auschwitz, and an archipelago of concentration camps—a thousand points of darkness—stretched from Amsterdam to Kiev. In nearby Grunewald, on a remote stretch of track, I walked along a platform that memorializes the deportation point of Berlin Jews from as early as 1941.

Although the Soviets dominated East Berlin from 1945 to 1989, surprisingly little in the city recalls their presence. In a cold, penetrating rain, I found the Russian war memorials in the Tiergarten and at Treptow Park. As Walt Whitman might have said, the real war will not get into the soaring bronze eagles. Otherwise, the battle for Berlin would be recalled as a triumph of nihilism in which an army of rape and pillage defeated one that deployed teenage boys as antitank weapons.

As best as I could during my visit, I biked along the traces of the Wall, which even in its fragmentary state remains a Neolithic presence in an otherwise glamorous, modern city. From the East Side Gallery, where local artists have turned the Wall into a funky SoHo-like exhibition, I rode out to Karlshorst, the eastern suburb where Marshal Zhukov accepted the German surrender, in May 1945. (The Germans surrendered to the Western Allies in Reims, France.)

At the end, delirious in his bunker, Hitler issued orders to armies that did not exist and condemned to death a city that was 80 percent in ruins. The sycophantic Albert Speer was among those who encouraged him to self-stage a Wagnerian finale. As Beevor writes: "The Fall of Berchtesgaden did not have quite the same ring as the Fall of Berlin." Hitler died a suicide under what is now a parking lot, just off the imperial Wilhelmstrasse. The site of the Reich Chancellery now has a take-out Chinese restaurant—further notes, perhaps, on evil's continuing banality.

Buried hastily near the bunker, Hitler's remains were dug up by the Soviets, who divided various organs among intelligence bureaus and Moscow archives. According to Beevor, the rest of the body was stored in the East German city of Magdeburg until 1970, when, without ceremony, it was cremated and the ashes were flushed into the municipal waste system—yet another Berlin battle with history.

Polish Corridors

ONE OF THE MORE COLORFUL DIPLOMATS in American history, later ambassador to Russia, William C. Bullitt Jr. accompanied Woodrow Wilson to France at the end of World War I as a member of the U.S. delegation to the Paris Peace Conference. Bullitt had covered much of the Great War as a foreign correspondent, spoke excellent French, and knew well a number of European diplomats. He was among those in the American delegation who thought the views of Soviet Russia ought to be represented in the peace, and when President Wilson agreed to a back-channel approach to the Bolsheviks, Bullitt was selected to lead the small team to Moscow. There he found Lenin "genial" and recommended that the United States give diplomatic recognition to the Soviet Union, a proposal that Herbert Hoover blocked on the grounds that the new Russian government governed by murder. Bullitt returned from Moscow to Paris, but resigned from the U.S. delegation over the proposed terms of the Versailles agreement. "This isn't a peace treaty," he wrote. "I can see at least eleven wars in it."

To understand the legacy of the Versailles Treaty, at least its consequences for Poland, I recently traveled by train from Berlin to

Warsaw, and then to Krakow and Budapest—cities that were the winners and losers when adding up the score of Wilson's Fourteen Points. How did a statement of such lofty goals, which even read today appear so reasonable, lead to such destructive consequences? Here, for example, is Wilson's Point 13: "An independent Polish state should be erected which should include the territories inhabited by indisputably Polish populations, which should be assured a free and secure access to the sea, and whose political and economic independence and territorial integrity should be guaranteed by international covenant." Who should have known, other than William Bullitt, that it would sow the seeds of so much bitterness after 1919?

The Berlin-to-Warsaw Express: *crossing the Oder*

FOR REASONS NEVER EXPLAINED, my Berlin-to-Warsaw express train started only at Lichtenberg Station, one of the main stations in the former East Berlin, and left half an hour late, not exactly a model for German efficiency. Earlier that afternoon I had come to the station, checked my bag, and taken a local bus through a neighborhood of worker housing (where some of the streets were named for the American Great Lakes) to a museum that commemorates the German surrender to the Russian army and the war in the East.

The Karlshorst Museum is located on a suburban side street, and it has a mounted T-34 Russian tank in the side garden. When the Russians invaded Germany in winter 1944-1945, they came with thousands of such tanks, and they breached the defensive line on the Oder River and then crashed into Berlin, which was laid to waste in the senseless struggle for the German capital. The battle cost some 500,000 lives, and it ended with a surrender in the main hall of what had been a school, until the Russian Marshal Georgy Zhukov made it his army headquarters.

Stalin had been incensed that the Germans had surrendered to the Allies in Reims, and he wanted his own ceremony, led by his own marshal. So for the second time in a week, the German high command capitulated, and this time were led away as prisoners of war. Zhukov, celebrated as the leading Russian general of the war, later served as the Soviet proconsul in the nascent East German puppet government.

Although the museum concentrates on the war's end in Eastern Europe, the displays that I found most compelling were those that explained the origins of Hitler's hatred toward the Russians and the Jews. On the first floor I looked at a series of posters, from the 1920s and '30s, condemning Soviet Russia for its links to "an international Jewish conspiracy." One poster shows a Jewish gold merchant being paid coins for having delivered Germany to Communism. Under his arm is the map of Germany, on which is stamped the hammer and sickle. Another poster warns of "Der Bolshewismus," the idea being that international Jewry was in league with the Bolsheviks, and that Germany could not live in peace until both were eliminated.

A short walk from these billboards of hate was the table-sized map of "Ansatz Barbarossa," Operation Barbarossa, the 1941 German invasion of Russia and the Ukraine that condemned so many Jews living in the Pale of Settlement, those lands of sorrow between Poland and Russia. More than the invasions of France and Holland, the attack against the Soviet Union allowed Hitler to articulate his racial theories with armies that stretched along a thousand-mile front.

To get to Warsaw, I had chosen a train that would cross eastern Germany and the Oder River in daylight, as it struck me that so much of European history has played out on this nondescript stretch of prairie farmland. The train, on which I had a window seat in a closed compartment, passed to the south of Seelow Heights, which in 1945 was the scene of the last large infantry battle of World War II. After crossing the Oder, the Russians encircled the Ninth German Army near Seelow, then raped and looted their way into Berlin, sixty miles to the west. Delirious in his Berlin bunker, Hitler had ordered his generals to make a stand on the river. He was sending orders to "armies" that were only the size of divisions. Once the two-million-man Russian army made its moves in mid-April, the German army broke, and only a few formations withdrew to Berlin. Many regiments were cut off and captured. My train passed through forests where in 1945 German stragglers attacked Russian soldiers for their bread and others died of starvation. There was bitter house-to-house fighting in and around Berlin, and 500,000 soldiers and civilians died in the battle. Once the Russians had crossed the Oder, the outcome of the war was never in doubt.

To take a picture of the Oder, I stood in my compartment, as if solemnly marking the occasion, and came away with a grainy image that shows the river, swollen in spring, through the fleeting girders of the train trestle. When his armies were dug along the eastern bank, Stalin formulated the plans that were to change the shape of modern Europe. He decided to deceive the Western Allies—claiming that the target of his offensive was the Elbe and not Berlin—and plotted to encircle Berlin before Eisenhower's forces from the Rhine could get to the German capital. Nothing indicates that Eisenhower had reason to doubt Stalin's objectives. According to the agreed plans, the Allies attacked toward the Elbe and farther south into Bohemia, to thwart the possibility that the German army might try to hole up in the mountains around Salzburg. Closer to Berlin, Eisenhower held back his troops from taking the city, and that left Stalin with a strong voice in postwar Germany, which he chose to leave divided.

Around sundown, the train stopped in Poznan, and then raced through the darkness to Warsaw. At this point in the journey, I was interested to see where, in September 1939, the German army had launched its blitzkrieg and overwhelmed the Polish defenses in a matter of days. In my mind, I had assumed that in those years the German-Polish border was a vertical north-south line, perpendicular to the Baltic Coast. Later, when I bought a map showing the 1939 Polish frontiers, I saw that even after Versailles, Germany had long borders with Poland in the southwest, west, and north of the latter country. When Hitler unleashed his panzers in 1939, they came at the Poles in nearly all directions. The attack ended with the fall of Warsaw and the closing of what was known as the Kutno Pocket, a concentration of Polish forces near Warsaw. What sealed Poland's fate was shown in another photograph that I had seen in the Karlshorst Museum, that of a smiling Stalin shaking the hand of Germany's foreign minister, Joachim von Ribbentrop, in 1939, on the occasion of the German-Russian Non-Aggression Pact. That treaty allowed Stalin to march west while Hitler was attacking east. In little more than a month, independent Poland, founded in 1919 at Versailles, ceased to exist.

The main Warsaw railroad station still feels like it's shunting trains behind the Iron Curtain. A large modern box, as if to pay tribute to Stalin the architect, it has a cavernous waiting hall and then subterranean warrens filled with sandwich shops and kebab outlets. It did not feel sinister so much as out-of-date, something that would have been East European vanguard in 1972, when construction began. I learned later that the shoddy workmanship had much to do with rush orders put out to coincide with a 1975 visit to Warsaw by Soviet First Secretary Leonid Brezhnev, and plans have circulated for a while to build a new station.

At one time Poland had three national railroads, which, like the country itself, took identities from Germany, Russia, and Central Europe. During the Russian invasion of Germany, the Red Army laid a Russian-gauge line from the Vistula to the Oder, mirroring a recent initiative of Russian Railways, to build a broad-gauge line to Vienna. Russian tracks are five feet wide, as opposed to standard gauge of 4 feet, 8.5 inches. Trains that cross from Poland into the former Soviet Union need to be jacked up and equipped with wider axles.

I changed money—Poland is part of the European Union, but has its own currency—and then stared at a map in the half light, trying to get my bearings as to where I would be spending the night. On an Internet website, I had located a Warsaw bed-and-breakfast that I thought would be across the street from the station. When I started walking, I realized that the scale of my Warsaw map was more suitable to a globe, and I hailed a taxi to take me to an adjacent neighborhood, which was turning white in a late-winter snowstorm. The driver dropped me on a side street, and I walked up several dark flights of stairs to an apartment, which was doubling as the bed-and-breakfast. Either because I had a view of snow falling on the street or because my room had everything I could want—Internet, mineral water, a desk, and shower—I felt at home there, and passed the rest of the evening answering emails and listening to the news on the BBC.

Remembering Communist Poland: *biking in 1986*

MY FIRST VISIT TO POLAND came in autumn 1986, when my wife and I decided to ride our bikes around the country. Then Poland was Communist, the president was Wojciech Jaruzelski, a military strongman, and Lech Walesa was still working at the Gdansk shipyard. We had decided on Poland for a bike trip after reading Aleksandr Solzhenitsyn's *August 1914*, a fictional account of the World War I battle near Tannenberg, in the Masurian Lakes region. We had a number of friends in New York who had Polish relatives, and they had encouraged the journey, which struck non-

Polish friends as mad. Nevertheless, together with our bikes, we flew from New York to Warsaw, and toured a city that had few cars and even fewer tourists. We met ancestors of the great Polish writer Joseph Conrad, looked for the remains of the Warsaw ghetto, had warm dinners in the homes of Solidarity members, and tried to recreate, in our minds, what happened during the Warsaw Uprising, when in 1944 the Poles had tried to break the German occupation, and failed.

In 1986, Warsaw was a broken city. The old town, destroyed in the war and the Uprising, had been rebuilt, and the city had its elegant parks and graceful boulevards. Power shortages kept the streets dark at night, hot water was spotty, and there were few restaurants, even on Nowy Swiat, Warsaw's most elegant address.

Even in those dark days it was a great pleasure to bike around Warsaw, a flat city with wide boulevards. We found the Jewish cemetery, outside the main part of the city, but failed in any way to connect with the ghetto, which the Germans destroyed in house-to-house fighting in 1943. To me it lives in the photographs of Roman Vishniac, who captured that vanished world in the thousands of pictures he took in the 1930s on journeys around the ghettoes and shtetls of Eastern European. He was living in Berlin, and traveled with his camera, taking portraits of everyday life in the Pale. His main interest was street scenes—peddlers with their carts, children leaving school, etc. Although most of his pictures were lost in the Holocaust, a number of negatives were smuggled out of occupied Europe, by way of Cuba, and are now preserved at museums in New York. In 1986, his photographs were the only glimpse that we had of what was lost in the ghetto's destruction. Prewar Poland had three million Jews. In 1986, the number was down to about 6,000. The area that had been the ghetto had high-rise worker housing and drab shops. I remember checking and rechecking both a current and an old map, finding it hard to believe that nothing from the ghetto would have survived. Nothing did, although I am told now that a monument has been erected in its general vicinity.

The most ambitious moment of the bike trip came in Gdansk, the home of Lech Walesa and Solidarity, which started around the Polish shipyards. We had taken a train to the former "Free City" and biked out to Westerplatte, the spit of land where the first shots of World War II were fired by a German battleship, *Schleswig-Holstein*, at a Polish garrison in the harbor. Then we hit upon the idea of riding to the Gdansk shipyard and sitting near the front gate. Our aim was shake Walesa's hand when he left work at noon. Friends had told us it was possible that we would meet him, and that he might take heart to hear English spoken to him, given all the recent crackdowns that the government had aimed at the union movement. (It was only in 1989 that the military regime fell and Poland started to enjoy a new birth of freedom.)

Just before noon we found the main gate of the shipyard, locked our bikes to a rack, and waited for Walesa. We missed him. About a thousand other Polish ship workers, looking almost identical to Walesa, with his trademark walrus mustache and frumpy appearance, poured out of the gate. Leaving work, the parade of identical workers, in our minds anyway, confirmed that Solidarity was not the creation of one man, but the work of thousands, many of whom went past us in their overalls and blue industrial jackets. We were disappointed not to have recognized him, but, in other ways, it was thrilling to discover that Walesa was Everyman.

Warsaw Rising and Falling: *another Polish partition*

DURING MY RECENT STAY IN WARSAW I had limited ambitions. I wanted to visit the new Warsaw Rising Museum, dedicated to the 1944 revolt, and I wanted to find the house where Joseph Conrad had lived when he was in Warsaw. In the end, the weather did not cooperate with my plans for excursions. I found myself walking around in a mixture of sun, sleet, and snow, and Warsaw's sidewalks, despite all the improvements, still have the uneven qualities of a country road. By the time I found the Rising Museum, a mile or so from the main train station, my socks and feet were damp, and I had my hood pulled up over my head.

Although the new Warsaw Rising Museum is now the most popular in the city, and its layout through a number of old industrial buildings is in keeping with the best in architectural design, I often found it confusing. I had a map, and before entering I knew the outline of the story well: In August and September 1944, the Polish resistance had risen against the occupying German forces and fought a house-to-house, street-to-street battle to recapture Warsaw. Although the resistance fought with homemade weapons and used cellars and abandoned houses for shelter, it took many German casualties and had the chance, if resupplied, to succeed. Stalin, however, held his armies on the east bank of the Vistula River, which runs north-south through Warsaw, and the German counterattacks against the resistance proved too much. After two months of fighting, the Polish underground army was crushed and marched out of the city as prisoners, to the fate that awaited them in the concentration camps. Only after the Germans had put down the rebellion did the Russian armies attack west and capture Warsaw. As in 1939, the Germans and Russians again were partitioning Poland.

Just because I found the museum confusing does not mean the story it tells isn't eloquent or accurate. The exhibits, showing how the resistance fought and lived through the siege, unfold in darkened loft spaces throughout the old factories, much the way the resistance army would have lived during 1944. I watched home movies of fighters moving across streets filled with rubble, read the biographies of resistance officers killed by the Germans, and studied maps on the walls that showed the neighborhoods that the uprising initially held. Once I had lost the chronological track of the museum, I found myself wandering back and forth across time, studying display cabinets about the Lublin Committee (Stalin's puppet government) when the street fighting was still undecided.

In the past year I have been to a number of World War II museums—in China, Germany, England, and now Poland—and many reduce the war to a docudrama suitable for a television audience. Many of these exhibitions have political as much as historical agendas. In Nanking, the message is that Asia needs to watch out for resurgent Japanese militarism; in Nuremberg, the point is that the Germans are contrite and apologetic; and in the Warsaw Rising Museum the case is made that the legitimate Polish government comes from the wellsprings of the resistance, not the Stalin organs of the Red Army.

If I had a particular interest in the museum, it was to recreate in my mind the diplomacy of Yalta that led to the Polish partition after World War II. To what extent could a free and independent Poland have emerged from the fighting in World War II? Was it inevitable that, with the Russian army on the ground, the postwar government had to be Communist, dooming Poland to another forty-four years of occupation?

I got to thinking about this question when my daughter took a college course on the origins of the Cold War, and I sent her a few cryptic emails about Russian power politics. (In the words of Stalin, "How many divisions does the Pope have?") In the museum there's an enlarged picture of Roosevelt, Churchill, and Stalin, with the implication that the Poles were sold down the river at Yalta. The storyboards reduce the tragedy to clichés—that Roosevelt was sick; that Churchill was weakened politically; that Stalin was in the catbird seat. The backstory, however, around Poland at Yalta is more complicated.

The irony of World War II is that the British and French went to war to restore Polish independence and, having won the war, delivered the country to the prison yard of the Soviet bloc. Scandalizing public opinion, the Oxford historian A.J.P. Taylor in his book on the origins of the conflict argued that British and French diplomatic incompetence, as much as Hitler's aggression, had caused the war. He argued that the failure of the Allies to make a stand in Czechoslovakia's fortified mountain redoubts doomed Poland, which had little high ground on its thousand-mile border with Germany. He wrote: "The blame can be put on Hitler's nihilism instead of on the faults and failures of European statesmen—faults and failures which their public shared. Human blunders, however, usually do more to share history than human wickedness."

Blunders, as much as Stalin's grabs for power, may also explain Poland's diplomatic failures before and at Yalta, leading to the Cold War partition. For example, during the war the Polish government in London refused all overtures to ally themselves with Russia, despite Churchill's advice that it might secure their eastern front. Nor did they reach any accommodation with the so-called Lublin Committee, Stalin's mouthpiece in the postwar order. Polish diplomacy remained incensed, perhaps correctly, at Stalin's 1939 betrayal, invasion, and later massacre of Poland's officer corps in the Katyn woods. In turn, by the time Stalin arrived at Yalta and Potsdam he had lost his eagerness to deal, and, because Russian troops occupied the country, Poland disappeared behind the Iron Curtain.

Another view of Yalta comes from Curtis Roosevelt, FDR's oldest grandson and a good friend of mine. His mother, Anna, accompanied her father to Yalta, which proved a grueling trip for the ailing president. Especially hard was the long drive, over terrible roads, to Livadia Palace, where the Yalta Conference was held.

The conditions prompted Churchill to remark: "If we had spent ten years on research we could not have found a worse place in the world than Yalta..." When I wrote to Curtis about Poland's losses at Yalta, he wrote back a detailed answer:

> To put it simply—the fate of Eastern Europe after WWII (better than the term Cold War) was pretty well a done thing by the time of Yalta. Look at the notes on the Tolstoy meeting (October 1944, I think) in Moscow between Churchill and Stalin—the U.S. was only an observer—wherein WSC [Churchill] tried to reinstate the traditional diplomatic style of "spheres of influence." Stalin rebuffed him (but later used it to rationalize his refusal to support the Communist uprising in Greece). Stalin knew that the USSR troops would be in place before the end of the war to gain whatever they wanted in Eastern Europe. He didn't need to bargain. The communique issued at Yalta regarding free elections in Eastern Europe was just eye wash, and each of the Big Three knew it—FDR for the Polish vote in the States, Churchill for his Conservative party backbenchers in Parliament, and Stalin just for amusement.

Perhaps the best postscript about the future of Poland came from Churchill, who said of the deal that was struck at Yalta: "This was the best I could get." In many senses Stalin shared the attitudes of Tsar Nicholas I, who is reported to have divided the Poles into two groups: those he hated and those he merely despised.

Versailles Poland: *big, but not strong*

FROM THE RISING MUSEUM I walked back into central Warsaw and found the house on Nowy Swiat, where Joseph Conrad lived briefly. Among the Polish cities, he has a deeper association with

Krakow, and he spent most of his adult writing life in England, befriending the likes of T.E. Lawrence (of Arabia) and Henry James. I cannot profess to have read even half of Conrad's books, but in the ones that I have, what is striking is the complexity of the English and the absence of any references to his native Poland. He was born in what is now Ukraine, in a small town near Kiev, and went to sea in his teens, where, like Herman Melville, several years before the mast gave him material for a lifetime of books. Among my favorites are *Heart of Darkness* (I think of it every time I walk along the Thames, imagining Marlow beginning to tell his tale), *The Secret Sharer* (about the ambiguities of leadership and how our fates can drift on unseen currents), and *Lord Jim* (which plagued me on every summer reading list in grammar school, and thus went unread until I was in my thirties). In Warsaw on a windy late winter day, it is almost impossible to connect the Polish Conrad with his books and their South Seas, just as in a place like Karachi or Penang, it is hard to imagine that the creator of Mr. Kurtz grew up on a fashionable street in bourgeois Warsaw.

From Nowy Swiat I caught a taxi to the main train station and bought a ticket on an afternoon express to Krakow. I would have liked to spend more time in Warsaw, but the late winter weather was raw, with snow showers and a strong wind, and all I wanted to do was read my book, Richard Watt's *Bitter Glory*, a diplomatic history about "Poland and its fate: 1919-1939."

The Warsaw train station was now familiar, but still I had to visit a number of kiosks to assemble lunch for the train. I ended up with coffee, a sandwich, cole slaw, and homemade cakes bought from a woman who might have baked them near the Masurian Lakes. Even though she was indoors, she wore a shawl and weighed the cakes on a scale, as if we were in a rural market.

The train left from a dark platform that had a swarm of travelers, all of whom rushed the train, despite having reservations for the seats. Some habits die hard, and apparently rushing departing trains is one that Poles still enjoy. I found my seat in a compartment that had only one other traveler, a student from Krakow. With room on adjacent seats, I spread out the map I had bought at the museum—one showing Poland's 1939 borders—and brooded about the Treaty of Versailles that drew them, as the train raced across a flatland of isolated farms and desolate forests, the same faceless landscape that for five hundred years has made it so hard to define where Poland begins and ends.

John Maynard Keynes, who was present at the Paris Peace Conference in 1919 and was disgusted with the outcome, remarked that "Poland is an economic impossibility with no industry but Jew-baiting." Watt writes about how Poland, which had not been a country since the late eighteenth century, emerged from Versailles as the sixth largest country in Europe, and one that had more than 3,000 border miles to defend against hostile neighbors. Of the nearby countries, including Germany, Lithuania, Czechoslovakia, and the Soviet Union, only Romania did not bear a grudge against the emergent nation.

Watt describes the lineup of hostility: Germany was furious about the losses in East Prussia, that fact that Danzig was a free city, and over the Polish Corridor, which ran through traditional German lands; Russia, which lost the 1920 Russo-Polish war, resented Poland's eastern borders, its occupation of Lvov (now Lviv), and the terms of the Treaty of Riga, ending the war; Czechoslovakia and Poland feuded over the Duchy of Teschen, southwest of Krakow, which Versailles awarded largely to the Czechs, who thus absorbed a Polish minority and some of the most productive coal mines in the region; Lithuania cut off diplomatic relations with Poland after the Poles took Wilno (now Vilnius) in the Russo-Polish war and refused to give it back to the Lithuanians. Only with Romania—and they shared only a small border—did Poland remain on friendly terms. That hardly mattered when the rest of its neighbors were sworn to Poland's destruction.

As a buffer against this collective hostility, Poland had one diplomatic card, its alliance with France, which saw the Poles as a counterweight to German or Bolshevik expansion. In such a relationship, Poland invested everything. Watt writes: "Poland had only to enter into an alliance with France in order to achieve complete security against its principal enemies." From an Allied perspective, an independent Poland was a linchpin in the collective security arrangements of the Treaty of Versailles and the League of Nations. In 1918, Britain, France, and Italy had declared that "the creation of a united and independent Poland with free access to the sea constitutes one of the conditions of a solid and just peace." At the Versailles conference, when the French foreign minster, Stephen Pichon, was asked what Poland should be like, he answered, "Very big and very strong."

The problem with the French alliance was that not all threats against Poland came just from an expansionist Germany. Poland had difficulties on all its borders, and increasingly that made France reluctant to threaten war, should, for example, the Lithuanians seek redress over Wilno. In 1925, at the Treaty of Locarno, France altered its alliance with Poland, pledging that it would go to war, on behalf of Poland, only if so authorized by the League of Nations. (The headline in the *New York Times* read: "France and Germany Bar War Forever.") Poland's defense rested on the collective will of European nations, few of whom had any interest in future wars. They worked hard to defuse the Polish hair trigger, trip-wired to Paris. In the same vein that year, British Foreign Minister Austen Chamberlain said that "For the Polish Corridor no British government will or can ever risk the bones of a British grenadier." From that point until war broke out in 1939, Poland was on its own and surrounded by enemies.

By Train to Krakow: *the Polish winter*

SEEN FROM A TRAIN CAR WINDOW, rural Poland looks like a landscape painting, perhaps one by the artist Brueghel the Younger. We passed small farms that looked medieval against the snow-covered ground, wisps of chimney smoke, and barnyard animals standing motionless in paddocks. Watt describes one of the problems in independent Poland: Inheritance laws reduced Polish farming to increasingly smaller lots, leading to insufficient yields as the world headed into the Great Depression.

The biggest problem of inter-war Poland was how to position the country for survival. The president, Josef Pilsudski, the hero of the Russo-Polish war and the autocrat of Polish politics, had hoped to create a federation of neighboring countries—almost a United States of Eastern Europe—that might be an effective counterweight against Russian or German aggression. But none of Poland's neighbors wanted to ally themselves with Poland. Nor could the Polish government ever decide whether Germany or Russia was the greater threat. Of nonalignment, Watt writes: "The policy of pursuing 'equilibrium' between its great neighbors proved a failure."

At times the Poles would get closer to either Germany or Russia, but the problem was the many minorities, all nursing grievances, that had been swept into Versailles Poland. The one alliance that might have saved Poland, and perhaps Europe, from the outbreak of war would have been a mutual assistance pact between Poland and Czechoslovakia, backed by Britain and France, or even Russia. That was lost in the Duchy of Teschen, through which later that day my train would be traveling.

After the Munich capitulations and after Hitler moved his troops into the Sudetenland, Poland used the moment to recapture its lost territory in Teschen. Watt recalls: "The Poles were determined that they should obtain concessions from Czechoslovakia

84

identical to those extracted by the Germans." (The Czech general who surrendered Teschen remarked that, before long, the Poles would be turning it over the Germans.) While the rest of Europe did nothing, the Poles marched troops into Teschen, ending any chance of a *rapprochement* with the Czechs, something that would haunt Poland during the desperate search for allies after the German-Russian Non-Aggression Pact of 1939.[1]

At least by that point Poland had assurances from Britain that it would come to its defense, if the Poles were attacked. Watt writes: "For Britain to give such a blank check to a Central European nation, particularly to Poland—a nation that Britain had generally regarded as irresponsible and greedy—was mind-boggling." The British had chosen not to defend Czechoslovakia, with its Maginot-like line of fortresses along the German border. Instead it threw its lot in with the Poles, who had 3,000 miles of borderlands, most of which were ideal for tank attacks. Watt is sympathetic to the aspirations of independent Poland, its balancing acts in a dangerous world of nearby tyrannies. But he feels that the Poles, when Germany and Russia were weak after World War I, had reached too far for territory. He concludes: "An ethically homogenous Poland would have had a lot fewer problems to solve."

Auschwitz Remembered: *the voice of Primo Levi*

ALTHOUGH IT WAS ALMOST the first day of spring, I arrived in Krakow during a cold soaking rain, the kind that instantly gets

---

1   In Alan Furst's historical novel *The Spies of Warsaw*, set in prewar Poland, a French diplomat tells a Polish counterpart: "If the worst happens and it starts again, you must be prepared to stand alone. A map of Europe tells the story. It's that, or alliance with Russia—which we favor but Poland will never do—or alliance with Germany, which we certainly don't favor, and you won't do that either."

into your shoes and socks. I had not recalled the station from my wife and my 1986 travels, when we took a night train directly from Gdansk and arrived just after daylight. The father of a friend had come to pick us up, but he had not anticipated or imagined that two Americans would show up with bicycles, and there was no room for them in his tiny Eastern European car. Instead he drove at a slow speed, like the pace car at the start of a bike race, and we rode behind, as he navigated the old streets of medieval Krakow.

On this 2010 trip to Krakow, I first had to collect my ticket for the overnight sleeper to Budapest. The agency had sent it to me care of the station post office, and I had complicated directions explaining how to find the correct window. In the rain I made a few wrong turns, but finally lined up at the post office and collected an express envelope, in which I found, perfectly in order, my ticket for the night train. For me, a lovely byproduct of the Internet era has been the ease with which it is now possible to buy night train tickets in foreign lands. In earlier eras, I had to hope that I could buy the tickets on arrival at the station, often on the day that I wanted to travel. It led to many disappointments, especially if the agent said that the train was full. Now thanks to the incomparable the Man in Seat Sixty-One web site, I can find links ahead of time to all sorts of railroad ticket brokers, national companies, or tour operators. The site has opened up night trains in China, Russia, Romania, Malaysia, and now Poland. After dinner in Krakow, I was heading overnight to Budapest.

In Krakow I hoped to connect with Henryk Wozniakowski, the editor-in-chief of one of the largest publishing houses in Poland. In 1986 my wife and I had met him in New York, before we had gone to Poland. On that trip, after arriving in Krakow, we had called him, and he had taken us around Krakow and to nearby Auschwitz (called Oswiecim in Polish). In the 1980s, Auschwitz was desolate, only a museum and memorial in a few places. The rest was not much different from when the Russians had liberated the camp. We walked around as if we had stumbled across a ghost town in the American West. I remember seeing no other tourists. We walked a long way along the tracks that entered through a main gate and terminated, in many senses of the word, not far from the camp's wooden barracks.

On that first trip, we were reading the memoirs of Primo Levi, and I still recall his description of his arrest in Italy, his rail odyssey across Central Europe, and his fate in the shadows of death. Although hundreds of thousands died in the Auschwitz crematoria—in 1986 they looked like abandoned swimming pools in a dark underworld. Levi survived as one of many slave laborers sent to a nearby rubber factory around the town of Monowitz. In January 1945 an illness had him confined to the camp, and that spared him the death march when the Germans, together with many prisoners, fled the approaching Russian army.

Until planning for Poland, my wife and I had never read Primo Levi. Before and after our trip, we read a number of his books. Less than a year after we were back, I remember how stunned I was to hear that he had committed suicide. At his home in Turin, Italy, he had thrown himself down a stairwell. Until that moment I had thought that his was a voice of fortitude and hope. Then I realized that the inspiring courage of his writing was more like one of painter Edvard Munch's screams of desperation.

Since 1986, I had seen Henryk Wozniakowski only once, in 2000, when I was passing through Warsaw and his publishing house was hosting a talk by the historian and *Guardian* columnist Timothy Garton Ash. I had been invited to attend the lecture, and remember how impressed I was that Garton Ash had been able to do much of his talk in fluent and confident Polish. He had spoken about the intellectual origins of Solidarity, and how that movement (Catholic, laborite, anti-Communist) had shaped the political parties that emerged in the post-Berlin Wall countries of Eastern Europe, which were racing to integrate with the rest of Europe. Already in 2000, Warsaw looked like a modern European city. In 1986, it had felt like a city that had yet to come in from the cold, and the half-lit streets were redolent of burning coal. Fourteen years later it had rooftop neon advertising signs, Mercedes taxis, and smart restaurants and cafés.

After Garton Ash spoke, many in the audience walked to the apartment of Wozniakowski's sister, who gave an elegant buffet dinner party in honor of the writer. I was a bit awed by the cosmopolitan air of the gathering (Polish ministers, editors, lawyers, and artists, all elegantly dressed), and recall that I ate dinner with some of the children present, as they were attending an American school and spoke to me in unaccented English. Afterwards when I left, I was in the company of the government's economics minister, and we stood together for a long time, hoping to catch a taxi. Around that time, Poland had applied to join the European Union, but at the last minute the application had been deferred, prompting the minister to vent some frustration as we stood under a street lamp. I made sympathetic small talk in response, confident that soon Poland would be part of Europe. Mostly what I remembered was 1986, when we got back from Poland and someone asked my wife what there was in Polish stores. She answered, "Apples."

An Evening Drink in Krakow: *'every day is wonderful'*

ON THIS OCCASION Henryk Wozniakowski found me in a Krakow cafe, where I had come in from the rain. Not just my socks, but my shoes and pants were soaked, and I had my jacket drying on a nearby chair, as sailors do with their gear when they come off watch. That afternoon Henryk had been a judge on a panel that was awarding a literary prize, and he had not been sure how long it would last. I thought maybe I would see him only briefly at 8 p.m., before my train left. But we were together by 6 p.m., and during a break in the rain we walked to another bar, which had an arching indoor solarium, set in what earlier might have been a small old-town garden. As we walked, Henryk pointed to a church, easily four hundred years old, with a façade that evokes so much about the historic center of Krakow, and said: "I was baptized in that church. It's very special."

The way he said it recalled his deep connection to old Krakow, the Catholic Church, and the printed word, and it reminded me that his publishing house had been among the most daring, in the era of Solidarity, in bringing out books that made the links between the Church and Poland's new birth of freedom. During the 1980s the Catholic Church could easily have sided with the established order of martial law, but many of its priests, such as Father Jerzy Popieluszko—later killed by the secret police—had spoken eloquently about the need for political freedom, and Henryk had published many of their testaments. For many in Poland, the breaking point with the communist regime had been the attempted assassination of Pope John Paul II, who, when he had been the archbishop in Krakow's Wavel Castle, had been known as Karol Jozef Wojtyla, a native son who was eighteen years old in 1938 when he moved to the city.

Over two glasses of beer, Henryk and I talked about books and authors, about our families, and mostly about the changes in Poland. I was curious to hear about Lech Walesa and how he was regarded in modern Polish politics. Since leaving the presidency, Walesa had served on a number of foundations and charities, but he had also been dogged by the suggestion that, as a young ship worker, he had collaborated with the secret police. He had even sued President Lech Kaczynski over the insinuation. Walesa had not been the most popular of presidents, and often his manner was thought to be brusque. Henryk made the point that for Walesa's role in Solidarity his legacy was assured, even if now, at age 67, he was something of a marginal political figure. He was sympathetic with Walesa over the allegation that he might have once cooperated with the security services. He said such an allegation must be examined in the context of the era, which was 1970, when Poland was firmly in the grip of a repressive regime. Walesa was a twenty-seven-year-old shipyard worker, and its possible (although the courts have exonerated him) that security agents might have coerced him into cooperation.

More poignantly, Henryk described his own detention in the 1980s by the security apparatus, and how hard the agents had threatened him to sign documents, to inform on friends, to confess to something, even things about which he knew nothing. He had been picked up for questioning because of his publishing activities and taken to a station house, where for hours the agents had told him that, to gain his freedom, all he had to do was sign a few papers. Henryk refused, and he knew that his family's influential friends would be working hard to get him released. Hour upon hour the police asked the same relentless questions. Thirty years later I could tell that the experience had been searing. When I asked him how he had survived it, he explained that his father, who founded the publishing house, had often talked about how friends had overcome a detention, and he knew that what was most important was to refuse to sign anything. Now he wondered if Walesa, not the son of a prominent publisher, would have had the preparation to withstand such an assault. Even during the worst of the interrogation, Henryk had the belief that he could hold out until pressure was brought to have him released. He was among the lucky ones, and many in his situation vanished without a trace. That good fortune explained another answer he gave while we were talking. I asked how life was now in Poland, and he said: "You have to remember, I grew up and spent much of my adult life living under a repressive Communist government. So now every day is wonderful."

Once More to the Katyn Woods: *crimes of war and peace*

IN THE MAIN SQUARE of old Krakow, a space that evokes Teutonic Knights, Polish kings, cobblestoned history, and the Central Europe that largely vanished in the world wars, I said good-bye to Henryk. He was headed home to dinner, and I had my train to catch. It was only after our visit that the plane, carrying much of the Polish government, crashed in the fog near the Katyn woods, killing President Kaczynski and many of his senior advisors. When it happened, I wrote to Henryk, wondering if he had known any of those who were on the doomed flight. He responded: "Yes, I had a few friends in the plane. One of them, Janusz Krupski, chief of the office of veterans and victims of repressions, left his wife and seven children. The state will stand the loss of personnel, but the families are wounded forever."

I found the tragedy haunting, given the importance of Katyn in the memory of the Polish nation. To put it in perspective, imagine much of the American government, on its way to a reconciliation meeting with Japan after World War II, dying in a plane crash at Pearl Harbor. At Katyn, which is outside the Russian city of Smolensk, the cream of the Polish officer corps was murdered in 1940 on Stalin's order. They had been taken prisoner after the 1939 partition of Poland and sent to camps within Russia. Almost worse for the Polish nation was the fact that for fifty years, even though the general facts in the tragedy were known, Britain and other Western allies refused to probe for the truth in the matter—fearful that it would rupture relations with Soviet Russia. Even the government of President Lech Walesa had trod softly around the Katyn graves and had not pushed to bring war-crimes charges against surviving Russian officials who bore responsibility. Others were less forgiving. The 2010 memorial service between President Kaczynski and Russian Prime Minister Vladimir Putin was arranged to bury the ghosts of Katyn between the two countries, and might have succeeded, had not the Polish president's plane crashed in the fog and added more victims to the tragedy. I still find the events around Katyn, past and present, worthy of a Shakespearean drama.

I first heard the story of Katyn in 1975, when I was taking a course in Vienna about the political history of Eastern Europe. The professor, Max Peyfuss, told the class of American foreign students about the massacre, and how it prevented a reconciliation between Poland and Russia. After the semester ended, he organized a student trip to Russia for members of the class. Although the schedule had called for visits to Moscow and Leningrad, the Intourist hotel reservations were lost in translation. Instead of bright lights near the Kremlin, we were shunted on night trains around western Russia.

During our wanderings—no hardship in high summer—we spent three days in Smolensk. Alas, the regional city, beyond a visit to the Napoleonic sites, did not hold much appeal for American college students, and one day we went in the countryside, to swim in a lake. It was a glorious day in June, and we lay in high grass and swam in a pond. During that afternoon, the guide mentioned to me, quietly and in passing, that the Katyn woods were nearby, but that it was a subject best left unexplored.

A few years later, I became friends with Lord Nicholas Bethell, the British historian and member of the House of Lords, who had written extensively to keep alive the memory of Katyn, even when his own government wished that it would remain in eclipse. At one of our early lunches, he told me about his work to have a memorial to the tragedy erected in London and how British politicians, notably Anthony Eden, had for years implied that the massacre was the work of the Nazis, and not the Soviet government. In his memoirs, Bethell writes:

> The horror of Katyn is thrust upon anyone who knows Poland and its people. It encapsulates the nation's feelings of outrage at fifty years of cruel foreign occupation, Nazi German and Soviet Russian. The story was told to me in every detail during my visits there in the 1960s, researching my biography of Wladyslaw Gomulka. It was Russia's great crime against Poland, something that could never be forgotten.... It was the touchstone of the Polish predicament, the most vivid example of their ill-treatment at the hands of their eastern neighbor. It symbolized their long service as Russia's satellite and their betrayals by Britain during and after the war. It showed how Soviet Russia had decapitated and subjugated their entire nation—and how no one, not even their British allies who had guaranteed their integrity in March 1939, had seemed anxious to care about it.

After the plane of the Polish president crashed on its way to the remembrance ceremony, a number of commentators spoke about how Russia, and in particular Vladimir Putin, had responded with empathy, over both the loss of the president and in trying to face up to the earlier crimes at Katyn. Like everyone, I wanted to believe that the new tragedy, if it showed a compassionate Russia, might heal the older wounds. My fear, however, is as Shakespeare wrote, that there is "a tide in the affairs of men," and around Katyn it always seems to ebb. In *Julius Caesar*, he has Marc Antony grieve:

> *And Caesar's spirit, raging for revenge,*
> *With Ate by his side come hot from hell,*
> *Shall in these confines with a monarch's voice*

Cry "Havoc!" and let slip the dogs of war,
That this foul deed shall smell above the earth
With carrion men, groaning for burial.

The Night Train from Krakow to Budapest: *more corridors*

As I HAD SEVERAL HOURS before the train left at 10:30 p.m., I decided to walk to what had been the Jewish quarter of Krakow, which was now, according to Henryk, lined with trendy restaurants. On the way, during a brief rain shower, I huddled in an open bookstore and drifted into the antique map collection, which showed how Poland had come and gone through history. One map had the so-called "Congress Poland," the rump state that emerged from the Congress of Vienna.[2] Another showed the combined kingdoms of Poland and Lithuania, which in the fourteenth century had been the largest nation in Europe. On many of the historical European maps, however, Poland was simply a duchy or an ideal.

Perhaps the most amazing outcome of World War II, when Poland was steamrollered from several directions, was that it emerged as a modern nation, even if it had Soviet overlords. Maybe Yalta did succeed in saving the Poles? For better or for worse, the maps of 1945 and 2010 look surprisingly like that of 1939, which led to so many conflicts. The difference now is that since World

---

2   Throughout history, whenever peace conferences have allotted new lands to Poland, they have come at the expense of Germany, Austria, and Russia, who are then determined to recapture what had been lost. At the Congress of Vienna in 1815, as at Versailles in 1919, Poland's enlargement—to serve as a buffer against Russian and German expansion—sowed the seeds of future wars. According to Harold Nicholson, at the Congress of Vienna British Foreign Minister Lord Castlereagh believed "that the establishment of a large Poland would be only beneficial to Europe provided three essential conditions were fulfilled. In the first place Poland must be absolutely independent. In the second place she must be strong enough to maintain that independence. And in the third place the enlargement of Poland must not entail undue compensations to Austria or Prussia." That configuration was no more successful in Vienna than it was later at Versailles.

War II ethnic Germans have been purged from East Prussia, the Polish Corridor, Gdansk (Danzig), and Wroclaw (the once German city of Breslau). Similarly, the Poles in places like Lviv (the former Lvov) are no more. Ethnic cleansing is a long-established European tradition, and not just in Poland.

Had I been organizing a night out with friends, I would have chosen any of the restaurants in the Jewish quarter, which has narrow, attractive streets, many of them at odd angles, recalling an Isaac Singer short story. They all looked warm and inviting, and my socks were still damp. Often when traveling I find it depressing to eat alone in a restaurant (many friends love it, I know). Despite the choices in this renaissance neighborhood, I preferred to walk back to the station and to eat a picnic in my train compartment, where I could change my wet clothes, drink a beer, and take in the atmosphere of a night train, among my happiest experiences.

The main station in Krakow is divided into two parts, not unlike Polish history. There's the old main station, which dates to a period when Krakow was a city of the Austro-Hungarian Empire (until the Little Treaty of Versailles gave it to Poland in 1919), and the newer, Communist-era platforms that might well have been footnotes in a five-year plan. In front of the old station is a statue in honor of President József Pilsudski. Watt writes of Pilsudski's government that "It was neither totalitarian nor fascist, but it was certainly authoritarian. It was not notably efficient, but it did enjoy the general support of the Polish people, who had never known any better system."

Inside the main concourse there were a few kiosks selling water and candy. I retrieved my luggage from the consignment room and carried my patchwork picnic to the train that, on its doors, showed the route of the train from Krakow to Oswiecim (Auschwitz in German), Bratislava, and finally Budapest. I was sorry that I would be going through the Duchy of Teschen in darkness. At least I had in mind words that British Prime Minister David Lloyd George had spoken, fatefully in retrospect, to parliament: "How many members have ever heard of Teschen? I do not mind saying that I have not."

I settled into my train compartment, which I had to myself, by unpacking my bag and arranging my books, as if setting up the train library. The train left on time, but I was still awake an hour later, with the lights turned off, when we stopped at Oswiecim, along a platform forlorn in the half light. Before World War II, it had been an important rail hub, linking lines from the east, west, and south, and the reason the Germans chose it for genocidal importance was because it could handle many trains. Now it looked forgotten. On this evening, no one got on or off at the ghostly station, which I took to be another hopeful sign for Poland's future.

Across Romania to Transnistria

My first visit to Romania came in spring 1975, when my father and younger sister came to visit me in Vienna, where I was studying as part of my junior year abroad. In those years, while locked behind the Iron Curtain, Romania had aspirations to do business with the West, and my father had cultivated connections in the wholesale paper bag business, the kind used in the shipment of sugar and cement. Before heading east, the three of us spent several days together in Vienna. Toward the end of the week, we rode the train to Budapest, spent the day among the many museums, and then after dinner headed to Keleti Station, where we were to catch the night train to Bucharest.

Although I had been to Yugoslavia on a family vacation in 1970, this night train was my first journey to the far side of the Iron Curtain. On an earlier weekend in Vienna, I had tried to ride the train from Austria to Hungary, but was turned away for lack of a visa—someone had told me, incorrectly, that they were issued at the border.

Although now it is at the center of a reunited Europe, in those darker days Vienna was a cul-de-sac of the Cold War, the end of the lines that began in London, Paris or Zurich. The Russian occupation of Vienna had ended formally in 1955, and twenty years later the city still had the feel that it had yet to come in from the cold. My student room was heated with a coal furnace, and my classes were held in a palace that had been attached to the Hapsburg court. Because of the losses in the first and second world wars, the city's population was tilted toward widowhood, and a common sight on the sidewalk was an older woman, dressed warmly in a Loden coat, leading a small dog on a leash. Sometimes I saw these women sipping afternoon tea in one of the city's many cafés, where I would go after classes to meet my friends or read the newspapers. I was drawn to Vienna for its history and because I thought it might be a springboard to Eastern Europe, although until my father arrived with rail tickets and I had figured out the visa application forms, the Hapsburg lands of the East were as remote as Lenin's Finland Station in St. Petersburg.

By Train to Romania: *spring of 1975*

AMONG THE COURSES that I took that spring was one from a professor named Max Peyfuss, who gave a seminar that overlapped the disciplines of literature and history. His subject was the politics of Eastern Europe, and for case studies and narratives he selected books that had been published only in the underground. We read authors such as Aleksandr Solzhenitsyn and Boris Pasternak. More often than not, the assigned reading was a grainy manuscript that looked as though it had been copied with a spy camera.

Along with his teaching duties, Professor Peyfuss was the co-editor of a literary magazine that collected stories from the Eastern European underground. During classes he would often interrupt his lectures to describe a furtive trip to Prague or Krakow, and how he had returned with a short story hidden in the false bottom of his suitcase. He had particular admiration for Solzhenitsyn, who the year before had been deported to the West and whose account of the Gulag was then being published in translation. Only in their underground literature were Eastern Europe and Russia democratic and free, and it was in this republic of letters that Peyfuss encouraged his students to travel. Although I don't recall talking with him about our trip to Bucharest, I am sure that I did and I am sure he recommended a dimly lit café or bookshop for us to visit.

After dinner in Budapest in a restaurant that looked down from the Buda hills on the Danube, my father, sister, and I arrived early at the station and huddled our luggage on the platform from which the train was announced to depart. My sister was thirteen and curious about the world. As we waited on the platform, the conversation shifted to my father's experiences, when he was in college, to what was called "riding the blind." Like hopping freight trains, riding the blind involved climbing on board a moving train and riding in the space between the coal tender and the first or "blind" baggage car. During the Great Depression, everyone from hoboes and drifters to Ivy League college students (in my father's case) rode the blind. After graduation, my father and his close friend Bob Lubar (who later became managing editor of *Fortune* magazine) rode the blind from New York to California. These memories of the blind, alive in our conversation on the platform in Keleti Station, prompted my father to teach his children how to board a moving train. As the station had many trains coming and going before ours departed for Bucharest, we took turns practicing on the Hungarian trains that were shunting around the station, which amused us, and no doubt some bemused Hungarian travelers who were waiting to board the overnight express.

Our compartment on the train, which we boarded while it stood still in the station, had only two berths. My sister slept on the floor, so that we would be together through the night. We had been warned that the border crossing between Hungary and Romania was severe, and expected that our luggage would be searched and our passports scrutinized. Nor were we to carry in any currency other than travelers' checks or U.S. dollars, as Romania and Hungary, in those days, had strict laws on the circulation of their money.

The border crossing came sometime in the middle of the night. True to form, the guards had a menacing look, although they processed our visas and had a look through our luggage without ever figuring out that the lump on the floor, fast asleep, was my sister. Sometime after 5 a.m. the train stopped in Brasov, one of the cities of the Transylvania region. All I recall now is that the platform was encased in a thick fog. We were eating breakfast when we went through Ploesti, about an hour north of Bucharest. I had never heard of the city, but my father spoke for a long time about air raids during World War II that had targeted its oil storage. Adolf Hitler had, in part, fueled his Reich with Romanian crude oil, pumped out of the ground around Ploesti, and the Allies had sent waves of bombers, many of which were shot down, to attack its refineries. His account turned a morning station stop into a battlefield tour.

In 1975 Bucharest had only a few hotels that would allow foreigners. One was an InterContinental, housed in the city's only high-rise building. The other was the Athenée Palace, where we stayed. It was located on the city's main square, but seemed unchanged from the 1930s when Bucharest had the reputation as "the Paris of the East." The hotel furniture was threadbare, and the lighting somber, as though the lobby were a funeral home. I recall the many forms that were required before we were given our key, and how the rooms looked as though they had hosted delegates to many five-year plans.

Because we were in the shade of the Iron Curtain, whenever we talked about my father's business or the stories I was reading for Professor Peyfuss, we would run water in the bathroom and point to the chandeliers, as few Americans in those years, other than Richard Nixon, were interested in doing business in Romania. Eager for a friend in the world, especially after Watergate, President Nixon had cozied up to Romania's party boss and president, Nicolae Ceaușescu, who in turn had distanced himself from the Soviet Union, at least in encouraging trade with the United States. Nixon had granted Romania what was then called "most favored nation" status, meaning that American tariffs on Romanian goods were preferential. No doubt this lull in the Cold War explained why my father was trying to import Romanian paper bags into the world market. Before leaving office, Nixon made a last-hurrah journey to Bucharest, and Ceaușescu obliged his friend by ordering thousands of people into the streets of the capital to celebrate the U.S. president's arrival, although Romania's jubilation did little to make Americans forget about Watergate. I am sure, however, it explained our visit.

Bucharest in the 1970s had more in common with the socialist East than with Paris, although many of the older buildings evoked a bourgeois elegance that was unusual in a Communist country. The buildings in the old city and those around the university gave an otherwise somber Bucharest the hint of an elegant past. To get around we walked and took taxis, but I remember that we were unable to find a restaurant for dinner, except for a smoky bar where everyone ate sausages standing up. On our walks we would often pass the presidential palace and other ministries, but guards were posted everywhere to shunt pedestrians in other directions or to discourage loitering and pictures. Ceaușescu had yet to build the palace for which he is remembered—a building on the scale of the Pentagon—and ran his government from downtown Bucharest. I don't recall that my sister and I went with my father to the paper-bag ministry. His meetings lasted a day or two, after which we had decided to take the train to the Black Sea resort of Constanza. Although he had never been there, my father had talked it up as

Romania's Miami Beach, and the journey was given the air of a family holiday, the children's reward for jumping moving trains in Budapest and eating standing up in Bucharest.

The Morning Train to Constanza: *taken for a ride*

INCREDIBLE AS IT NOW SEEMS in memory, for our trip to Constanza we were joined by my sisters' godmother, Marjorie Stauffer, who was in her mid-seventies. She had worked with my mother in the 1940s and remained a close family friend. She had never married, but during the 1930s had lived in what she called Peiping, now Beijing. As we were growing up, she had an air of internationalism that I am sure all of us later sought to imitate. In college I had stayed at her apartment in San Francisco, and it was decorated with objects from her travels, especially in China. I recall many small teapots and birdcages. Although the details are now lost to me, I think she was in London or Paris when she heard that the three of us were taking the train to Bucharest and Constanza. At the last minute, she decided to join the expedition. None of us were surprised, although I think we wondered how her elegant bearing would mix with Ceaușescu's Romania.

I was waiting in the lobby of the Athenée Palace for her taxi to arrive from the airport. The first I knew she had arrived was when she came through the hotel front doors in what English novels would have called "a fright." Her luggage was still in the car, and the driver was chasing after her, waving his arms. As the story later unfolded—over several glasses of nerve-calming Romanian brandy—she had decided that the driver wanted to settle the fare with romantic favors, and that had prompted her to sacrifice her luggage, as opposed to her body. During the uproar, I had retrieved her bags from the car and seen off the driver, with the help of the doorman, who assured me that the driver had only wanted to be paid in dollars, nothing more. Apparently something in his sign language had gotten lost in translation.

When all of us left for Constanza, it was aboard a 7 a.m. train. To have breakfast, we sat in the diner, surrounded by more bottles of Romanian brandy, which at the tables around us flowed like orange juice. The diner lacked the holiday air of the *East Coast Champion* (a once popular train to Miami) and felt more like a labor convention, with men in somber suits smoking, talking, and eating. The train ride took about four hours. At some point during the morning we crossed the Danube, which flows into the Black Sea in a series of tributaries north of Constanza. Because it was a gray March morning, more winter than spring, Constanza appeared as the end of the line. All it shared with Miami was a series of high-rise hotels and apartment buildings, although these had the drabness of George Orwell's *1984* more than the Art Deco trimmings of South Beach. I had never before seen a worker's paradise, and this one, along with the rows of anonymous buildings, had a working port next to the vacation homes. Think of Norfolk with a Black Sea beach. We checked into a hotel that could easily have entertained thousands of vacationing Romanians and spent the next few days gazing at the Black Sea, which in the March gloom seemed well matched to its name. In subsequent years my father was reminded of Constanza whenever he would bring up other destinations for family vacations that involved the word "paradise."

Return to Bucharest: *an imaginative whirlpool*

MY NEXT TRIP TO BUCHAREST came thirty years later, when I was living in Geneva and was given an introduction to a Romanian businessman, alas, in real estate, not paper bags. He was looking for foreign investors, and it interested me to dig into the Romanian economy, to see how far it had come since my father, my sister,

Aunt Marge, and I had flown from Constanza to Bucharest and Vienna. Those flights became memorable when immigration officers at the main Bucharest terminal searched all of us at gunpoint, in sequestered little areas, like changing rooms in a department store. They were not looking for anything in particular, and we had nothing to hide, as Romanian shops had yielded up only a tablecloth and some napkins.

In 2005, the Bucharest airport felt like many around Europe, and I was relieved not to be strip-searched on arrival. I found a hotel in the downtown area, although for several days I felt like the only guest. I met my business connection for a long lunch in the courtyard of the Athenée Palace, which since the 1970s had been renovated and was now part of the Hilton chain. No longer were guests treated like spies (or anxious matrons) coming in from the cold. Hilton had transformed the hotel so that it looked like its counterparts in Buffalo and Copenhagen. On the menu of the courtyard café were such local Romanian dishes as club sandwiches, American beer, and hamburgers. At least in a culinary sense, ketchup had ended the Cold War.

Although his goal was to sell me an office building, my business friend painted a picture of the Romanian economy that was encouraging. He said that Romania still produced some oil and gas from around Ploesti, and the company working there was in partnership with Lukoil, the Russian energy conglomerate. The country had $8 billion in foreign currency reserves, about six months' worth of imports at current levels. The country earned $2 billion in foreign exchange from the export of metals, forestry products, and steel products. He didn't mention paper bags by name, but I assumed the business was still thriving. Despite these exports, Romania still had a trade deficit that amounted to 7 percent of gross domestic product (GDP), then estimated at around $40 billion to $50 billion. To balance the budget, the government had sold off $1 billion in state assets, and workers living abroad remitted another $2 billion from their hard-currency jobs in Germany and elsewhere. (Italy was Romania's largest trade partner and foreign investor.) Foreign debt was still less than $20 billion, or well under 50 percent of GDP. Corporate and personal income tax rates were fixed at the flat rate of 16 percent.

The biggest companies on the local stock exchange, Petrom and Rompetrol, both linked to the oil business, had a combined market capitalization of about $3 billion. In short, he painted a picture of a national economy—despite its relative small size and reported corruption—that was living within its means and well positioned to join the European Union within the next year or two. My business friend's goal was to package index funds around the rising values of local real estate, and, with the funds raised in the market, to reinvest in other properties. Lehman Brothers had the same ideas for the U.S. real estate market. When the crash came after 2007, Romania's economy contracted by almost 10 percent.

Our meetings tended to be clustered around meal times at the Athenée Palace. In between, I was free to tour around Bucharest and see how it had changed in thirty years. The city streets had fewer potholes than in the 1970s, and the black sedans parked in front of the Senate were from Mercedes. I noted the rise of what I took to calling "casino capitalism," the penchant among emerging economies to promote nightclubs with flashing arrows, which pointed toward cellars or attics, if not roulette wheels. Words like "discretion," "relaxation," and "escort" dominated the handbills of these establishments and were found everywhere: in the back seats of taxis, hotel lobbies, and Irish bars (where it still appeared that Romanians preferred to eat standing up). I was reminded of Jonathan Harker's Journal, which is published in Bram Stoker's novel, *Dracula*, set in Transylvania. He writes: "I read that every known superstition in the world is gathered into the horseshoe of the Carpathians, as if it were the centre of some sort of imaginative whirlpool; if so, my stay may be very interesting. (Mem., I must ask the Count all about them.)"

Ceauşescu's Magic Kingdom: *democracy is very expensive*

ONE FREE AFTERNOON I hired a taxi to drive me to the Parliamentary Palace, the symbol of Ceauşescu's rule, which ended in late 1989 when he and his wife, Elena, were tried and executed after they failed to escape the country in a helicopter. Earlier, on December 17, 1989, he had ordered the security forces to open fire on demonstrators in the city of Timisoara. Sixty-two people, many of whom were striking miners, were killed, which touched off the hunt for Mr. and Mrs. Ceauşescu, who in the tradition of fleeing monarchy had lined their suitcases with gold and jewels. Their helicopter was forced to land, after which their bodyguards commandeered a car and started driving north. Eventually they were captured at an army roadblock and taken to a military base near Targoviste, where they charged with "counterrevolutionary activities," "gathering of wealth," and having organized the death of thousands of demonstrators. As their trial lasted less than a day, I can only assume that the defense didn't call many witnesses or that the revolutionary council did not find them "credible." The Ceauşescus were lined up against a wall. Apparently the army commander had hundreds of volunteers to fire the shots. Nicolae prepared for the end by singing repeatedly the "Internationale." One wonders if he knew the second verse. The eager troops began shooting before they were ordered. Later that day the grisly scene was shown on Romanian television.

When Ceauşescu fled from Bucharest, it was from the Parliamentary Palace, which he had built to remind Romanians that he was the life of the party. My taxi dropped me a long way from the entrance, which, in a building slightly smaller than the Pentagon, was difficult to find. It took me half an hour to locate the right door and buy a ticket for an organized tour, which left when there was enough to justify the ramble. The guide, a cheerful young woman, greeted us with the words "Democracy is very expensive," although I wasn't sure if she was referring to the costs of the Romanian revolution or the expenses that Ceaușescu took on when he engaged 700 architects and 20,000 workers to construct a presidential Magic Kingdom.

The theme-park palace overlooks Bucharest at the end of an imperial boulevard, on a hillside that looms over downtown. Moscow has a number of Stalinist, wedding-cake buildings, including the old Ukraine Hotel, but they could be guest quarters when compared with the Ceaușescu palace.

During the tour, I jotted down some of the guide's statistics, all of which I still find hard to comprehend. The palace employs 300 cleaners and has some 22,000 square meters of carpeting (most of which is that ruby red of socialism), five tons of chandeliers, and acres of silk wallpaper. Building costs were estimated at 40 percent of Romania's GDP. Unification Hall is 2,200 square meters, although the only known event to have taken place here was the marriage of the Romanian Olympic gymnast Nadia Comaneci. The world-touring former president, George H.W. Bush spoke here in 1995, and Israeli Prime Minister Shimon Peres had used the palace to meet Yasser Arafat. (Did they play hide and seek?) No one had any ideas on what to do now with the building. When I was standing on the stage where Miss Romania had been crowned, the guide gave me a serious look and said, "It can be rented." I assumed she meant the cavernous hall—lined with marble and portraits of Mr. and Mrs. Ceaușescu, not Miss Romania.

The palace has an entire room, complete with an orchestra pit for an adoring band, in which Ceaușescu planned to sign international treaties of friendship. The palace is without air conditioning, as Ceaușescu feared that his enemies might use it as a conduit for poison. All the marble steps in the building, and there are thousands, are shorter than normal so that the diminutive Ceaușescu could be photographed as if he were of normal height. Only 3 to 5 percent of the building is occupied, mostly having to do with the meetings of the parliament, although the guide said the deputies meet in a secret chamber, not the lavish Hall of Deputies. The guide made the point that Ceaușescu did not live long enough to see the building finished, and that after his death no one knew how to use the space. Michael Jackson gave a concert from the balcony that had been set aside for presidential addresses, like those Hitler gave at Nuremberg. Jackson's concert plays on a television loop in a corner of the palace. His first words to the crowd were "Hello, Budapest." I guess if you are the king of pop, someone else deals with the small print on the itinerary.

Shadows of the Past: *the village museum*

I NEXT CAME TO BUCHAREST in 2009, although by then I had lost interest in the local economy, which had become a ward of the European Union. Romania had joined in the common market in 2007, with expectations that its economy would integrate into that of Western Europe and that its currency, the lei, would soon be exchanged for the euro. Instead, the global bubble in real estate had burst along the seams of speculation, especially in places such as Bucharest, which had been growing at more than 10 percent annually, largely on the strength of schemes that allowed building developers to tap into the easy money of international banking. Funds that held properties around Romania had been spread around the counting houses of London and Paris. When the construction dust was settling in 2009, few were happy with their half-built office buildings on the edges of Bucharest.

Instead of kicking investment tires on this trip, I restricted myself to a due diligence of Romanian history in the late nineteenth and twentieth centuries. I knew that Romania, like other Balkan countries, had emerged from the wars of the Ottoman succession, but I was hazy on the contributions that Transylvania or the Treaty of Berlin had made to its independence. In 2009, however, the course of history seemed like a better deal than the initial public offerings then being flogged at a discount in secondary exchanges around Eastern Europe.

Instead of Michael Jackson, the concert attraction during this visit was Madonna, who was playing at a stadium not far from my hotel. Her arrival had stalled city traffic and closed one of the national highways, so to get from the airport to the Hotel Rembrandt, I took a shuttle train to the Gare du Nord and the city metro, which left me on the edge of Lipiscani, the old city of Bucharest, now getting a makeover with new cobblestones, cafés, boutiques selling skimpy dresses, and mobile phone outlets.

By threading my way through the narrow streets on makeshift sidewalks, I found the Hotel Rembrandt, which is located in what was once a bank. The building is tall and narrow and, because the owner is Dutch, has the feeling of an Amsterdam townhouse. I was given a room with a single bed in the eaves and could look out at the cityscape, a mixture of buildings that borrowed from French and Stalinist schools of architecture. Near the hotel were several Orthodox churches with Byzantine arches and cool courtyards, where in the midday heat I could sit with my book and water, pleased that I had found a corner of Europe that was little changed from the 1920s.

On this trip I thought about an excursion to Transylvania, the struggle for which defines modern Romania, and even plotted with my maps and timetables the best way to visit Dracula's castle or the vineyards around Sinaia, said to be among the most promising in Eastern Europe. The guidebooks speak of Transylvania as the "Switzerland" of Romania. As I live near Geneva, I had decided to venture farther east, to Bessarabia, and to confine my Transylvanian travels to books and museums. Even though Bucharest is in the Wallachia region of Romania, throughout the city it is easy to find traces of Transylvania, in the history and art museums, and at what is called the village museum, a collection of rural houses reminiscent of Colonial Williamsburg—had Vlad the Impaler been a member of the Virginia House of Burgesses.

To get to the open-air museum, I took a bus and walked through a wooded park until I found a restaurant near the entrance for lunch. Afterward, I strolled among the houses, which have been collected from the regions around Romania, including Bukovina, Bessarabia, Moldavia, and Transylvania. Many of the exhibits had been simple farmhouses, and some looked like Swiss chalets, with shingled roofs and spare lines. My wife has a passion for wooden houses, so I took many pictures of hand-carved fences, some topped with thatch, and old kitchens with open chimneys. To understand better the story of Transylvania, beyond what I recalled from *Dracula*, I needed to read several of the books I had brought with me. As it was a hot late-summer afternoon, I took advantage of a shady bench at the museum, overlooking a small lake, and read until closing time, happy that I had found an oasis free from city traffic, not mention Madonna's wailing.

The Transylvania Question: *great powers head to the mountains*

As a flashpoint of European history, Transylvania has all the prerequisites of disputes that turn on nationality, religion, language, and power politics. Roughly understood as the mountainous region northwest of Bucharest and stretching to the city of Cluj-

Napoca, through the nineteenth century it was a mining region of the Austro-Hungarian Empire, principally for the salt found in its hollows. The predominant landholders were Saxons, who were Protestant and spoke German, although in the towns and village there were many Hungarians and Romanians.

The medieval Hungarian empire ruled Transylvania for centuries until the Ottomans pushed against the gates of Vienna and Budapest, leaving Transylvania as one of the many contested borderlands between Islam and the West. Princes such as Count Dracula ruled their fiefs from imposing castles—none of which are on display at the village museum—but they rarely agreed on which of the great powers should hold sway in the remote valleys and mountains that were far from the rival capitals of Vienna, Budapest, and Constantinople. In the dissolution of the Austro-Hungarian Empire, Transylvania became one of the contested battlegrounds of Europe, less well known than Alsace or the Sudetenland, but with the same ingredients to lead larger powers into wars.

After the revolutions of 1848 threatened the Austrian foundations, Hungarian nationalists dreamed of reconstituting Greater Hungary, including Transylvania. When the Austrian monarchy was divided with Hungary in 1867, it was decided to leave Transylvania beyond the direct control of Budapest. István Lázár writes in *Transylvania: A Short History*:

> When forging the Compromise of 1867, one of the Hungarian demands was the re-establishment of the 1848 union. But, as we can recall, the union did not have the endorsement of the two principal Transylvanian nationalities, the Romanians and the Saxons, and therefore the new Hungarian state, now an integral partner in the Austro-Hungarian Monarchy, decided to proceed cautiously. Thus, Transylvania was not immediately integrated into the motherland.

Transylvania was an autonomous region of the empire—a mix of Saxons, Hungarians, and Romanians—until 1907, when Austria rearranged its imperial deck chairs, annexing Bosnia and integrating Transylvania into Hungary. Ironically, both fractured regions had become coveted chess pieces in the great games being played among Britain, France, Germany, Austria, Russia, and Turkey. When the guns of August sounded in 1914, ambitions for Transylvania played a determining role in how the empires chose sides in the war.

In 1914, King Carol I of Romania wanted to side with Berlin and the Axis powers. Originally a German noble, he had sat on the Romanian throne for thirty-three years and believed that the Germans would win the war. Such a victory would leave Transylvania as part of Hungary. A.J.P. Taylor writes in *The Struggle for Mastery in Europe*: "All Rumania's national ambitions were concentrated on Transylvania; and she would do nothing to help a Habsburg victory." Romania remained neutral for the first two years of the Great War, until August 1916, when it attacked Transylvania with an army of 500,000 men. When I went to the military museum in Bucharest, I saw grainy photographs of the offensive, led by cavalry and horses pulling pieces of field artillery.

The campaign might have succeeded had the Allies pushing north from Salonika, Greece, made better progress and had the Germans not reinforced the Hungarians. Like so many attacks in World War I, this Romanian offensive stalled, and a German counterattack captured Bucharest. After Russia dropped out of the war in 1918, Romania was forced to conclude a separate peace with Germany, and with it signed away its ambitions to regain Transylvania. Lucian Boia writes in his history, *Romania*: "Romania lost Dobregea and the Carpathian ridges (as the Austro-Hungarian border pushed forward). But history was now out of control, and it offered unexpected solutions."

In spring 1918, no one expected that, with Russia out of the war, Germany would lose the war in the West. But she did in November 1918. Boia writes: "Austria-Hungary crumbled in defeat, and new political enemies emerged from its ruins. Bukovina united with Romania in November 1918, and Transylvania on 1 December, by the vote of a great Romanian assembly held at Alba Iulia." At the Paris Peace Conference, the Allies tried to redraw the maps of Europe along the continent's ethnic boundaries. The Treaty of Trianon, which dismembered Austria-Hungary, awarded Transylvania to Romania, which, despite its many battlefield losses, emerged from the peace conference as one of the war's winners. Taylor writes: "Wilson was as much a Utopian as Lenin." The more determinant element in Romania's diplomatic triumphs was the presence at Versailles of Queen Marie, a granddaughter of England's Queen Victoria and the Russian czar Alexander II. On paper she was married to King Ferdinand, but in practice she was a royal courtesan of the first rank, who deployed her considerable seductive assets in the cause of Greater Romania.

In the 1920s and '30s, the fragile state of Greater Romania found itself at odds with Hungary over Transylvania, where the dogs of World War II would find more bones on which to chew. Nor did it prove capable of diplomatic policies that would rise above shameless cynicism, even if it found itself caught in the vise between Germany and Russia. Lázár writes: "While both the claimants for Transylvania, Hungary and Romania, entered the war on Hitler's—and each other's—side, they did this largely to obtain and keep Transylvania." To Romania's unease, Hitler's denunciations of Versailles resonated in Hungary, which at all costs sought the return of Transylvania.

After the Molotov-Ribbentrop Pact of 1939 partitioned Eastern Europe, Romania allowed the deposed leaders of Poland to take refuge in its country, and King Carol II hoped to remain neutral in the fighting. Hitler rewarded the Hungarians for their loyalty by granting them what was called "Northern Transylvania." By the terms of the 1939 nonaggression pact, the Russians took northern Bukovina and Bessarabia.

After a coup in 1940 deposed Carol II (Marie's son) and installed in Bucharest the strutting fascist government of General Ion Antonescu, Romania saw its future as an Axis power—to maintain its hold on Transylvania and to drive the Russians out of Bukovina and Bessarabia. After Germany invaded Russia in June 1941, Romania served as a willing executioner in Hitler's wars of the East, including its own holocaust against the Jews. Romanian armies swept through Bessarabia, occupied Odessa and the Crimea, and served on the front lines at Stalingrad. In 1944, when the Russians drove the Germans out of the Soviet Union, Romania abruptly changed sides in the fighting and joined the Allies. At the war's end, as compensation, Romania was given northern Transylvania, although it never regained Bessarabia or northern Bukovina, and the Russians occupied Romania until 1958 and, to this day, view the country with suspicion.

The Night Train to Moldova: *changing gauges*

To get to Chisinau, the capital of the nearby country of Moldova, I took the overnight train that left in the early evening from a platform baking in late summer heat. I had bought my ticket from a window marked "International" at Gare du Nord and gambled that I might have the compartment to myself. I was early to the station and passed the time buying cold water and snacks. Around the platform were a number of Gypsy families, some of whom were eating picnic suppers on the station benches. Gare du Nord, like so much in Bucharest, was built in the 1930s from French inspiration. From the outside it has the feel of a Parisian *palais.* The interior is less classical. There are numerous kiosks that sell water and sandwiches, a McDonald's, and many newspaper racks. I watched the *Prietenia*, the train's official name, back into the terminal and joined the scrum of passengers searching for their berths or seats.

The overnight train is one of the few ways to go from the capital of Romania to that of Moldova. A bus makes the run in twelve hours, but not every day, and flights are sporadic. I found my compartment and spread out my maps, book, and cold water, but after a while I felt like I had joined a comedy theater instead of a night train. Clearly, more than a few of the other passengers wanted my compartment, which had air conditioning and two beds.

Every so often someone would peer into my room, take stock of its comforts, and launch into a soliloquy about how I would be happier in another car. When I refused to budge, they would return with the conductor, who made it a great exercise to review my ticket and berth reservation, both of which were in order. To some of the more determined claimants, I asked to see *their* tickets and reservations, adopting the tone of voice that I had learned from the conductor. That usually sent them slinking off down the corridor. None of these conversations were hostile or threatening. I could imagine all of them thinking, "Who knows, maybe this foreigner is dumb enough to give up his compartment?" I stuck to my berth. Once the train departed the station, no one challenged my claim. I passed a pleasant night, sleeping and looking out the window, until the train stopped at the Moldovan border town of Ungheni.

The dramatic aspects of the border crossing involved changing the gauge of the axles on the train, which was jacked into the air and dropped onto another set of bogies, ones suitable for Soviet tracks. Romanian tracks are standard Western gauge, while Moldovan rails are five feet apart, as is true across Russia. It took more than an hour to change the undercarriages. I watched the railroad workers change the sets from the door at the end of my car until the porter chased me back to my room.

All sorts of customs and immigration officials paraded through the train, giving me the impression that relations between Romania and Moldova have yet to come in from the Cold War. At one point border guards walked the length of the train with a mirror device pointed under the cars, in case any irredentists had it in mind to sneak into Moldova. A few months earlier, riots had broken out in Chisinau, and the Moldovan authorities blamed Romanians for the street violence. Moldova, once a part of historic Bessarabia, is a mix of Romanians, Ukrainians, and Russians, all of whom feel like a persecuted minority in a country that emerged from the collapse of the Soviet Union.

I fell back asleep between Ungheni and Chisinau, a run of several hours, and felt groggy when the train arrived and the passengers walked to the station past a restored Russian steam engine, which has been preserved in snappy colors. I had come to Chisinau without a hotel reservation and the hope of visiting the breakaway enclave of Transnistria. A guidebook listed some of the local hotels, but was more discouraging about a day trip across the border, describing the "autonomous region" as a cross between Pyongyang and Abkhazia.

Luckily, in the jostling at the Chisinau station, I struck up a conversation with a man who offered his services as a driver and tour guide. His name was Wlady, and for some moments I didn't know whether to trust him, and he didn't know if he should trust me. We discussed the fare for the day and settled on $60, provided he was willing to make a run at the difficult border. He said he would try, and I paid $30 in front money.

Before setting out on our tour, I checked into the Hotel Turist, which dates to one of Moldova's early five-year plans (one that omitted hot water). For $50 I got several rooms of furniture that looked borrowed from Khrushchev's waiting room and a full breakfast of bread, eggs, and dried meat. In years to come, as memories of the Soviet Union fade, it will be harder and harder to find hotels like the Turist, which even had desks for *dezhurnaya*—Russian den mothers stationed on every floor—there to serve tea, chase down keys, and report on revisionism.

Bessarabia: *neither here nor there*

BEFORE HEADING to the Transnistria border, Wlady insisted on taking me to several monasteries on the edge of Chisinau, one of which, Capriana, was said to be a presidential favorite. During the Soviet era it had fallen on hard times. I had printed a page from the Internet about its past, which reads:

> On June 29, 1940, a day after the conquest of Bessarabia by Soviet troops, the whole estate of the monastery was confiscated. The last abbot of the monastery was the Superior Eugeniu (1952-1962) and the last church oration was solemnized on October 25, 1962. A day after the activity which lasted more than a half of the millennium, the monastery was closed, monks took refuge in other parishes, monks and brothers being driven banished.... The Soviet State declared the Capriana Monastery an architectural monument governmentally protected, but at the same time the monastery began to be foraged and crashed.... After 1962, the monastery was transformed into a sanatorium for sick children. The monastery refectory was transformed into a club where dancing parties, good cheers and weddings were organized.

After Moldova left the Soviet orbit in 1991, the monasteries were restored, and Capriani, when I was there, was overrun with day-tripping families out for the sunshine. As we drove to yet another monastery, Wlady talked to me about his family. His parents were Russian and had settled in Moldova in the 1960s, because they could find work. After the collapse of the Soviet Union had led to Moldovan independence, citizens of Russian origin, even if their children had grown up in Moldova, were treated as outcasts. They could neither go back to Russia nor apply for Moldovan citizenship. Wlady was lucky, because his family had a car that ran on natural gas and he could work as a driver.

Wlady talked about the April 2009 riots, during which protesters set fire to the parliament and presidential palace. They had also waved Romanian flags and denounced the election that had returned the local Communist Party to power. He believed that Romania had helped to organize the riots. ("They were a horde of 10,000 outside agitators, shipped in from Romania. Now they fix everything.") Why else was the Romanian flag hoisted over the smoldering parliament, if only for a brief time? Personally, Wlady felt more Moldovan than Russian, as he had grown up in the country and never lived in Russia. He felt that the Russians "left behind" after the collapse of the Soviet Union deserved recognition and protection, especially from Romanians who, when they had the chance alongside the Germans, had invaded Russia.

Because Wlady had agreed to make a run for Transnistria, we drove the car east to a bridge over the River Dniester at Dubăsari. On a clear day, we passed through a rolling forest, and for a while I thought that the crossing might be easier than what was described in the guidebook. As we got closer to the bridge we could see cars, waiting to get across, backed up for a kilometer. For the next two hours we crept in line across the bridge, while each of the cars ahead of us was searched and the occupants forced to fill out a stack of customs and immigration papers. In the meantime, we waited on the bridge over the River Dniester, which cuts through Moldova in a dramatic valley. To the west were forests and hills; to the east, the black earth of the steppes and Ukraine. It struck me as a deep and natural divide. We had slowed to crawl over the frontier that separates Europe from the East. No wonder the Russians had occupied a meaningless strip of land on the far shore. Transnistria was Checkpoint Charlie, dressed up as an autonomous region.

The Slow Road to Transnistria: *Europe's natural divide*

THE POLITICAL GENEALOGY of Transnistria feels like an except from *The Gulag Archipelago*. Even physically, and with barbed wire on its borders, it resembles one of those desolate islands of the Soviet Union. As part of his gerrymandering of various nationalities, Stalin created the Moldavian ASSR in 1926, an autonomous region within the Ukrainian Soviet Socialist Republic, no doubt to check the eastward expansion of Greater Romania. In 1940, following the Molotov-Ribbentrop Pact, Stalin annexed Bessarabia and North Bukovina and folded all the region into the Moldavian Soviet Socialist Republic, the precursor of the modern Republic of Moldova. As described, Transnistria, the far shore of the River Dniester, was overrun in June 1941, when German troops launched Operation Barbarossa against the Soviet Union.

Under Romanian control, Transnistria became a killing ground for Romanian Jews deported to the frontier or others caught in the vise between the Germans and the Russians. Some 185,000 Jews died in the areas around Transnistria. After the Russians swept over the area in 1944, Transnistria—known also as Trans-Dniester, Transdniestria, and Pridnestrovie—was restored to the Moldavian SSR. When the Soviet Union fractured in the early 1990s, many Moldovans sided with Romania, with which they shared a common language. Those in Transnistria, however, had more sympathy with Russia and Ukraine, and feared joining an independent Moldova as a minority.

Since 1990, Transnistria has existed in a diplomatic nether world, neither East nor West, a remnant of Stalinism that enjoys the protection of the Russian army around its borders. On September 2, 1990, it took the name Pridnestrovian Moldavian Soviet Socialist Republic, which befits a rump state that has the air of a model village. Under international law, Transnistria is part of Moldova, but nevertheless it claims Tiraspol as its capital, circulates its own money, and flies its own flag, even though the population is only 500,000.

Initially, as Moldova was declaring its independence from the dissolving Soviet Union, a war of border skirmishes was fought between Moldova and Transnistria, until in 1992 a cease-fire was negotiated. That agreement allowed for the presence in Transnistria of Russian troops, who can be found on tanks near the border crossings and in larger numbers stationed in the old Turkish fortress at Bender (which was fought over in the Russo-Turkish War of 1877, which gave Romania its independence). Russian troops were to have withdrawn from Transnistria in 1997, but they stayed on, as they have in other Soviet enclaves such as Abkhazia and elsewhere in the Caucasus, such as South Ossetia. Russia thinks of its forces as peacekeepers, although they look more like the kind of ceremonial guards that goose-step around the Kremlin.

At the far end of the Dubăsari bridge, our car got close enough for me to head into a small office, full of immigration officers, and fill out the paperwork needed to enter Transnistria. I was handed the same forms that used to be routine around the Iron Curtain: one for immigration, explaining the reason for my visit; a second for customs, wanting to know all the money in my wallet. I checked the box marked "Tourism," which a series of armed guards accepted without question. To visit Transnistria for tourism is like heading off to Albania for wine tasting. None of the other boxes—Medical, Job, Business, Government—seemed to apply. I counted my money, filled in the blanks, and handed in the forms, which were passed from officer to officer while others ransacked the car and trunk and went through my briefcase. None of the officers, however, were rude or aggressive. After the last inspection, Wlady and I were waved into Transnistria, and we drove in the direction of Tiraspol.

Along the Dniester Valley to Tiraspol: *a Soviet showroom*

BY NOW IT WAS LATE AFTERNOON, and we had the main north-south road to ourselves. To our right, as we drove south, was the plunging Dniester Valley, so deep that only on occasion could I see the twisting river. To the left stretched what looked like the Russian steppe, vast tracts of farmland that had rich black soil and a sense of eternity as it approached the far horizon. Along the two-lane road were graceful trees, like you might find on an American parkway. Nowhere to be seen were tanks, soldiers, or traces of officialdom; that was left behind at the river crossing. Transnistria is a snake of a country, which on a map looks to have shed its skin from Moldova. For the next hour, we drove across a pristine landscape, as if on a motoring holiday.

Even for an ambitious tourist, there was little to visit in Tiraspol, the erstwhile capital, a sleepy Balkan town dressed up as a seat of power. I had the idea of stopping to buy postage stamps for my son Charles' collection. Wlady chortled with amusement at the suggestion that we might find an open post office or that we could find local money to buy anything. Apparently Tiraspol is a variation on a company store, and neither of us had any scrip. Wlady did, however, loop through the downtown, otherwise a sad socialist housing project. We got caught behind a marching band, celebrating some military achievement, and we passed near the railroad station, where I have read passengers on international express trains are routinely shaken down for $25 "transit visas." Trains from Chisinau to Odessa, Moscow, and Kiev go through Tiraspol, but it's little more than a speed trap.

I found it difficult to place Transnistria's political coordinates on any map of the twenty-first century. Unlike Moldova's Latin alphabet, Tiraspol's signage uses Cyrillic lettering, much the way many of the population speak Russian or Ukrainian, not Moldovan or Romanian. Psychologically, the capital appeared to be closest to Moscow, whose troops were there to keep outsiders from entering or locals from leaving. From Wlady I got the impression that the enclave had few jobs and that most people lived as wards of Moscow. On many side streets there were the hulking remains of socialism, as if Stalin's will had yet to be probated. Farming might make some money, but the only markets were local. Transnistria looks like a satellite, but one far from normal orbits.

Except as a model village for a Soviet *risorgimiento*, Transnistria did not look to have much of a future. The country is landlocked, and hostage to the suspicions of Ukraine and Moldova. It lives off its collective farms and heavy industries, not to mention black-market profiteering. In exchange, it stands as proof that the sun has yet to set on the Soviet empire.

Leaving the autonomous region was easier than our arrival. We returned the many forms and were continuing on our way until my American passport caught the attention of a border guard. He took it in his hand, whistled to himself as if he had found a false bottom in my suitcase, and motioned for Wlady to pull the car over to the side. Clearly, he wasn't amused with the idea that the breakaway republic was attractive to Western tourists, especially one from such a bourgeois republic as the United States. Wlady spoke to him softly in Russian, although it did little to calm the performance.

The border guard waved his arms—I was reminded of Khrushchev and his shoe at the United Nations—and denounced (I guess) revisionism, capitalism, decadence, Bush, the United Nations, etc., until even he tired of his histrionics and gave me back my passport, with a faint smile.

The Five Dollar Train to Iasi: *remembering Pushkin's exile*

LEAVING TRANSNISTRIA PROVED easier than getting out of Chisinau. I spent my last morning in the capital at the Pushkin Museum, the house where the poet lived in exile in the 1820s. It was located just behind my hotel, on a side street away from city bustle, and I found it behind a large tree, said to have been planted when the poet was in residence. I was the only guest that morning, and was followed closely by several members of the staff, all of whom were eager to show artifacts from the poet's life in Bessarabia.

Czar Nicholas I had sentenced Pushkin to exile for what amounted to free thinking, but he was allowed to choose the warm climate of Bessarabia over the winter freeze of Siberia. By all accounts, including Pushkin's letters on display in the museum, he enjoyed his time in Chisinau, especially in summer, when he fell in love with a young woman living on an estate in Dolna. To her he dedicated some of his most heartfelt poetry, and it was in Chisinau that he began writing *Eugene Onegin*. Such was the leniency of Pushkin's exile that he was free to travel. On the wall of the museum is a map that shows the path of his tour around the contours of Bessarabia, taking in Odessa—the kind of trip that would have interested me, had I had an easier time figuring out how to leave Chisinau.

My hope had been to catch a train to Bucharest or even the old Bessarabian capital of Iasi (pronounced Yash). From my schedules

I knew that there might not be daily service to Romania, but I had hoped to relay myself on local trains to Ungheni, and then across the border. The main train station was quiet on a Sunday. Chisinau's station has been completely renovated, and its stone arches evoke an Ottoman influence while the cool marble floors and walls suggest a more traditional Slavic terminal. I lined up at several windows to learn what I suspected from timetables and the departure board: that no trains were running that day.

I tried the adjacent bus station, but nothing was heading west. A dispatcher suggested I try the minibus terminal, to look for a van heading toward the Romania border. I took a taxi across town to a parking lot that was alive with minivans and small buses, serving towns across Moldova. I bought lunch and cold drinks, and idled hopefully near a bus platform marked for Iasi. Nothing came or went in the next hour. Finally a clerk told me I was foolish to think a bus would take me to Romania. Didn't I know the border was closed?

I was forming that impression, as well as getting tired of waiting around the crowded bus station. Maybe the buses were canceled because of the riots? For $40 I hired a taxi to drive me to the Romanian border. It was a two-hour drive, and the driver enlivened the journey with stops along the way at the homes of his relatives, as if to boast of his good fortune at bagging a wealthy tourist. We chatted in a smattering of different languages. My good fortune was that he didn't abandon me to the fates in Ungheni, which I knew had no road connection to Romania and at best spotty train service. We drove to the city station and found a shuttle train leaving in an hour for Iasi. The fare was $5, and the train, towing cars roasting in the hot summer sun, looked like the New York City subway, from the age of graffiti.

I bought my ticket and took a seat, the only passenger on what looked like a ghost train to nowhere. Still, I was happy to be away from the bus station and out of the homes of my taxi driver's family. About thirty minutes before we were scheduled to depart, an immigration officer asked me to return to the station to clear border formalities. This time, when asked the reason for my trip, I thought I could say "tourism" with my head held high. That answer went nowhere with the strident Moldovan immigration officer, who was scrutinizing my passport and demanding to know which monasteries I had seen in Moldova. Normally I would have instantly forgotten the names of the Capriani and Curchi monasteries. Under interrogation from the snarky guard, I remembered them and delivered an impassioned soliloquy on the Pushkin exile. The agent's rude questions infuriated others in line, fearing I might have influence in tourist circles. No one quite believed the officer when she handed me my passport and said "Come again." On the rail trip over the border to Iasi, my new friends were eager to point out local points of interest, knowing that I was sure to remember them.

Commissar Class to Bucharest: *Romanian compartmentalism*

THERE WAS ANOTHER LONG LINE in Iasi to clear immigration. I was last, until one of the Romanian border guards asked me to follow him. I figured I was in for more questions about Moldovan monasteries, if not a discourse on Queen Marie's behavior at the Paris Peace Conference. All he wanted to do, however, was move me to the front of the line and wish me a pleasant evening in Iasi. I had six hours before the night train left for Bucharest, and few plans other than to buy a ticket and, I hoped, reserve a berth.

The easygoing immigration officer explained that intercity trains left from another station and suggested a taxi might be the easiest way to get there. I followed his instructions and found the main terminal on the edge of the historic downtown. Trains were listed for many cities around Romania. I watched an 8:42 p.m.

sleeper, elegantly appointed, depart for Timisoara, wishing I were on it. Instead I lined up inside for a Bucharest ticket, only to be told that they would not go on sale until 9 p.m. Since I had two hours to kill, I decided to hire a taxi and tour the old capital of Bessarabia.

By luck, I found a driver who spoke a few words of English and who was as motivated as I was to make the most of the drive. We cruised to the city's main square, saw the former royal palace, now the city hall, and other elegant buildings, which echoed the splendors of Vienna, if only on the scale of a provincial capital. In the main park I bought a small painting from an artist, and the driver stopped in front of the university so I could peek my head into the library. I strolled around the lobby of the Traian Grand Hotel, which dominates a city square with its elegant and soft lighting, and wished I had a reason to spend several days in one of its suites, reading about the Bessarabian Question. Best of all, the driver took me to the home of a famous poet, assuming I had some citizenship in the republic of letters. The surprised but gracious family of the poet (now dead) showed me his desk, books, and grave, and hoped I would stay for dinner. I explained that I needed to get back to the station.

The agent handling my file, to use a European expression, was a guardian angel. She was attractive, bright, spoke good English, understood her job, and clearly liked selling train tickets. She confessed that the sleepers on my train were sold out, but her solution was ingenious. She said that if I could wait until 10 p.m. to buy my ticket, she might be able to give me the compartment normally reserved for high officials of the Iasi government. They had priority, but if they failed to turn up, she was free to sell the space, and I was first on the waiting list.

I ate a bad dinner in the station restaurant, the price for staying close to the ticket window. At 10 p.m., in exchange for $28, I was given a first-class berth on the last overnight train to Bucharest, which before midnight backed into the Iasi terminal. Not only was my compartment lined with dark paneling, fit for a commissar, but it also had air conditioning and a shower, which I used to clean away the dust from my cab ride across Moldova and the twenty questions in the Ungheni immigration stall.

As I do on all trains I love, I unpacked my bag and arranged my books and maps, as if departing on a cruise. In a sense I was, across the plains of Wallachia, which under a full moon and in summer heat shimmered like Kansas in July. I wanted to stay awake, with my head propped against the bedstead, so that I could watch the tableau of Romania rush past the large window. The long day got the better of my comforts, and I slept until the first rays of the sun pushed through my window shade. I awoke to the breadbasket of wheat fields that lead into the Bucharest suburbs.

Romanian Bloodlands: *Jewish life in Bucharest*

ON MY LAST DAY IN THE CITY, I could have headed directly to the airport and waited there, maybe in some plastic café chair, for my flight home to Geneva. Instead, after breakfast back at the Rembrandt—thanks to an invitation from the owner Jerry van Schaik—I set off with my city map in search of the Jewish Museum. It was not located in a part of the city I knew. I walked in circles, through a modern housing project, in search of the correct address. In retrospect, I should have looked along the skyline for a synagogue, because the museum is located in one of the few that survived the war. When I knocked on the door, at first no one answered. Then an elderly woman said the museum did not open until later. When I looked disappointed, she motioned for me to come inside and turned on the exhibit lights. She returned to her desk. I was free to wander through the several floors of Romanian Jewish history, as sad as many similar stories in other Eastern European countries.

The museum is a chronicle of Jewish life in Romania dating to the twelfth century, although for much of that period Jews had few legal rights as citizens. In the nineteenth century, a ukase had denied rights to all non-Christians. After the revolutions of 1848, living conditions improved, but not the legal status of Jews, who even when Romania became independent lived with a myriad restrictions. Nevertheless, Jews fought with valor for Romanian independence and in World War I, in what was called the Romanian Unification War. Medals for bravery grace a number of display cases.

The museum showed early photographs of Jewish life in Bucharest, although the majority of Romanian Jews lived in Bessarabia and Moldavia, having drifted west from the pale of settlement during the pogroms of that time. Still denied rights in the early twentieth century, many Romanian Jews were attracted to Zionism, the subject of posters in the museum. The 1923 constitution did grant civil rights to Jews, and a census in 1930 showed their population as 756,930, or almost 5 percent of the Romanian population. In the cities, such as Bucharest, they made up almost 15 percent of the population and were predominant in professional classes.

The rise of Marshal Ion Antonescu and new laws against the Jews in 1940, followed by the German advance into Russia, placed the Jewish population in a vise of war that shifted back and forth across Bessarabia for more than three years. Although the Romanians carried out a pogrom in Iasi that killed three thousand Jews in June 1941, it was not until Bessarabian Jews were deported to Transnistria after July of that year that wholesale killings began in those bloodlands between Hitler's Germany's and Stalin's Soviet Union.

Estimates are that more than 100,000 Jews were killed or died of disease in those camps. As a museum map shows, in the northeast of the country the Hungarian government deported to German concentration camps thousands of the Jews who were living in northern Transylvania. Nevertheless, as the war went on the

Antonescu government resisted German calls for a "final solution." After the war, most surviving Romanian Jews left for Israel. The current Jewish population in Romania is less than 9,000.

The museum, set up in a synagogue, feels like a lonely island that has drifted away from its shores. When I went out the front door I was back in the Bucharest of high-rise apartment buildings and busy intersections, without a hint that previously this neighborhood had been among the most vibrant Jewish communities in Eastern Europe.

To collect my bag from the hotel, I picked my way across the Lipiscani, the old city now being renovated, although the results are haphazard. Some streets are lined with boutiques and small restaurants, while others look as if Communism was still in receivership. I paused at some of the marble plaques that are posted around the city, recording the names and pictures of the students who were killed on the streets during the 1989 fight for liberation from the Ceauşescu regime. Adrian Nutu was killed on Christmas Day, 1989, in his twenty-third year. The photograph grafted onto the wall tombstone shows a studious young man, with glasses, better prepared for biology class than for martyrdom.

Because I liked it so much, I made a last visit to the courtyard of the Stavropoleos Church, which struck me as the perfect synthesis of Romanian history during the recent centuries—a mixture of arches and mosaics that echoed the civilizations of Byzantium, Greece, Russia, Vienna, Turkey, and Rome. Each of these capitals had made claims on Romania, and the results had often been disastrous, especially for the Jews and lonely protesters, like Adrian Nutu. Heading to the airport, I wondered if the European Union might give Romania a respite from the wars, although Bessarabia, Moldova, and Transnistria have about them an air of unfinished business. Even at the end of *Dracula*, Transylvania is recalled as "the old ground which was, and is, to us so full of vivid and terrible memories."

OUTBOUND FROM THE FINLAND STATION

"God is too high, and the Tsar is too far."

—Siberian expression,
quoted in Harmon Tupper's
To the Great Ocean

The Trans-Siberian to Mongolia

In June 2008, I accepted an invitation to deliver several lectures to the passengers on board a Trans-Siberian train headed toward Mongolia, with stops in the principal cities of Siberia. Although the rolling stock of the train was a mixture of Ukrainian and Belorussian cars, the tour was privately organized and the passengers were English, French, German, and Swiss, all of them sharing my dream of taking the train across Russia. I did too, as I had never traveled by train east of the Ural Mountains, and not since summer 1975, when I went with a university class, had I spent much time on Russian rails.

On that student trip, about fifteen of us flew to Moscow, spent a few days hanging around Gorky Park, and departed on what turned out to be a railway odyssey. Sputnik, the Russian student travel agency, had failed to find us hotel reservations in Moscow and Leningrad. All they could think to do with our group of Americans was to book us on night trains, which shunted us through the short Russian summer nights. One night we traveled overnight to Smolensk, where Napoleon had fought and beaten the Russian armies in 1812. Some days later, we changed trains in Leningrad (now St. Petersburg) and ended up in Tallinn, the capital of Estonia. My first impressions of Russia were from the rails, with mornings spent gazing from my couchette at birch forests and evenings passed looking out the window as the midnight sun hovered on the horizon. On that trip I did not learn a lot about Peter the Great, the Russian economy, or the Russian Orthodox Church. I did learn to love Russia in summer and its railways, and have daydreamed ever since about returning to St. Petersburg's Finland Station.

The undergraduate class that made the trip was studying Russian dissident literature and wondering about the future of the Soviet Union. We spent much time reading Solzhenitsyn and debating *samizdat* literature—sadly, much of it awful. On this trip I was more interested in the fall of the czars, Russia during World War II, and the building of the Trans-Siberian, which struck me as a political as much as an engineering endeavor. From Napoleon's invasion to the Russian Revolution, I knew the procession of the czars, the dates of the Crimean War, and the causes of World War I. But it was hard for me to imagine Napoleon's retreat from Moscow, the reasons for the revolution, or the course of the fighting in World War II. I had collected a number of books about Russian history, but found little time to read them at home. Who has the concentration, after dinner, to dig into the details of the Russo-Japanese War or the history of the Octobrists, a group that pressed constitutional reforms on Nicholas II? Over the years, on business trips to Russia, I had read extensively about Stalingrad and the country's economic reforms. But by definition business trips are rushed.

Russian History: *"I am among the pupils"*

BEFORE THE TRANS-SIBERIAN left from Moscow's Kazan Station, I spent a week at a friend's apartment, located near the Kremlin. I could walk to Red Square in fifteen minutes. Like many Moscow apartments, mine was hidden behind a shabby courtyard and a dank stairwell, as if Raymond Chandler had been the lead architect on the project. Once I had mastered the various keys to the entrance and the elevator, and was inside the flat, I felt the pleasure of a Moscow interior, where I could drink tea, watch local television, scatter my maps, and work on my computer. On my first afternoon, I shopped in the subway station—yes, it's a Moscow thing—for eggs and bread, some coffee, and a few cans of beer. I was impatient to see the city again, and abandoned domestic chores to visit the State History Museum, located on Red Square.

Entering the museum, I had a long conversation with several of the guards, who tried to find an English guidebook, explaining to me that the restaurant was closed (although it was full of people). I started my rounds in a room devoted to the life of Peter the Great (1672-1725), who ruled Russia in the early eighteenth century, when the splendors of St. Petersburg were conceived and, to the outside world, it looked as if Russia would develop much like France, if only with colder winters.

On the first floor I found Peter's sleigh (like the Roman emperor Hadrian, he spent his imperial time on the road), and his portrait (he had the eyes of a Machiavellian prince). Among the objects that recollected his life were things that he brought back from Western Europe on his many travels. He collected writing instruments, books, looking glasses, clothes, pictures, and china, as if he were a philosopher of the Enlightenment sent west on a shopping spree.

In his history of Russia, Bernard Pares writes: "[Peter's] real object was to study Europe and bring back to Russia a teacher of all those arts of which his country was most in need; the crest of the mission bore the words, 'I am among the pupils, and seek those who can teach me.'" He had qualities that Americans admire in Thomas Jefferson: a restless curiosity about the confluence of politics and science, and a conception of government as a vast university, there to instruct the student population. Pares writes: "Peter was first of all a mechanician. His first toys were pieces of machinery. He not only shaved his courtiers' beards; he was his own court dentist and kept in a little bag the teeth which he had extracted; but the object to which he applied all his technical knowledge was the possession and extension of power." He made his own boots, which, in the Kremlin museum, look to have been left behind by a giant. The Romanov side of his disposition believed in the concentration of power, much as did Louis XIV, and he left behind an empire.

I spent so much time in Peter the Great's room that when I left it I assumed that the museum had closed, and that one of the guards would soon ask me to leave. It was 4 p.m., and I was alone in the museum. Seeing no one, I feared that the museum had shut for the night and that I would be accused of hiding among the display cases, perhaps with revolutionary intent. A curator entered the room where I was looking around. I asked if the museum had closed. Her English was good, and she said, with what I assumed was bureaucratic logic: "The museum is open, but we are no longer selling any tickets." I thought of all the museums that I had seen in a scrum of tourists; now I had the State History Museum to myself. Better yet, the curator trailed behind me, answering my many questions. She showed me around some of the rooms, which, despite Communism and the liberalism of *perestroika*, breaks down Russian history according to the lives and times of the czars—what one historian summed up as "muddle and intrigue followed by negation."

Death of the Czars: *"a defective Russian gene"*

STARTING IN THE WORLD of Catherine the Great (1729 –1796), who in her portraits looks like Margaret Thatcher, I spent the next two hours footloose across Russian history. I found a painting that showed Poland on a child's seesaw, balanced between Russia and Prussia, and a Catherine quote about Warsaw: "There is there, a happy anarchy with which we can work at will." I saw images of Catherine in her study. She was said to rise early, light her own fires, and work fifteen hours a day. She was kind to her servants and expanded the borders of Russia to include the Crimea, parts of Ukraine, Belarus, and the Baltic states. I drew no conclusions, nor did the museum, whether she had a hand in assassinating her husband, Peter III (he was killed in a coup in St. Petersburg that put her on the throne). She consumed young men as lovers in astonishing numbers. It was said: "To be Her Majesty's lover was equivalent to having an appointment at court." After leaving her suite of rooms, I thought about how many subsequent czars, including her son Paul, died from assassination, as if it were a defective Romanov gene.

I didn't know much about Czar Paul, until I stared at his portrait, in miniature form, and then read through the long list of his assassins, who in 1801 found him hiding behind some palace drapes and ran him through with a sword. When Paul was a child, Catherine had ignored him. Later, if she noticed him at all, it was to belittle him. After she died in 1796, his reign was brief, yet mercurial. Unhappy with one regiment, he ordered it, in full dress, to begin marching toward Siberia.

Paul turned against his mother's court, and the Russian aristocracy, for treating him like a footman. His portrait shows an effeminate young man, someone resembling the young Catherine in drag. He was terrified of revolution. On the throne, according to Pares, Paul "recalled Russians on a Bourbon passport, excluded European books and music; he forbade costumes suggestive of revolutionary Paris; round hats, frock coats, high collars, if shown in the streets, were snatched or torn away; he proscribed the words *society* and *citizen*. All this was addressed to the aristocratic Russia reared by Catherine on French culture." Paul was succeeded by his son, Alexander I, who was in the palace when his father was murdered and knew of the assassination plans, something that would haunt his own rule. When the French foreign minister Talleyrand heard that Paul had died of "an attack of apoplexy," he said: "The Russians should invent another illness to explain the death of their emperors."

Alexander I Saves Europe: *"there is a piece missing in his character"*

THE MUSEUM PORTRAITS of Czar Alexander I show him on a horse, liberating Paris or defeating Napoleon at Leipzig. Despite saving Europe from French tyranny and enlightenment, Alexander was a reluctant warrior, the home-schooled product of a Swiss tutor, Frédéric-César de La Harpe, who drilled his pupil in the liberal arts. At the time, critics said that what Russia needed was "a Tiberius or a Genghis Khan," but La Harpe brought up Alexander closer to the traditions of the Enlightenment. Henri Troyat, one of Alexander's biographers, writes: "He aspired at one and the same time to political power and to retirement on the banks of the Rhine."

For a while Alexander exchanged intimate letters with Napoleon, and in 1807 they met on a raft in the middle of the Niemen River. The museum has a huge canvas of the ceremony, which Troyat describes: "Napoleon, who was fond of dramatic settings, had had a great raft anchored in midstream bearing two superbly decorated pavilions of white canvas. The larger structure, in which the sovereigns were to meet, had a gigantic A painted on the side and on the French side an N of the same size. Napoleon had deliberately omitted the initials of the King of Prussia, who, naturally enough, took offense at the slight." The wellsprings of the Cold War might be found in the Niemen.

In signing the Treaty of Tilsit (a town on the Niemen), the two emperors look like they are on a summer camping trip. After 1807, neither trusted the other. Napoleon thought Alexander had a screw loose. He said: "No one could have more intelligence than the Emperor Alexander, but I find that there is a piece missing in his character, and I cannot discover what it is." On his side, from his classical La Harpe education, Alexander should have responded to the liberal ideals of the French Revolution, except that they conflicted violently with his family obligations to power, not to mention his own demons. He wrote to Princess Sophie Mestcherski: "Our purpose is to counteract the empire of evil, which is spreading rapidly by all the occult means at the disposal of the satanic spirit which directs it." A biographer wrote: "When he mused on the past, Alexander wondered whether Napoleon had not been the ideal enemy for him, a friendly enemy."

In Napoleon, Alexander discovered evil. After Tilsit, Troyat writes: "Despite their good intentions, neither of the two Emperors could make his acts accord with his principles." Alexander was dismissive of Napoleon's threats to invade Russia, saying, "I have space and I have time on my side....If Napoleon goes to war and fortune smiles upon him, notwithstanding the legitimate goal pursued by the Russians, he will have to sign the peace on the Bering Strait." Napoleon may have broken his empire with his Russian invasion. Nevertheless, before retreating in the snow, he did leave his calling card for Alexander, by burning Moscow to the ground. I enjoyed the rooms devoted to Napoleon's Russian invasion. A large painting shows the French emperor, at the head of a column, trudging through a plain of snow. Later, from the train as it left Moscow, I discovered that such depictions were allegorical, because much of the terrain around Moscow is a mixture of forests and bogs. The better image of Napoleon's retreat would be to show his men knee-deep in frozen mud, as if caught in quicksand, or lost in the woods. At least Alexander was correct when he said: "Our climate, our winter will fight for us."

Besides looking at some Napoleonic artifacts left in the retreat, I passed in front of the cabinets that contain the personal effects of Grand Marshal M. Kutuzov, who fought the French at Borodino, the battle that Leo Tolstoy describes in *War and Peace*. Kutuzov said: "Napoleon is like a torrent that we cannot stop. Moscow will be the sponge that absorbs it." If the museum is accurate, Kutuzov went to war with very little: a tattered leather briefcase, a gilded dinner set, some letters, an icon, and a samovar. Yet Kutuzov outwitted one of the largest armies ever assembled on the planet.

Troyat describes him: "Lazy, fond of good food and sensual pleasures, he indulged himself at table, enjoyed himself with his mistress, a big Moldavian peasant whom he dragged with him everywhere disguised as a soldier, and very often fell asleep in the middle of a discussion, with this chin on his chest and potbelly protruding. But in spite of his tendency to be drowsy or absentminded, his judgment was still very keen. He was cunning, patient, and endowed with a rough common sense that always showed through the polish of Western culture."[1]

Alexander ended the first reign of Napoleon's terror when he led Russian forces across the Rhine and into Paris. He was the man on horseback, marching in with his glittering troops, until the Congress of Vienna diverted his attention. At Vienna, sounding more like Stalin, Alexander said: "I shall keep what I occupy." (He also said that the Congress "dances but does not take one step forward.") It did, however, with his consent, agree to an independent Poland, under a constitutional monarchy, as if his old tutor

---

1   The French writer in exile Madame Germaine de Staël said of the general: "Looking at him, I was afraid he would not be equal to the struggle against the strong and ruthless men who were swooping down upon Russia from every corner of Europe; but the Russians, who are courtiers in St. Petersburg, became Tatars again in the army."

La Harpe had dictated the settlement. Pares writes: "Paradoxically, the Czar thus granted the Poles what he refused the Russians. But, he thought, the Poles had long experience of a constitutional regime, while in Russia such an innovation would lead to mad dreams and rumblings of rebellion." That concession was the high-water mark for Alexander I's liberal compassion.

Until he died of malaria in 1825, Alexander I turned increasingly mystical and reactionary. The goal of his rule, he wrote, was to "to unmask and punish the Voltarians, the Martinists, the Freemasons; to decapitate 'the seven-headed hydra of illuminism.'" He said: "Have no illusions, there is a conspiracy among all these societies…all these anti-Christian sects, which are founded on the principles of the so-called philosophy of Voltaire, have sworn relentless vengeance upon all governments." Some suggested that he faked his death in the Crimea, so that he could live out his life as a hermit in Siberia. The same rumors circulated about Stalin.

To the Crimea: *the hero of my tale is truth*

I SHOULD HAVE SPENT MORE TIME in the State History Museum rooms concerning Czar Nicholas I and gotten a better understanding of his dark personality. (The Russian writer Alexander Herzen said: "I know nothing so terrible, nothing which could banish hope as those colorless, cold pewter eyes…") But I was impatient to find the cabinets that showed the topography of the Crimean War, and the coordinates of the Light Brigade's charge. Alfred, Lord Tennyson ends his epic with these words:

> *Honour the charge they made!*
> *Honour the Light Brigade,*
> *Noble six hundred!*

141

The British cavalry are less esteemed in the museum, which takes the view that the Crimean coalition (that of the Allies ganging up against Russia) was to be avoided in the future. The war began in 1853 when Russia threatened the existence of the Ottoman Empire, which limped along on the goodwill of France and Britain. Weak herself, the Austro-Hungarian Empire stayed away from the fighting. The British and French came ashore above and below Sevastopol, in the Crimea, and threw themselves at the Russian defenses, which included battery officer Leo Tolstoy. When he wrote about Borodino, he had Sevastopol in mind. "You will also see," Tolstoy wrote about the Crimea, "that danger, misery, and suffering in the war will have imprinted on these faces the consciousness of their dignity, of high thoughts, of a sentiment."

A painting of the defenses shows Russian gunners around the Sevastopol parapets, like those under which Tolstoy served. Lost in the hero worship of the Light Brigade is the fact that Lord Cardigan spent most nights of the war living on his yacht, which was anchored off the Balaklava shore. In the tragic generalship of Lord Raglan can be seen the self-destructive heroism of the British Empire—one Crimean witness said: "I never saw people die with such a dreary perseverance"—that took so many casualties for such little gain. As a result of the war, the Ottomans were propped up, although Russia took confidence from its stout defense and later pushed the Turks out of Europe. By then, Tolstoy had retired to his estate at Yasnaya Polyana. In his *Sevastopol Sketches* he writes: "The hero of my tale… is the truth."

In Moscow I had wanted to visit Yasnaya Polyana and went so far as to find a tour that spent the day at his house and included lunch. I regret not going, but the tour was "temporarily canceled." Yasnaya Polyana is about three hours south of Moscow, just past Tula. I did visit Tolstoy's sprawling wooden house in Moscow, and loved looking at his writing table and drawing room, where he would read aloud to guests what he had written during the day. According to the guide who took me around, Tolstoy spent only an hour each day writing (mostly in the mornings, but sometimes after lunch), a fact I find difficult to comprehend, given the length and complexity of his writing. He had the legs on his desk chair cut down so that his nearsighted eyes would be closer to his manuscripts. It took Tolstoy almost eight years to write *War and Peace*. A picture I saw in his house shows the inn at Borodino where he stayed when conducting his research. After the trip, he wrote to his wife: "God grant me health and peace and quiet, and I shall describe the battle of Borodino as it has never been described before."

Count Witte Travels East: *on the rails to revolution*

ALEXANDER II (czar from 1855 to1881) is a fork in the road of Russian history, with one way leading to a constitutional monarchy and closer ties with the West and the other leading to Lenin and Stalin. Nevertheless, he gets little play in the State History Museum. Anarchists got him with a bomb in 1881, near the Winter Palace, but earlier he had signed the declaration that freed Russia's serfs (the ceremonial pen from 1861 is preserved). A fatalist, his assassin Grinevetsky said: "It is too early to thank God." Pares writes: "The bomb that killed Alexander put an end to the faint beginnings of Russian constitutionalism."

Alexander II had hoped to right an injustice and to increase agricultural production, but the emancipation of the serfs, as with many acts of the czars, had the effect of stalling political and economic progress. Instead of redistributing land to freed serfs, the emancipation kept it in the hands of the gentry, who either rented it to their former slaves or sold it to the local community. The gentry were no longer landed, which undercut a power base for the czar.

Russian agriculture remained inefficient and backward, as the serfs could do little more than subsistence farming on their small plots. For the constitutionalists, the hopes of self-government centered on local assemblies and dumas (*zemstvo*), although as with many czarist decrees these bodies had a bigger say in school hours than in the secret police. Russia drifted. Anarchism became one of the few growth sectors in the economy.

Lenin was eleven when Alexander II died. The event that changed the path of his life was the execution six years later of his older brother, who was charged with plotting against the life of Alexander III. (One account reads: "He became, as his younger brother Dmitri later observed, 'grimly restrained, strict, closed up in himself, highly focused.'")

A physically imposing man, Alexander III ruled Russia during a period of industrial expansion. To think about his years, I went into a room that explains "Industrial Russia." Among the cabinets with railway bonds and factory models, I found a portrait of Count Sergius Witte, the financial genius behind the Trans-Siberian Railway. Before becoming minister of finance in 1882 he had run a number of railways, and would later be instrumental in the financial structure and plans for the Trans-Siberian. He would also serve as the czar's negotiator in the Treaty of Portsmouth, which ended the Russo-Japanese War of 1904-05. His diplomatic skills reversed some of the losses that Russia suffered in the war. When I was home, I tracked down a copy of his engaging (if self-serving) memoirs, which are written with the frankness of the political and financial advice that he provided to several emperors, including his favorite, Alexander III. "It is my firm belief," he writes, "that had Alexander III been granted a longer life, he would have inaugurated an era of liberalism, but God called him away before this could be."

For all that Witte is associated with Russian expansion in the Far East, he lobbied against the war parties, for example those that believed in 1904 that the way to avoid revolution was to wage a "small victorious war." Witte's views were close to those of Otto von Bismarck, who said: "Russia has nothing to do in the West; she only contracts Nihilism and other diseases; her mission is in Asia; there she stands for civilization." Witte is credited with the revolutionary truism of 1905 that "The Japanese will not enter the Kremlin, but the Russians will."

Witte was a mercantilist who saw Russia's future as a trading bloc between Europe and the Pacific Ocean. He was less successful in navigating the transition between Alexander III and his son, who became Nicholas II and led Russia into World War I and then revolution. Witte had fueled Alexander's dreams of industrial self-sufficiency, and admired the czar for looking east, especially when Russia found itself shut out from Constantinople and rebuffed as a European power. ("Thus I argued that to uphold the territorial integrity of the Chinese Empire, it was necessary for us to have a railroad running along the shortest possible route to Vladivostok, across the northern part of Mongolia and Manchuria.") Both were proud when the crown prince Nicholas, in 1891, laid the cornerstone of the Trans-Siberian Railway in Vladivostok. But when Nicholas was czar, Witte found him weak and vacillating.

Witte describes the day of Nicholas' coronation, when a stampede on Moscow's Khodynka Field caused the death of five thousand celebrants. Witte writes in his memoirs: "A few hours after the Khodynka disaster, their Majesties attended a concert conducted by the celebrated Safonov....A gorgeous evening party was scheduled for the same day, to be given by the French Ambassador, Marquis de Montebello. We expected that the party would be called off... [but] it took place, as if nothing had happened, and the ball was opened by their Majesties dancing a quadrille." Such behavior foreshadows the czar's reaction during the Russo-Japanese War, when he got the news that Russia's Baltic fleet had been sunk in the Strait of Tsushima, with most ships lost. The czar was playing tennis when given a telegram with news of the defeat; his answer was to keep playing.

Witte negotiated the so-called 1896 "Treaty of Integrity" with the Chinese that established a defensive alliance against Japan and allowed Russia to construct the Chinese-Eastern Railway (CER) that cut across northern China from Lake Baikal to Vladivostok. The agreement was signed in secrecy, and terms of the treaty were not revealed until the Soviets published them in the 1930s. They set Russia on a collision course with Japan that lasted well into the twentieth century.[2]

When Nicholas was the crown prince, Witte liked to compliment his graciousness, saying: "I have never in my life met another with nicer manners." Those traits, however, were part of his undoing. Pares writes: "Nicholas had a conquering personal charm, the source of which was an extreme delicacy of thought, almost feminine in kind; but he was hopelessly weak." It was said that he would have been better suited as the director of a boys' summer camp than as emperor of Russia. Witte quotes a minister, Pyotr Durnovo: "Mark my words: Nicholas II will prove a modernized version of Paul II."

Hitler Invades Russia: *the ghost of Napoleon stood at his elbow*

WHILE IN MOSCOW I tracked down the sites associated with the city during World War II. At an Ikea store near the airport, a monument marks the farthest penetration of the German armies

---

2   In his *Memoirs* Witte writes: "The agreement was an act of the highest importance. Had we faithfully observed it, we would have been spared the disgrace of the Japanese war and we would have secured a firm foothold in the Far East. Anticipating upon the course of events, I may say here that we ourselves broke the agreement and brought about the situation which we are now facing in the Far East. It was an act in which treachery and giddy-headedness were curiously mingled."

on their 1941 attack into Russia. Some of the mosaics that adorn the Moscow metro depict themes of World War II. At various stations I found the themes of glory and defense of the homeland etched into ceilings and corners, lost to rushing commuters. One mosaic shows a dirigible over Red Square, although I could not tell if it was part of a German attack or a Russian five-year plan.

The biggest exhibits about the Great Patriotic War are in a memorial park that is some distance from downtown, surrounded by fountains, victory columns, dates of major battles, and great halls of marble. I went there on a cool summer Saturday, laden with swirling clouds and stiff breezes. I lingered over the dioramas that showed such epic struggles as the battle of Stalingrad, the siege of Leningrad, the tank battles at Kursk, and the fall of Berlin. The German Reichstag is shown engulfed in flames and surrounded by advancing soldiers.

Absent from the remembrance storyboards is the extent to which Russian soldiers raped and pillaged their way into Berlin, in retribution for what the Germans did to the Russians after they attacked on June 22, 1941. For example, by September 1941 the Russians had suffered two million casualties in the German invasion. Another two million would die in extermination camps, set up in the rear of the front-line German forces. The territory squeezed between Germany and Russia, in the words of historian Timothy Snyder, became the "bloodlands" that would consume fourteen million individuals.

Because I did not have many dinner meetings during my stay in Moscow, I spent most evenings in local cafés, answering emails and reading Alan Clark's *Barbarossa*: *The Russian German Conflict, 1941–1945*. Growing up, I had seen the book on my father's shelves, but never read it, until I was hunting for books to take with me to Russia. Clark was a Conservative member of the British parliament who published diaries that were savored for their accounts of his serial love affairs. Earlier in his career, his books were more conventional military histories, including this one, which was published in the early 1960s. His thesis is that the German invasion was doomed from the start, even though it carried to the banks of the Volga and the outskirts of Leningrad and Moscow. He writes: "But the hard fact remains that the Germans, even at this early stage, were attempting too much. Their mobile forces were not strong enough, or numerous enough, to support three simultaneous thrusts."

Clark is strongest in analyzing how Stalin's policies in the late 1930s decimated the Russian officer corps. The dictator's purges and show trials took the following toll on the army: "Every commander of a military district had been executed by the summer of 1938. Thirteen out of fifteen army commanders, fifty-seven out of eighty-five corps commanders, 110 out of 195 divisional commanders, 220 out of 406 brigade commanders, were executed." By the time Hitler attacked the Soviet Union, the only option available to Stalin was to trade lives and space, in the hope of exhausting the German attackers. In the first months of the war, Russia suffered two million casualties, had 18,000 tanks destroyed, lost 22,000 artillery pieces, and had 14,000 aircraft shot down or disabled. Clark writes: "Stalin believed that space was more important than fixed defenses, but he ignored the fact that the Army was not trained in the sort of fluid defensive battle that alone makes use of space profitable."

What saved Russia from annihilation in the fighting, according to Clark, was Hitler's decision to forgo a direct attack on Moscow and to press forward on three broad fronts, which, as they moved deeper into Russia, were too thinly spread. He describes Hitler's indecision as his armies moved east: "The ghost of Napoleon stood at his elbow, as it did at some moment for every German officer in the East, and he was determined to resist the temptation of a March on Moscow until he had laid (as he believed) a secure strategic foundation."

By not encircling Moscow in a "super Cannae" (that is, by going around behind it), Hitler allowed his three-pronged invasion to stall along a front that stretched more than a thousand miles. Clark concludes: "From November 1942 on, the posture of the Wehrmacht in the East was fundamentally a defensive one." Evocatively, he quotes a German colonel: "The German army in fighting Russia is like an elephant attacking a host of ants. The elephant will kill thousands, perhaps even millions, of ants, but in the end their numbers will overcome him, and he will be eaten to the bone."

From the war memorial, I took the metro to Moscow's military museum, which had out front the T-34 tanks that were so pivotal in stopping the German offensive. Some German panzer tanks might have had more mobility than the T-34, but the comparable production numbers favored the Russians. In 1943 and 1944, the Germans produced 6,000 and then 9,161 tanks, while in the same two years the Russians made 11,000 and then 17,000 tanks, the result being the victory at Kursk, which in 1944 ended the German invasion and broke open the long eastern front.

For some bureaucratic reason the military museum was closed that afternoon. In my disappointment I started walking until, by consulting a guidebook, I found the nearby boyhood home of the great Russian writer Fyodor Dostoyevsky. His father was a doctor at a Moscow clinic, and the apartment where Dostoyevsky grew up is on the grounds of a sanitarium. There were no signs for the writer's house. I wandered the grounds, poking into empty buildings, until I found the exhibition on the early days of the writer, whose life spanned much of the nineteenth century.

Dostoyevsky died about the time Alexander II was assassinated in 1881, and his lifetime included long stretches of exile in Siberia, which shaped his views of individual and government powers. His childhood room shows a bed, desk, and small coal stove. The apartment is surprisingly cheerful for someone whose writing would capture the underworlds to which the czars and Stalin would doom so many Russians. (*"If he has a conscience he will suffer for his mistake. That will be punishment—as well as the prison."*) Imagine how his novels would read if he had had to take account of the crimes and punishments that engulfed Russia in World War II.

Russian Railways: *a shortcut to Shanghai*

THE TRAIN LEFT on time from Kazan Station. Normally the Trans-Siberian leaves from Yaroslav Station, but as this one was privately chartered, we left from a station that has the grandeur of a czarist palace. I could imagine Witte dedicating the frescoed waiting room or supervising the station's construction.

I was early for the train and wandered into the railway museum, which had models of early Trans-Siberian engines, which were powered by steam, painted black with red trim, and had first silver and later red stars. I also met with a public-relations manager of Russian Railways. I had gotten his name from the Internet, and he agreed to meet me. We went to a café around the corner from the railway headquarters, not far from Kazan Station. Although it was a summer day, it felt like October. I was happy to have a pot of hot tea to nurse as he told me about the strategic plans of the railway, one of the biggest companies in the world.

What interested me most was to hear about the freight service that is shortening the time it will take to deliver a shipping container from, say, Shanghai to Berlin. In the past, because of political tensions between Russia and China, and then the kleptocracy that was dominant in Russia, not many shippers wanted to send their containers overland from the Far East to Western Europe. Instead, they loaded their goods on container vessels that went around the Cape of Good Hope or used the Suez Canal to enter the Mediterranean. Depending on the stops, the voyages take about three weeks.

Because of the improvements at the Russian Railways, the company can compete with many shipping companies that offer liner service from the Far East to Europe. A freight train can make the run from Shanghai to Berlin in two weeks. Shanghai to Beijing is a day, Beijing to Moscow is nine days, and then another two to three days are needed to connect into a European rail yard. If the gauge of Russian rail were the same as those in China and Western Europe, the time could be even less, as boxes from China now need to be hoisted onto Russian flatcars, a process that is duplicated when the Russian trains cross into Western Europe. To improve the service, Russian Railways is extending its five-foot-gauge tracks from the Russian border to Vienna, which will mean that the boxes, and even passenger trains, would not need to change over to the European system.

Another bottleneck in the system stems from the fact that there is only a single track across much of Mongolia, the logical freight line from China to Russia. Mongolia is a vast, open steppe of a country, with high mountains in the background. It fears Chinese penetration as much as it does Russian influence. The idea of double track raises geopolitical fears, as much as it would facilitate expanded East-West trade. Across Russia, the lines of the Trans-Siberian are double-tracked, with marshaling yards and sidings in the many cities and towns along the route. Even with double tracks, Russian Railways operates at full capacity on the line between Irkutsk and Omsk, with a train every fifteen minutes in both directions. Adding another track to the Trans-Siberian route would alleviate the freight congestion, but Siberia is vast, and transcontinental construction epics were the dreams of the nineteenth century, not the twenty-first.

Although the joint-stock company of the Russian Railways dates only to 2003, it is already a world railroad leader for size and innovative strategic plans. At my meeting I collected brochures and annual reports of the company. Since then I have spent many happy hours daydreaming about some the new routes that the railroad is proposing. Already the company has 82,000 kilometers of track, 11,100 locomotives, 624,000 freight wagons, 24,100 long-distance passenger cars, and more than a million employees. Each year it carries more than a billion passengers, and accounts for 41 percent of intercity travel within Russia, despite the distances. From these figures, the assumption could be made that the Russian Railways is a staid bureaucracy, the kind of cumbersome venture dreamed up in a five-year plan. Instead, the company bristles with innovation.

The railway has introduced high-speed service between Moscow and St. Petersburg, cutting the travel time to less than four hours. (The track between the two cities is famously straight.) It has similar high-speed plans to connect St. Petersburg and Helsinki, Finland, with customs and immigration done on the train. Another plan is to renovate the line that cuts across the Korean peninsula, from Russia and North Korea to Pusan, a port in the South. Cost estimates are $8 billion to refurbish this line, which would allow freight to move exclusively on the Russian gauge, if not bring peace to the peninsula.

The company has exciting plans that would extend the "North-South Corridor" to include rail links to the Persian Gulf, India, and China. Already it is possible to travel along a steel "Silk Road" from Moscow to Beijing. (My friend Tim Littler, who operates GW Travel, offers such a journey in luxury cars.) In partnership with other lines, Russian Railways has hopes of through service to Hong Kong and Singapore. (It will need to finish the line that crossed the River Kwai.) Within Russia, it wants to improve commuter rail around Moscow—notorious for its traffic congestion—and build a new corridor through Kursk down to Adler.

When I first rode the Russian railways in summer 1975, the cars and stations felt worn, and I remember how passengers would come and go from our couchettes, anonymous as characters in a Russian novel. Now the main terminals across Russia are elegant and vast. Even in remote Siberian cities it is not uncommon to find stations on the scale of New York's Grand Central.

From and to the Kazan Station: *expelling Lenin*

FOR THE TRIP TO ULAN BATOR, Mongolia's capital, I was assigned a compartment in the last car. My bedroom had two parallel bunks, on either side of a large window, and a desk in between. On the folding table I set up my computer, notebook, map, and timetables. Along the empty berth I arranged what I called, "the train library," a collection of books I had carried to Russia. I even had a documentary film of the last czar and a rail map with Russian names. For the next week this compartment would be home. I never tired of coming back to my room, ordering tea from the porter, and watching Russia unfurl as the train picked its way east. Later, I liked to joke with my son Charles, "The problem with the train trip was that it lasted only eight days."

Because it was high summer, the sun set after 10 p.m. and rose early. I rarely lowered the shade, fearful that I might miss something outside: a wooden dispatcher's hut, a collective farm, a city, or a river. In truth, there is little to see between Moscow and Kazan, the first stop. The landscape is swampland, like parts of the American South, and the vegetation is gnarled, as if home to alligators. I thought often of Napoleon's retreat through such a festering landscape. Pares describes it: "They were not regiments on the march but twenty tribes of nomads, weighed down with booty and united by fear, dragging themselves across the steppe."

The other travelers in my group were English. We met in the late afternoons around the bar, when I would talk for an hour about some aspect of Russian history. Leaving Moscow, I talked about the aftermath of the Napoleonic wars and the Congress of Vienna. Before leaving, we had toured the Kremlin and seen the embellished cannons that Napoleon had dragged to the gates of the city.

The next morning the train stopped in Kazan, the capital of the Autonomous Republic of Tatarstan, a Muslim enclave within Russia, and a center of oil wealth. We toured the city in a cold rain and took a boat ride on the Volga River, which at Kazan is wider than the Mississippi, more the size of a large lake. Because of prevailing winds, the west bank of the river is hilly, which explains why, farther down the river at Stalingrad, the Russians defended that side of the Volga.

I liked the humor of the local guide, who said: "It used to be that I took my guests to Lenin statues and museums. Now I take them to Orthodox cathedrals." He explained that Lenin had attended law school in Kazan, until he was expelled for attending a political rally, reinforcing the point that his anger at the monarchy sprang from the execution of his older brother, stemming from the plot against Alexander III. The guide added, "Whether the city is happy or sad that he was expelled from the law school depends on the prevailing political situation."

Kazan has a historic Kremlin, similar, if smaller than that in Moscow. Turkic nomads who preceded Genghis Khan, the Tatars often fought battles of religious frenzy around Kazan's fortress. (In response, the Russian princes said defiantly: "When there are none of us left, then all will be yours.") Later the city was the capital of what was called "the Kingdom of the Khans of the Golden Horde," which Ivan the Terrible liberated in 1552. Maybe that explains why the president's palace is locked behind high gates? Politically, the local parliament "suggests" a presidential candidate to the Russian Federation, which then "ratifies" the choice. In other words, Vladimir Putin appoints the local leader. As best as I could determine, the job of the president of Tatarstan is to stand around reception halls, of which there are many across the city.

At the center of Kazan, along with cathedrals and icons, is a brand new mosque, which looks as if it were lifted, minarets and all, from the Persian Gulf. Iran paid $300 million for its construction, completed by the Turks. In the mosque I climbed to a balcony that looked down on the segregated women's prayer room, as incongruous in the middle of Russia as would be horsemen of the Golden Horde, bearing down on some tourist buses. Mosques in Tatarstan are one reason why Moscow opposes so violently the separatist claims prevalent across the Caucasus and Central Asia.

Across the Urals to Ekaterinburg: *the last days of Nicholas and Alexandra*

WHEN I WOKE UP the next morning, the train was snaking a course through the Urals, the chain of mountains that separate Europe from Asia, at least in geography textbooks. I had expected something similar to the Alleghenies or maybe the Alps. From the train window, the Urals looked like pleasant rolling hills covered with lakes, birch, and pine. No wonder they offered little protection during the Mongol invasions.

Ekaterinburg, where the train stopped for the day, was until recently a closed city, meaning it was off limits to foreigners for military reasons. During the Communist era it was known as Sverdlovsk, named after an early party warhorse, until the city was opened and resumed having the name that came from the wife of Peter the Great. The reason that Ekaterinburg had military significance is that, after Hitler invaded Russia, Stalin ordered that heavy industry be relocated behind the front lines, and many plants were dragged to the city. At the station the guide said, in the patter of her trade: "As you can see, Ekaterinburg is a city of great transport." All I could see was a dusty city that had none of the oil revenue that has given Moscow and Kazan their sheen.

Western travelers come to Ekaterinburg to take ghoulish stock of where the last czar, Nicholas II, and his family were executed in June 1918. After the czar abdicated his throne in March 1917, the family refused asylum in Germany, which, after all, was the enemy, but they had no way to transit to England or France. Instead, the provisional government sent them to live along the Volga, not far from Rasputin's home village. In 1918, fearful that advancing Czech and White Russian forces, moving west from Siberia, might link up with the Romanovs, the Bolsheviks arrested the former royal family. In their last week, the Romanovs were held in the house of Ekaterinburg's governor, under Bolshevik guard. At the end, the family, along with a doctor and several attendants, were herded into the basement and massacred, including the famous Anastasia.

The czar's family had meekly descended into the darkness because the guards had said they wanted to take their picture. This was the first royal family to have grown up in the glare of flashbulbs and celebrity. Instead, they were stabbed and shot. Their remains were driven to woods outside the city, burned, and buried, although in two separate plots, which explains the theories that some members, notably Anastasia, had escaped and perhaps were living in New Jersey. In 2007, the last of the remains were unearthed. (A chapel marks the location, although there are demands for a full-blown cathedral.) All the bones of Nicholas II and his family were interred in St. Petersburg, at the Saints Peter and Paul Cathedral. A new cathedral, Our Lady of the Blood, was built in Ekaterinburg, where the Romanovs were killed, and to mark Nicholas' sainthood. Oddly, the Orthodox Church has rejected the assertion that the bones found locally are all those of the royal family, and have called for a criminal investigation of the murders, so that new details of the killing could be learned. Like the mosque in Kazan, the new cathedral in Ekaterinburg must have cost millions of dollars to construct, and it looms incongruously large in the city.

Without the losses in World War I—3.8 million Russian soldiers were casualties in the first year—Nicholas II might have muddled through and not met the violent fate of so many Romanov czars. The 1905 Revolution could have led to a constitutional monarchy, and allowed the czar his proper role in Russian society, that of a genial figurehead and a symbol of continuity. Instead, the declaration of war in 1914 exposed the weaknesses not just of Russian society—the legacies of serfdom, the absence of a middle class, an aristocracy that equated governance with a masked ball—but those of the czar as a wartime leader. During the war's first months, at Tannenberg in the Masurian Lakes region of Poland, the Germans surrounded several Russian armies, which suffered a million casualties. The German commander Hindenburg said of Russian losses: "Five or eight millions? We have no idea. All we know is that sometimes in our battles with the Russians we had to remove the mounds of enemy corpses from before our trenches in order to get a clear field of fire against fresh assaulting waves." In the campaigns that followed, across the broad fronts of Poland and Austria-Hungary, the czar's generals deployed these strategies of suicidal attrition, which exhausted Austria's empire and that of the czar.

In *The Fall of the Russian Monarchy*, Pares writes about the last czar: "Everywhere there is humor, good sense, a compelling kindness, a quick intelligence and an excellent memory. Nowhere is there strength. The quality was one of appeal; it was as if he were almost asking you to be pleased in his company." Witte, who died before the war, nevertheless takes a darker view of the czar's inabilities, arguing that he was not just weak and "feminine," but also callous and arrogant.[3] Witte recalls: "When, in the course of my official conferences with His Majesty, I referred to public opinion, His Majesty often-times snapped angrily: 'What have I to do with public opinion?'"

Guchkov Stands Up for Russia: *dueling with its enemies*

WHEN CZAR NICHOLAS ABDICATED in March 1917, in favor of his brother, who had no interest in the job, he handed his letter of resignation to Alexander Guchkov, who had earlier rallied the democratic opposition in the Duma parliament. There is no photograph of the abdication, but in Moscow, before leaving on the Trans-Siberian, I found a painting of the scene at the Museum of the Contemporary History of Russia. It shows the czar, dressed in a long robe, handing a letter to Guchkov, who looks as if he is standing up from a desk in a hurry to receive the sovereign, who might have entered the room unexpectedly. (Pares writes of the scene: "Guchkov was full of pity at approaching his archenemy at the moment of his deepest humiliation.") I was pleased to find the painting because, through my work, I had spent many years working with Guchkov's grandson, Jean Goutchkoff, who grew up in Paris and later moved to Geneva.

Over the years Jean and I had traveled together, at times in Russia. Often our conversations had touched on his grandfather, whose dramatic life from 1860 to 1936 represents a path not taken in Russia—toward democracy, constitutional monarchy, and a

---

3   It was said about the czar: "He hates everyone whom he fears, and there is no one whom he fears more than [the German Kaiser] William."

Western economy. Certainly Alexander Guchkov's life is worthy
of Tolstoy's fiction. He was chairman of the Duma, volunteered
in foreign wars, managed a large fortune, and fought numerous
duels. In his trilogy about the Russian revolution, *The Red Wheel*,
Aleksandr Solzhenitsyn includes his character at length, having
read much of his unpublished correspondence. Eager to hear more
about Guchkov's tempestuous life, Solzhenitsyn invited Jean to
meet with him.

The grandson of a serf, Alexander Guchkov grew up the son
of a Moscow industrialist who made his fortune in insurance,
trading, and other industries. His son Alexander inherited his
father's company and fortune, but also a temperament for bold
action and risk that is difficult to fathom. He was present in
China during the Boxer Rebellion in 1900, at which time he rode
a horse along the Great Wall. During the Boer War in South
Africa, he volunteered to fight against what he perceived to be
English imperialism, and he served the Boers with distinction.
Several years later, in the Russo-Japanese War, Guchkov stayed
behind in Mukden to treat the Russian wounded in the climactic
last battle. (Pares writes: "When the hospital operations in progress were completed they escorted him back to the Russian lines,
which involved a walk of six days.") After the 1905 Revolution,
he was elected to the Duma, where he later served as chairman
and, in opposition to the czar, as the leader of the reformers,
known as Octobrists.

During World War I, Guchkov was the head of a War Industry
Committee of businessmen who supported the war. He was also
a senior official with the Red Cross, dealing with the millions
of casualties that resulted from the czarist orders that sent men
forward in battle, at times without weapons. After the disastrous
Battle of Tannenberg, Guchkov went forward into no man's land
to seek the fate of the Russian general Samsonov, who, he learned,

had committed suicide behind the Russian lines, an event that Sol-zhenitsyn describes in tragic detail in *August 1914*. Solzhenitsyn's subsequent volume, *November 1916*, explores the possible conver-sations that Guchkov might have had on the subject of removing the czar from power. Solzhenitsyn has Guchkov saying: "Well, winning the war with such an incompetent government is indeed impossible!"

After his heroics in the Russo-Japanese War, Guchkov had been close to the royal couple, but his opposition in the Duma strained the relationship. Never awed by pomp, Guchkov denounced the influence of Rasputin as a charlatan. Not surprisingly, Czarina Alexandra came to despise Guchkov and disparaged him in her letters (many of which were found in a trunk in Ekaterinburg). She wrote, "Hanging is too good for him." On one occasion she asks, "Could not a strong railway accident be arranged in which he alone would suffer?"

From the left, Leon Trotsky denounced Guchkov as an accom-modating capitalist. In his history of the Russian Revolution, Trotsky goes on at length about Guchkov's fawning obsequies over the assassinated prime minister, Stolypin, notorious for his repres-sive policies. After the czar abdicated in 1917, Guchkov consented to join the transitional government as minister of war, and did his best to avoid the collapse of the army. He resigned in May 1917, citing the inability of his colleagues to enforce civil law. In a tribute to his friend, published in 1936, Pares describes Guchkov's last speech: "Beginning with the now discarded word 'Gentlemen,' he told the story of his life's work for the Russian army, and of all that was portended by its dissolution. When he ceased, there was a long hush, and then, even in that hostile audience, a tremendous outburst of applause; but the next minute Zinoviev was preaching Marxism from the same tribune, and so that particular record of achievement was allowed to slip away into history."

In 1918, after the Bolsheviks seized power in the Russian civil war, Guchkov fled to Paris, where he lived until 1936. His last words were: "Read me what they are writing about Russia."[4] The ironies of Guchkov's life are that he was a strong Russian patriot, yet opposed to the rule of the czar; he was a man of arms and the army, yet opposed to the slaughters of World War I; he was an anti-imperialist, yet believed strongly in the Russian empire; he was a democratic parliamentarian, yet respectful of the monarchy's traditions and continuity; and he was a revolutionary figure, in terms of advocating a constitutional government, but without any illusions about how the Bolsheviks would rule Russia. Before the October Revolution, he said presciently that "power would fall to those who had made the revolution."

Pares says of him: "Guchkov has a large dose of adventure in his composition; and it was his political defect that he was often overdoing his cleverness and attempting too much." Solzhenitsyn asks: "Perhaps in a career of uncompromising awkwardness he had bumped his head against too many walls?"

My friend Jean never personally knew his grandfather, but to anyone who knows Russian history, his last name evokes respect and admiration, among all political classes. Even the current prime minister, Vladimir Putin, praises Guchkov as one of his "childhood

---

4   In exile, Guchkov was close to Professor Pares, who in the 1920s and '30s was the foremost western scholar of czar's last government and the revolution. In *The Fall of the Russian Monarchy* Pares writes at length about his achievements: "Guchkov's chief quality was a daring gallantry; he was at ease with himself and enjoyed stepping forward under fire with a perfect calm whenever there was anything which he wished to challenge; his defect was his restlessness; without actually asking for it, he was instinctively always in the limelight, always trying to do too much. He had the easy organizing ability of a first-rate English politician; he was quietly proud of his democratic origin, and all his actions were inspired by an ardent love for Russia and the Russian people, in whose native conservatism, common sense and loyalty he fully shared. He was an enemy of class privileges, and at this time he claimed for his country some measure of consultation as was secured for Germany by the Reichstag. Guchkov led the Octobrists or party of patriotic reform, and for them no less than for the Cadets the political model was England; but while the Cadets preached English political principles, the Octobrists were much more akin to the ordinary instincts of English political life."

heroes." Trotsky called him "a liberal with spurs." Guchkov's legacy is summed up in his confession to his friend and literary executor, Boris Elkin, that for him "A love of Russia was his religion." As postscript to his friend's passing, Elkin added: "The tragedy of a great man is the tragedy of Russia."

Across Siberia to Krasnoyarsk: *bears are available*

AFTER THE TRANS-SIBERIAN left Ekaterinburg, there wasn't much to do for the next several days along what is called the Great Siberian Post Road. In the train's dining car I found a perch that was an open door guarded by a wrought-iron railing, which allowed me to ride with my head tilted outside the train, as I were if a steam engineer. The kitchen staff even brought me coffee, and were amused that I could spend hours communing with the empty landscape.

Western Siberia resembles the Great Plains of Kansas and Nebraska, with prairie stretching to the horizon. I was surprised at how few farms there were on the endless landscape. Occasionally, near some of the stations, I saw the hulking remains of collective farms, reduced to abandoned warehouses or forlorn sidings with a few outbuildings. Across vast stretches of Siberia, there is little evidence that anyone is working the land, except the summer sun and winter winds. In Moscow I had been told that private corporations owned much of the arable land and that Russian farmers were trudging to the cities. John Steinbeck writes in *The Grapes of Wrath*: "But this tractor does two things—it turns the land and turns us off the land. There is little difference between this tractor and a tank. The people were driven, intimidated, hurt by both."

Each day the train stopped for a few hours, in cities such as Novosibirsk, where we rode on buses and took trips along some of the Siberian rivers that have the vastness of the Mississippi or Missouri rivers. At the Ob River, which passes through Novosibirsk on its three-thousand-mile run from the Altai Mountains to the Arctic Sea, one of the guides explained how Huns, Turks, Mongols, Tatars, and Cossacks had fought their way across the river, which was a huge obstacle in the construction of the Trans-Siberian Railway. The guide at the Academy of Sciences spoke about the vast deposits of oil, gas, coal, gold, diamonds, and other minerals. Gesturing toward the forests, she added: "Bears are available."

If I had a favorite among Siberian cities, it was Krasnoyarsk ("... *third city in Russia in terms of city fountains*"), which is on the banks of the Yenisei River. I could have done without the band of folk singers who regaled us on the river, as we passed under a sprawling party edifice that, so the guide claimed, had won the same architectural award once given to the Eiffel Tower. Otherwise, I warmed to the city's history, more than its Parisian-Stalinist architecture. In a park I found a memorial to the more than one million Ukrainians and Germans who were resettled in Krasnoyarsk after Hitler's 1941 Russian invasion. Nearby was a plaque that recalls the Chernobyl residents who also were resettled in Siberia.

On the bus we passed near the house of local industrialist Gennadius V. Yudin, who in the nineteenth century collected 80,000 books about Siberia. The collection was valued at $114,000, but in 1907 he sold the books for $40,000 to the U.S. Library of Congress. They became the basis of its Siberian collection, and the irony is that, while here in exile, Lenin used the books freely to write *The Development of Capitalism in Russia*. He spent three years in Krasnoyarsk, traveling by the ship *St. Nicholas* to the city center. (Presumably he was spared the band.) He wrote: "There is nothing new I can write about myself; my life goes on as usual. I stroll to the library outside town, I stroll in the neighborhood, I stroll around to my acquaintances and sleep enough for two—in short, everything is as it should be." He makes exile sound like a postdoctoral fellowship.

The Building of the Trans-Siberian: *dependent on the railroad*

MOSTLY WHAT I DID while crossing Siberia was drink tea in my compartment and read Harmon Tupper's *To the Great Ocean: The Taming of Siberia and the Building of the Trans-Siberian*. It is another book that I knew from my father's bookshelves. It is much more than a railroad history. Tupper sets the Trans-Siberian in the political context of Russia's Asian ambitions as conceived by, among others, Alexander III and Sergius Witte. He describes, for example, how railroad politics obsessed Russia at the time of the Boxer Rebellion in 1900. He writes: "It was an open secret that from the very beginning of the campaign it was the desire of the military party not only to punish the Boxers but also permanently to annex Manchuria." Those positions pitted Witte against the war lobbies, as he writes: "After dealing with the railroad for forty years, I can say that in most cases the strategic considerations of our War Ministry regarding the direction of the road are pure fantasy. The country will be best off if, in building railroads, it is guided by purely economic considerations."

The continuous Trans-Siberian line wasn't finished until 1916, with the completion of the bridge at Khabarovsk; until bridges were in place, tracks in winter were laid across frozen Siberian rivers. Another shortcut was found in the 1901 completion of the Chinese Eastern Railway, which the Russians built across Manchuria to Vladivostok. A touch naively, Witte writes: "The Chinese Eastern Railway was designed exclusively for cultural and peaceful purposes, but jingoist adventurers turned it into a means of political aggression involving the violation of treaties, the breaking of freely given promises and disregard of the elementary interests of other nationalities."

In the Russo-Japanese War, however, the Trans-Siberian bottleneck around Lake Baikal kept Russian reinforcements from reaching the front lines at Mukden and encouraged the sending of the Baltic Fleet to rescue the beleaguered army—a move that cost dearly the navy, if not the monarchy. At the end of World War I, the progress of White Russian allies, moving west along the Trans-Siberian line, forced the hand of the Bolsheviks in executing the czar and his family. Throughout the 1920s and 1930s, the foreign relations among Russia, Japan, and China can best be understood as a struggle for the control of the Chinese Eastern Railway.

In theory, Russia wanted its classless society to return the line to the Chinese—in exchange for control over Mongolia—and did so officially in 1924. A year later, however, the Russians and the Japanese confirmed the terms of the 1905 Portsmouth Peace Treaty, and awarded Japan controlling interest in the South Manchuria Railway (nominally a Chinese asset). In the 1930s, Stalin sold the Chinese Eastern Railway to the Japanese, as part of the partitioning of Manchuria in 1933. They changed the rail gauge from Russian to standard, but war remained on the line.

In the early days of World War II, Stalin made the point that if a foreign army cut the Trans-Siberian, the Soviet Union "would be finished." In February 1945, much of the Yalta Conference dealt with the question of Russia's railroad interests in the Far East, and how a peace with Japan would restore them. After the war, Stalin pushed the line south through the border town of Naushki, south of Irkutsk, to expand Russia's presence in Mongolia and to link Moscow with Peking. A 1962 report concluded: "It is likely, indeed, that no major nation has ever been so completely dependent on the railroad as the Soviet Union is today."

Siberian Exiles: *from Solzhenitsyn to E. H. Harriman*

IN TELLING THE STORY of the railroad, Tupper describes the political effect of laying track across Siberia, which until construction of the line was accessible only by boat, sled, and dirt paths. "Its route in western and central Siberia," he writes, "roughly follows the fifty-fifth degree of latitude and passes through territory traversed since the sixteenth century by fur hunters, traders, Cossacks, freebooters, religious dissenters, gold and silver prospectors, and hosts of convicts, political exiles, and free peasant settlers."

Part of the reason Alexander III and Count Witte were so determined to lay track across Siberia was to keep it from falling into foreign hands, including that of the United States. Tupper describes the Siberian explorations of several Americans, including the namesake of the future diplomat George Kennan, who wrote home about the region's untapped riches. Kennan (1845-1924) published *Tent Life in Siberia*, from his travels, and later wrote a pioneering study of the exile system.

One consequence of Kennan's explorations across Siberia was to encourage the railroad magnate E.H. Harriman (whose biography he later wrote) to consider buying the Trans-Siberian and having it be part of a round-the-world rail network. In his book *Manchuria and Her Railways* (1917), Kennan quotes from one of Harriman's letters, written in 1905: "It is important to save the commercial interests of the United States from being entirely wiped from the Pacific Ocean in the future, and the way to find out what is best to be done is to start something." "Something" meant trying to acquire sections of the Trans-Siberian Railway, especially in Manchuria. Billionaire Warren Buffett, the new owner of the Burlington Northern Santa Fe, a successor to Harriman's Union Pacific, should have similar ideas.[5]

5　Kennan writes: "His plan was, first, to secure control of the South Manchuria Railway, which Japan, through fortunes of war, had just acquired from Russia…. No one who had studied Mr. Harriman's constructive and administrative methods can doubt that if he had ever acquired even partial control of the Trans-Siberian Railway, he would have doubled or trebled its carrying capacity."

The presence of the Trans-Siberian Railway made it that much easier for the czar to sentence petty offenders to exile. Between 1800 and World War I, more than a million Russians were exiled. ("*The Tsar's cow pasture is so large you can't get out of it.*") They included those convicted of "felonious assault, fortune-telling, vagrancy, prizefighting, snuff-taking, setting fires by accident, and begging under false pretenses…" In czarist Russia, it was a crime to own a copy of Ralph Waldo Emerson's essay on "Self-Reliance." In Omsk prison, part of the early exile system, Dostoyevsky was "thrashed almost to death because he complained of a lump of filth in the soup."

With the completion of the rail line, deportations could become wholesale. Much of the Trans-Siberian's second track was built from 1933 to 1935 with slave labor. After the war, Gulag prisoners, such as Aleksandr Solzhenitsyn, were also used to build the Baikal Amur Mainline, the so-called BAM line, which runs parallel to the Trans-Siberian, but to the north, thus far removed from would-be (Chinese) invaders. Perhaps from experience, in *The Gulag Archipelago*, Solzhenitsyn writes: "The line separating good and evil passes not through states, nor between classes, nor between parties either, but right through the human heart."

Even though the Trans-Siberian was an instrument of exile and deportation, the early trains were the definition of luxury until the Russian Revolution retired the standard equipment on the *Russian State Express*, which included: stationary bicycles, an "exerciser," a darkroom for photography, steam heat, ice boxes, electric fans, card tables, overstuffed armchairs, and a "gymnasium with dumbbells." Early ads for the service boasted of the reduced travel time between Europe and the Far East: "From London or Paris or Shanghai this will take 16 days, and cost £32 instead of the 35 days and £90 required by the present sea route. With the increase of speed of Siberian trains to the European limit, the overland journey between the Atlantic and Pacific will in time be reduced to 10 days."

The Trans-Siberian had water tanks for live fish, and the chef was praised for the "nominal" charges he would assess if asked to roast wild game bought at one of the stations. Along with speed and lavish comforts, the train also featured a "church car," complete with a priest, "icons, free-standing floor candelabra, and, outside at one end of the roof, a pair of church bells surmounted by the double-barred cross of the Russian Orthodox Church."

Irkutsk and its Rebels: *Lake Baikal's revolutionary waters*

TO GET FROM KRASNOYARSK TO IRKUTSK, we traveled through the summer night. Instead of the empty steppe between the Ural Mountains and the Yenisei River, the landscape became more varied, with elegant dachas outside Krasnoyarsk and colonies of small tenant farmers, who during the week probably lived and worked in the city. Irkutsk is a junction on the Trans-Siberian, with the yards full of containers from Korea and the Far East. For its neighborhoods of old wooden houses, which reminded me of the French Quarter in New Orleans, the city deserves UNESCO protection. Most houses are in elegant disrepair, as if awaiting urban homesteaders to transform Irkutsk into the next Brooklyn.

For a landlocked city, about thirty miles from Lake Baikal, Irkutsk is surprisingly international. A local explorer, Gregori Sherikov, discovered Alaska, thanks to funding from Catherine the Great and the Russian-Asian Bank, which also financed the Trans-Siberian. Sherikov explored the Aleutian Islands and founded the town of Sitka (now in Alaska), on the Inside Passage. Of the two hundred thousand Irkutsk residents who fought in World War II, only 120,000 survived. The places of worship in Irkutsk include mosques, Polish Catholic churches, and Orthodox synagogues, and the faithful extend to Buddhists, Shamanists, and Old Believers.[6]

Irkutsk is where the Decembrists were sent into exile—along with their pianos, books, newspapers, music, and art—after some of their ringleaders were hanged, in 1826, for plotting against Nicholas I. (One historian later said that it was "an attempt that appeared less like a revolution in the making than a premature and tentative rehearsal of the first act of a play, still uncompleted, enacted under open skies, with great crowd scenes against an architectural setting.") They had fought Napoleon in front of Moscow in 1812 and elsewhere, but later came to embrace the republican ideals of the French Revolution. I attended a concert at one of their houses, now a museum in a rambling wooden home, painted gray, as might be found on Cape Cod.

On display are the art and letters of the Decembrists, some of which came from the poet Pushkin to Maria Volkonsky, the so-called "Princess of Siberia," who voluntarily went into exile with her husband, a conspirator. Like Lenin, the Decembrists made the most of their exile, although it began with years in chains, as if in the Gulag. As their sentences eased, they filled their houses with laughter, children, music, and ideas, one reason why Tolstoy conceived, but never finished, a historical novel about them. A relative once complimented Maria on the "kingdom" that she had carved from the tundra, to which she answered: "A kingdom I bought with my tears."

Some mark the Decembrist attack as the first act of the Russian Revolution, and make the pilgrimage to Irkutsk, in homage to the aristocrats who, not unlike Guchkov, turned against the czar. One of their supporters, Peter Chaadayev, said: "We are not of the

---

6   Tupper describes the Raskolniki, or Old Believers: "Mercilessly persecuted as heretics, many settled over the years as forced or voluntary colonists in Siberia, where they exemplified industry, thrift, and religious fervor."

West or of the East, and we have the traditions of neither. Life is constantly putting to Russians the question: 'Where are you?'"

The prominent statues in Irkutsk are of Alexander III, to acknowledge his conception of the Trans-Siberian, and another, from the year 2004, to the White Russian commander Admiral Aleksandr Kolchak, in Tupper's words "a small, highstrung, and humorless former commander of the Black Sea Fleet, who proclaimed himself Supreme Ruler of Russia and assumed dictatorial powers." In 1920 Kolchak was killed in Irkutsk, after carrying the fight against the Bolsheviks as far as Kazan and then retreating along the Trans-Siberian. His legacy is divided between those who admire his opposition to the Communist leadership and those who despise his brutal autocracy, which alienated him from Allied forces operating in Russia, including 7,000 American troops, led by General William Graves. Neither Graves nor President Woodrow Wilson, who ordered the troops to Siberia, had much time for Kolchak, whose eagerness to fill concentration camps made him incompatible with the idealism of Wilson's Fourteen Points. In a great "what if" of history, had Kolchak been a less polarizing figure, it is easy to imagine that Russia might have been partitioned, along the lines of the Bolshevik and royalist spheres of influence.

The train left Irkutsk in the middle of the night and ran at slow speeds, so that in the early morning we were on the tracks of the Circum-Baikal Railway, which traces the southern edges of the primeval lake. The mainline of the Trans-Siberian used to end at Port Baikal on the western shore. There the cars and passengers were put aboard steamships, several of which had been shipped to Irkutsk in boxes from England. During the Russo-Japanese War, these lake steamships were unable to carry the volume of traffic needed to fight and supply a modern war, and tunnels were later dug so that trains could bypass the lake crossing.

Tour trains still use the Circum-Baikal Railway. In the morning our train stopped in a small village, so that the crew could serve a barbecue picnic and passengers could swim in the lake. The lake temperature was 38 degrees Fahrenheit. I made the plunge, on the promise that swimmers are guaranteed twenty-five more years of life. Leaving the water, I traded one of those years for a tall glass of vodka.

Lake Baikal offers a glimpse of what European or American lakes might have looked like in the Dark Ages. Except for Port Baikal, and a few factories on the southern shore, the lake is pristine. It is covered with ice from November to June. Some of the bears on its shores weigh 800 kilos. The bottled water from the lake is piped out at the depth of 450 meters. Visibility, although it wasn't something I checked during my swim, extends to forty meters. At the Limnological Museum, a collection of stuffed prehistoric animals, Tupper was told: "If not another drop of water entered and the Angara continued to flow out at its present rate, the lake would take more than five hundred years to run dry."

Into Mongolia: *Stalin loses faith*

THE NEXT MORNING THE TRAIN arrived in Ulan Ude, a city largely of Buryiats, a Mongolian tribe who ended up across the border in Russia. Before World War II, Stalin refused to let the Autonomous Republic of Buryiata link up with Mongolia, fearful that that the Trans-Siberian would then have to run through another country. To emphasize his point, Stalin purged thousands of Buddhist monks there in 1937 and closed the monasteries, as he did across the border in Mongolia. Stalin had other ways to achieve nirvana than to tolerate an Asian religion that worshipped the Dalai Lama.

After the war, when Stalin felt less threatened in Asia, he allowed some of the monasteries to open religious schools. Only in recent years has the Dalai Lama been welcome in Buryiata, or its capital, Ulan Ude, which lays claim to having the largest Lenin statue in the world. (Think of a bust that would be suitable in the Macy's Thanksgiving Day parade.)

The train crossed the border from Transbaikalia into Mongolia at Naushki, a small town crawling with border guards. The train spent hours at Russian customs, as if we were crossing into East Berlin. During the wait, on a beautiful summer night, the passengers walked up and down the platform. After it grew dark, we were confined to our compartments. I went to sleep with my clothes on, as I am uneasy when crossing a troubled frontier. During the night, my passport was stamped out of Russia and into Mongolia, and I struggled into my pajamas.

As much as I like traveling in Russia, it felt wonderful to be *out* of the country and to wake up as the train swept across a broad Mongolian plain, complete with yurts, that led toward Ulan Bator. (The Mongolian spelling of the capital is Ulaanbaatar, and the ubiquitous circular tents are called *gers*; the more familiar spellings come from Russian.) If Siberia is a cross between the Great Plains and a Vermont forest, Mongolia looks more like the American Southwest, with great valleys and high buttes along the far horizon.

To clear up linguistic confusion: the country sometimes called "Outer Mongolia" is simply Mongolia; "Inner Mongolia" is a region in northeastern China, across the border from the republic, but ethnically similar to Mongolia. The country has a population of 2.6 million, of whom more than a million live in Ulaanbaatar, despite the people's strong attachment to the land. Even inside the sprawling city, tents are everywhere. I heard that those who work in offices like to spend their evenings and weekends under the stars, as if they were still nomads.

From the station, built to Soviet designs, I joined a tour of the city, which included the natural history museum (which has dinosaur eggs), the palace of the last sovereign (Nicholas II gave him two musical chairs for his throne), and a large monastery (a third of the men in Mongolia, at some point, have lived as monks). Marco Polo never made it to Ulaanbaatar, although the image of the Khans, including Genghis and Kubla, are visible everywhere, notably in Sukhbaatar Square. Around the large city center are party headquarters, office buildings, banks, and the parliament, which is divided between democrats and Communists. When Mongolia was a People's Republic, until 1990, the image of Genghis Khan was banned. Now he is everywhere, and selling lines of vodka and beer.

The tour stopped at a war memorial reached by a long set of stairs, obligatory for tourists and for citizens on national holidays. From the top, Ulaanbaatar looks like Albuquerque, New Mexico, with high-rise buildings clustered around the downtown and dry mountains in the distance. Looking at the skyline, I asked the guide about the city's family economics, and she poured out a wealth of statistics. She said the average salary in Mongolia is about $300 a month. Apartments cost about $80,000. Tuition at the university is $500 a year. Ninety-five percent of Mongolians vote in parliamentary elections, which in 2008 turned violent when voters felt that the Communists were stuffing the ballot boxes. Most Mongolians are Buddhist, and the country has 800 monasteries. In his 1937 purge, Stalin liquidated about 17,000 monks. A car from Korea costs about $4,000. American hunters pay local governors $50,000 for a permit that allows them to shoot endangered long-horned rams. President George W. Bush, who stopped briefly in Ulaanbaatar to salute its independence, is the country's favorite foreign politician.

Mosaics around the memorial recall the Battle of Halhin Gol, which was fought in summer 1939, as Hitler was invading Poland. Few outside Mongolia remember it. Japanese forces from the puppet state of Manchukuo in Manchuria tried to seize disputed territory in eastern Mongolia. Stalin dispatched his "fireman," General Georgi Zhukov, who later commanded Russian forces in the offensive against Berlin. In Mongolia, he counterattacked the Japanese at Halhin Gol and killed 18,000 Japanese soldiers, with consequences that altered the course of World War II in Asia.

After Halhin Gol, the Japanese were leery of engaging the Russians along China's northern frontier, and scaled back their ambitions in Mongolia and Manchuria in favor of aggressive moves toward Southeast Asia and the Pacific. After the battle, Russia also agreed to an armistice with Japan, which settled the Manchurian border and avoided further confrontation between the two countries until 1945 when, at Yalta, Stalin agreed to attack Japan. Hahlin Gol was also the first large-scale military operation for the Russian army after the Stalinist purges of the 1930s wiped out the senior officer corps. From this victory, Stalin might have concluded that his forces were more capable than they were to prove when Hitler attacked in June 1941. Again it would be General Zhukov who would save Stalin at Stalingrad, and he accepted the German surrender in Berlin at the end of the war. The author Alan Clark writes about Hitler's end: "No ascent in history had been so meteoric, no power so absolute, no decline so complete."

Musical Chairs in Ulaanbaatar: *Sino-Russian bargaining chips*

I STAYED THAT NIGHT in a hotel on the edge of the city, and after dinner walked to a dry river bed, which had the feel of a nomadic encampment. The next day, the group from the train drove out to a national park, where there was an exhibition of wrestling and pony races. When the train left for Beijing, however, I stayed behind in Ulaanbaatar, because I did not have a visa to enter China. The invitation from the train company had not come in time for me to apply, and my two trips to the Chinese embassy in Moscow resulted only in frustration.

On my own I explored the capital and found a book that I grew to love, *From World Power to Soviet Satellite: History of Mongolia* by Bat-Erdene Batbayar, who goes by the pen name Baabar. He describes how Mongolia became independent in 1921, but its history is that of a buffer state between Russia and China, and an unhappy one at that, at least until the 1990s, when Soviet troops— who had been "protecting socialism from Chinese Communism"— left the country. Mongolia's modern miracle is that it survived a century of power politics to emerge independent. Its fate could easily have been that of Tibet, to which it is linked culturally and religiously.

Through the nineteenth century, Tibet was a "special interest zone" of the British, as a result of its war with Nepal in 1814–1816. Much of the Great Game between Britain and Russia was fought along Tibet's mountain ridges until an 1899 treaty between the two empires recognized Russia's spheres of influence north of the Great Wall, including Mongolia, and in Manchuria. In exchange, Britain was granted unrestricted trade access to the Yangtze River. Russia's treaty with Britain coincided with Sergius Witte's agreement with China in 1896 to build the Chinese Eastern Railway to Vladivostok and to block Japan penetration of the Liaodong Peninsula. Little wonder that Japan felt excluded from these great games.

In 1898, Russia acquired its lease to Port Arthur, triggering the Russo–Japanese War of 1904-05, although Count Witte inserted into the 1905 Portsmouth Peace Treaty a "Baikal Corridor" that divided East Asia between Russian and Japanese spheres of influence. The two powers codified the line in a secret 1907 Russo-Japanese agreement (known as the "Unequal Treaties") that explains much about the current configuration of Mongolia. Baabar writes: "It was a brand new map of Central and East Asia. Manchuria was divided into south and north Manchuria and Outer and Inner Mongolia were separated. In fact, this map sealed the fate of Mongolia in the twentieth century."

In 1907, China was too fractured to oppose the partition of its northern lands. In 1912, when Sun Yat-sen became the first president of the Republic of China, he asserted claims over both Mongolia and Manchuria, even though he was too weak to enforce them. Baabar writes: "Sun had neither money nor an army. The only thing he had was paper and pen, so he wrote his *Three Principles of the People* and *Plan of Government Building*." By 1913, Mongolia had a new king and was recognized as part of China, although it remained a Russian sphere of influence.

The 1917 Russian Revolution weakened Moscow's influence in Mongolia and the Far East. After World War I, China occupied Harbin, the critical Manchuria junction of the Chinese Eastern Railway, and, as Baabar writes, Japan argued in favor of a "Pan-Mongolia... to exert pressure on China and create favorable grounds for the Japanese occupation of the Russian Far East." Japan also had control over Vladivostok and southern Manchuria. To counter these moves, Soviet Russia created another buffer state, called the "Republic of the Far East," although the Central Committee promised to renounce the czar's secret treaties, notably the 1907 agreement with Japan to partition the Far East, and to cede the Chinese Eastern Railway to China.

In 1921, this aura of good feeling led to yet another Mongolian declaration of independence. But by the time the Russians agreed to the terms in 1924, it was demanding the restoration of its sphere of influence in Mongolia. Baabar writes: "Both Outer Mongolia and the Chinese Eastern Railway had always been exchange units in numerous previous Sino-Russian transactions."

The 1931 Chinese constitution declared Manchuria, Tibet, and Mongolia to be "territory of the Republic of China." Those noble intentions, however, conflicted with the military and commercial interests of Russia and Japan, which continued to divide Mongolia and Manchuria into their respective spheres of influence. Japan may have contrived its military intervention in Mukden in 1931, but Soviet Russia did the same when in 1929 it attacked Chinese forces in Manchuria (Hailar) and when it put forth the idea of the Mongolian People's Republic, in which the party was "the red corner of the state."

During the 1930s, however, Japan forced Russia out of Manchuria, and its designs on "Pan-Mongolia" caused Stalin, in Baabar's phrase, to "unleash a Great Terror." He followed up with purges and pogroms, especially against the Buryiats. Of Mongolia's 797 Buddhist temples, 760 were destroyed, and 17,000 lamas were massacred. "By the end of the 1930s," Baabar writes, "Mongolia had become a prison with walls of murder and fear." The battle of Halhin Gol drew a sharp line, like the 1907 secret treaty, between Russian interests in Mongolia and Japan's in Manchuria. Throughout the Chinese-Japanese fighting of World War II, Stalin's only interest was that neither power would cut the Trans-Siberian Railway. Then, at Yalta, he found the opportunity to gain revenge for the humiliations of the 1904–1905 Russo-Japanese War.

The Yalta agreements are associated with establishing Soviet dominance in Eastern Europe. Another way to read the agreements is as an update on the 1907 "Unequal Treaties," in that they would, yet again, divide East Asia into spheres of influence, to the benefit of the Russians. Earlier in the war, at the Cairo conference, the Allies spoke of confining Japan to its 1894 borders. At Yalta, the Russians staked their claims to the Chinese Eastern Railway and inserted a curious phrase into the final treaty, that "the status quo in Outer Mongolia shall be preserved." No one knew what that entailed. Baabar writes: "It is difficult to say whether it implies the borders of Mongolia, its state structure or the social system, or perhaps all of them taken together."

Before entering the war against Japan, Stalin made repeated requests for the United States to recognize the Mongolian People's Republic (as if it were part of the Soviet Union) and for control of the Manchurian ports, including Port Arthur. Those big power concessions, however, caused problems with both the Nationalist and Communist Chinese. In exchange for ceding Mongolia's "status quo" and the Manchurian railways and ports to Russia, President Franklin Roosevelt offered Chiang Kai-shek influence over French Indochina. The Generalissimo expressed little interest, saying it had never been part of China. Toward the end of the Chinese civil war, the Communists regained Manchuria, from the Nationalists and the Russians

Until the 1990s, Mongolia was a ward of the Soviet Union, although it was still claimed by the Chinese, who in the meantime annexed Inner Mongolia. During this period, the Russians stationed thousands of troops in the country. They withdrew after independence was proclaimed, yet again, in 1991. In all, Mongolia has proclaimed its independence in 1911, 1921, 1946, and 1991, after which it has often found itself as a bargaining chip in the rivalries among the Russians, Japanese, and Chinese.

The problem in East Asia is that with the fragmentation of the Soviet Union, Russia has enough problems on its borders (Chechnya, Georgia, Ukraine, etc.), without adding Mongolia to its lists of unhappy dependents or provoking a confrontation with China. Riding the train east, I had even imagined, with all its mineral wealth, that some day Siberia might make a claim of independence from Moscow, on the truism that "God is too high, and the czar is too far." The Decembrists encouraged similar independent thinking, and their stock is on the rise in the new Russia. In the meantime Mongolia has the advantages of space, which I saw as the flight headed west over snow-covered mountains. Mongolia is six times the size of France.

To get home, I flew over the route that Genghis Khan would have taken when he led his thirteenth-century invasions of Russia and the West. Now the only Mongolian horsemen are those putting on pony games for tourists, and they might not be enough to frighten the Chinese.

China in the Shadow of War

As if to confirm that I was flying to the Forbidden City, I spent many of the twelve hours heading to Beijing under the impression that I might be turned away at the front door. A year after crossing Russia on the Trans-Siberian, I was traveling to China during the sixtieth anniversary of the 1949 Communist revolution. A friend who was living in Hong Kong warned me that the capital would be off limits to tourists and foreigners. I had picked this travel window, not because I wanted to celebrate sixty years of Maoism, but because my tourist visa was about to expire, and I dreaded another trip to the Chinese consulate more than I feared a lockdown in the Beijing airport.

Instead of a police barrier at that airport, I passed through a series of checkpoints that were eager to test me for fevers and bird flu, especially as I was one of the few disembarking the China Eastern Airlines jet without a face mask. When the spot medical checks proved negative, I was free to present my passport to immigration, collect my bag, and follow the crowds to the airport rail link that would take me into Beijing. Not only was today the sixtieth anniversary of the Communist revolution, but it was also a Sunday, which explained why the metro was empty and why I stepped out of the system into a deserted boulevard.

In trying to warn me away from Beijing, my friend had made the point that the area around Tiananmen Square would be closed and that it might take me several days to check into a hotel. Instead, I rolled my bag along the wide sidewalk for about a kilometer, turned right, and found that my hotel, perhaps lacking some revolutionary fervor, was open for business. The women at the front desk were a team of cheerless clerks, who as a pack processed my credit card, handed me a key, and shooed me off toward an elevator at the back of the building.

Beijing by Bike: *into the hutong alleys*

To GET AROUND BEIJING I had decided to rent a bicycle, and had reserved one on the website of a company called Bicycle Kingdom, which I learned from my cab driver was on the forbidden side of the celebrating city. He dropped me at a police barricade, although it lacked the menacing qualities associated with armed forces and Tiananmen Square. I persuaded one of the policemen to call Bicycle Kingdom on his cell phone. That led to a conversation with George, the store owner, who agreed to bring my rental bike to the barricade. I waited with an official hostess, who was wearing a yellow T-shirt advertising the festivities. In a few minutes George arrived with my bike, which I rented by initialing a few papers and shaking his hand.

Because I had not slept on the flight, I was nervous about setting off on my own into the streets of Beijing. By now it was getting dark, even if Beijing had a party atmosphere. George sensed from my questions ("Which way is Tiananmen Square? Are there bike lanes?") that I was new to biking in Beijing, and suggested that I might join a night tour of the city. I opted for a private guide, named Johnny, who cost $40. Together we rode off in search of Beijing, unfazed by barricades, the police, and the occasional tank. In the urban jungle, bicycles are king, and Johnny and I rode everywhere until midnight, like a couple of lions on the prowl.

My Beijing bike had the look of a clunker. It had one gear, a large basket, and a U-lock, but it rolled like a dream across the expansive, flat city. Johnny was not bothered with many traffic regulations. I hugged his rear wheel as he hopped sidewalks, threaded his way down narrow alleys, and cut across Tiananmen Square, by then aglow with neon—Maoism as a Rose Bowl float. A number of the city's more prominent tourist sites were closed to cars and pedestrians, but Johnny always managed to find an open bike lane. We looped around the Forbidden City, stopped for dinner from a street vendor, headed north to the Olympic district, and cruised downtown Beijing, which is clogged with name-shops and high-rise hotels. To get where we were going, we weaved our way through the *hutong*, Beijing's neighborhoods of small alleys, which at night feel like landlocked sections of Venice.

During my stay in Beijing, I never grew tired of biking around the hutong, and I became so obsessive about seeing more of the city that I would set my alarm for 6 a.m., just to cruise through another neighborhood. Some hutong are six hundred years old, and they have communal showers and toilets, small tea shops, and street vendors, instead of supermarkets. A few of the hutong cater to upmarket tourists, with elegant restaurants and charming inns. The risk to Beijing is that the march of the new city, with its subway lines and high-rise office buildings, will engulf the hutong, like some blight taking over a protected forest. Sometimes at night I would get lost in the maze, but after a while I would stumble across a boulevard that showed on my map. Then I would continue on my way, usually along the city's segregated bike paths, which are the width of bus lanes.

As much as I loved Beijing by bike, I never warmed to the Olympic Park, which is north of the city center. The Olympic Park looks like a Big Ten campus, if not an amusement arcade out of season. Such landmarks as the Bird's Nest (the Olympic Stadium), and the Cube, where the swim meets were held, glow at night with pulsing neon. At all hours the park is awash with tourists lining up to see the Olympic interiors. When I asked Johnny if events were still held in the Olympic Park, he shrugged, as if to say that they remained only as shrines to the wealth of a nation that could afford to spend billions on arenas that were needed for games lasting three weeks. The Forbidden City had similar extravagances.

Around Tiananmen Square: *warlordism*

ONCE I GOT THE HANG OF BEIJING, I took my bike everywhere. The best time to visit Tiananmen Square is early morning. I spent several hours there, trying to imagine the events in 1989, when the Chinese government cleared the square of protesters, who died by the hundreds, if not the thousands. In the 1980s, the square was more a public park than what it is today, the world's largest intersection—a parking lot the size of New York's Central Park—around which are located the ministries of the Chinese government, the Communist Party, Mao's mausoleum, and the gate to the Forbidden City. The 1989 protesters who were camping in the square had turned it into a shanty town, Tiananmen Square's Woodstock.

The demonstrations lasted seven weeks. The crowds in the square—including Liu Xiaobo, who in 2010 won the Nobel Peace Prize—at times amounted to some 100,000 people, many of whom demanded greater economic and political freedoms. When the Chinese army deployed tanks and armored personnel carriers, which sprayed machine-gun bullets into the crowds, the protesters attempted to block the square with overturned buses and the skeletons of burned cars. On the night of June 3-4, the square was cleared of protesters, many of whom were killed. Others, including Liu Xiaobo, were arrested and put in prison. Because of the movement, or in spite of it, after 1989 China entered a period of unparalleled economic growth. In my many trips around the square, I could never make up my mind whether the Communists or the capitalists had been the winners in the Tiananmen battles.

I wasn't able to ride my bicycle into the Forbidden City—even Beijing has a few limits on cyclists. I walked around in a jet-lagged trance, made worse by the package tourists and the midday sun. The City is the old imperial court, to the north of Tiananmen Square. I paid my respects to many dynasties by poking my head into the Hall of Preserving Sanity, the Imperial Garden, the Hall of Mental Cultivation, and the Palace of Earthly Tranquility. I expected to find a Palace of the Missing Concubine, but that may have been the Hall of Supreme Harmony. I did like the gardens and a small house (the Study of the Cultivation of Nature) where the last emperor, Puyi, came for his English lessons. He was aged three when placed upon the throne, and cried at his investiture, a proper omen. Elsewhere the Forbidden City felt overrun with the ghosts of angry wives, jealous concubines, inscrutable advisors, and half-mad princes, all of whom appeared guilty of what Mao would later call "warlordism."

After more touring with an audio guide, I bought a bottle of cold water and wandered into a small courtyard, away from the crowds. In the shade I read from Jonathan Fenby's *The Penguin History of Modern China: The Fall and Rise of a Great Power, 1850-2009*. It has many accounts set in the Forbidden City, including one about Puyi's father, Emperor Yuan, which might explain why Mao's portrait, not someone from the Qing dynasty, hangs on the front gate. Fenby writes: "On 23 December, he stepped into an armored car at the Forbidden City to be driven to the Temple of Heaven [a few miles away]. The road was covered with imperial yellow sand. On arrival, Yuan transferred to a vermilion coach and then to a red sedan chair, on which he was carried up the steps to the altar." No wonder, to use Mao's cliché, that the revolution was not like a dinner party.

Leaving the Forbidden City at the north end, I had a long walk back to my bicycle. I was done with what might be called my "duty" touring. For the rest of my time in China, I did only those things or went to only those places that interested me—a peculiar list, I admit, that included train stations, battlefields, the homes of political figures, and the sites of political events. Although I grew more interested in dynastic Chinese history, I stayed away from temples, vase factories, and summer palaces, concerned that I would not be able to distinguish a Ming from a Qing, or that the vastness of the country would give me a permanent case of tired museum feet. For years, not wanting to join an organized tour or visit terracotta warriors, I had stayed away from China. Only more recently had I figured out that I was free in China to wander as I pleased.

In Beijing, I bypassed some of the famous museums to visit the Marco Polo Bridge, where in 1937 the war started between China and Japan. Instead of lingering at the Temple of Heaven, I pushed on to ride the new high-speed train between Beijing South and Tianjin (formerly Tientsin), the western entrepôt that was the heart of the Opium Wars, the Boxer Rebellion, and the American occupation in China after World War II. In Shanghai, I tracked down some of the places mentioned in J.G. Ballard's autobiographical novel, *Empire of the Sun*. Instead of watching an evening dance troupe, I took the train to Nanking, to learn more about the 1937 Japanese "rape" of that city. My interest was to see some of the places that, between the 1900 Boxer Rebellion and the 1949 Communist Revolution, had shaped modern China. I started in Beijing, and then went to Manchuria and the sites of the 1904-05 Russo-Japanese War, before heading to Shanghai and up the Yangtze River to Nanking. To get around, I decided to limit myself mostly to trains and bikes. For my guides I relied on the books that I had jammed into carry-on bag. At night I would stay in guest houses or sleep on trains. I knew that I might miss sumptuous palaces and worthy museums, but I would see Port Arthur (the objective of the Russo-Japanese War) and better understand the politics of Manchukuo, the puppet state of the 1930s. Best of all, because I wouldn't be led around on a leash, I would develop an affection for China, despite its repressive politics and polluted economic policies.

The Boxer Rebellion: *anti-imperial, anti-missionary*

LATE ONE AFTERNOON IN BEIJING, I rode my bike to the South Station, where high-speed trains depart every thirty minutes for Tianjin, the treaty port city formerly called Tientsin that is so evocative of the Boxer Rebellion, not to mention its causes. South Station has a small bicycle parking lot, where I could lock the frame to a railing. I rode long escalators into the station, among the newest in the world. The main waiting room is a vast cavern of glittering steel, girders, and sunlight. For a long time, wondering how to buy a ticket to Tianjin, I wandered around a concourse that is several times the size of the heavenly vaults at New York's Grand Central Terminal.

Before lining up at a ticket window, I tried my luck with a ticket vending machine that looked like cross between an ATM and a slot machine. I switched the language to English, reviewed a list of departing and returning trains, inserted a credit card, and instantly had tickets to get me back and forth to Tianjin. I ate lunch in a restaurant (plastic replicas of each dish were displayed in the front window) and wandered some more around the station, which, while a touch antiseptic, is nevertheless grand. In a waiting-area chair, with a coffee at my side, I also plowed ahead with Fenby's history of modern China.

Fenby writes engagingly about the subjects that interest me about China: the intrusion of Western capital, the 1895 Sino-Japanese War, the Boxer Rebellion, the Russo-Japanese War over Port Arthur, Sun Yat-sen, the occupation of Manchuria, the rise of Communism, civil war, Chiang Kai-shek, the Rape of Nanking and the war with Japan, and the 1949 revolution. About the 1900 Boxer rising against Western powers that controlled the ports and trade in and out of China, he writes: "Thus, though they certainly constituted a rising, the often-used description of the movement as the 'Boxer Rebellion' is wrong, unless one considers a Chinese attack on foreigners as the action of rebels."

The high-speed train covers the 100 miles from Beijing to Tianjin in thirty minutes. My train reached speeds of 332 kilometers per hour. I had a cramped seat by the window and watched the speedometer that was over one of the interior sliding doors. The train runs on elevated tracks, like a monorail. I felt few curves in the track bed, which in construction cut through villages, farms, and private property on its rush to the sea. Although the scenery outside was largely a blur, we passed the spot where after World War II, when U.S. Marines were on occupation duty along the rail line, there was a firefight between Chinese Communists and elements of the First Marine Division, an early encounter in the Asian Cold War.

The Marines had the mission to keep open the rail line to the port city, and Chinese guerrillas, feeling that the occupiers were supporting Chiang's Nationalist army, attacked the Marine guards, killing several. (During a similar skirmish in 1945 in Shandong province, Chinese Communists killed 1st Lieutenant John Birch, from whom the famous right-wing society took its name.) The 1946 encounter persuaded General George Marshall, who was trying to arbitrate a peace between the Nationalists and the Communists, that the United States did not have strategic interests in China's fight and that the Marines and other troops could be withdrawn.

Had I arrived at the station in Tianjin a hundred years earlier, I would have taken a rickshaw to one of the banks, legate missions, or clubs that line the main street of the historic downtown. A century later, I decided to walk, although as I crossed over the Hai He River, which cuts through the city, I came across the friendly owner of a trishaw (powered by a bike), who offered to ride me around the foreign concession. I had a list of buildings and places that I wanted to visit, and my guidebook listed them in English and Chinese. We worked our way down the list, as if on a treasure hunt that involved unlocking a Da Vinci Code to China's anger about foreign intervention.

In 1900, Tientsin was a foreign entrepôt where bankers, lawyers, diplomats, freebooters, soldiers, sailors, traders, shipping companies, and their accomplices gathered to buy, ship, steal, sell, or haggle over goods passing into or out of China's vast interior, beginning long before the Opium Wars that were fought so prominently around the city. In the Boxer Rebellion, Western troops, to restore order, landed at Tientsin and pushed inland to liberate Peiping's Foreign Legation Quarter, which I knew from my bike rides. The rebel Boxers were anti-imperial, anti-missionary, but loyal to the Qing emperor and the embodiment of later Chinese distrust for a foreign presence in China. President Hu Jintao's unease in foreign circles can be traced to the anger of the Boxers.

Modern Tianjin has high-rise office towers and a population of several million, who give the impression of having mastered the arts of capitalism. The old quarter retains the feel of the many

colonial ports that stretched from Aden on the Arabian peninsula to Nagasaki in Japan and that defined the Asian imperial
ambitions of the Western powers, including the United States.
My trishaw driver found the "Headquarters of the First National
City Bank" (now Citigroup) and the "Former American Navy
Club," plus European banks, churches, and trading houses, each
of which imported their local architectural styles to the Chinese
coast. In its heyday Tientsin would have looked like early images
of Macau, Goa, Hong Kong, and Shanghai. Always there was a
strong military presence in the city, and their mission—even that
of the Marines after World War II—was to guard Western capital.
Fenby writes: "For the Western powers, faith and trade were to
bring enlightenment to the Chinese."

For some years I have followed the path that the First Marine
Division cut during World War II, because my father commanded
a company during many of its bloody encounters on Guadalcanal,
at Cape Gloucester, and on Peleliu. When the war ended, he was
serving as G-3 (in charge of training) at Camp Pendleton, California, and thought that, with so many "points" from years of service
and combat, he would be among the first to be discharged from
service. Instead, a commanding officer asked, as a favor, if he would
take a battalion of replacement troops to Asia, where they would
serve in the occupation. He would then be free to return home.

On Liberty ships, my father took the replacement troops to
Hawaii, where in September 1945 he saw Pearl Harbor, and then
to Guam, where three officers, including my father, drew cards
to decide who would take troops to Japan and who would go to
China. My father drew the low card and headed off to Nagasaki,
where, despite all his points, he spent almost a year in the occupation, which was notable for the absence of any malice on the part
of the Japanese population despite having been partly destroyed
by an atomic bomb in August 1945. The two officers with higher

cards chose to go with their battalions to China, and they found themselves stationed in Tianjin and in sporadic combat with Chinese Communists. Nevertheless, my father regretted that he wasn't able to become a "China Marine."

China Marines: *a terribly lonely sensation*

THE FIRST DIVISION MARINE who made it to China after the war was E.B. (Gene) Sledge, who wrote a classic account of Pacific Island combat, entitled *With the Old Breed*, which later became one of the story-lines in the HBO mini-series, *The Pacific*. *With the Old Breed* describes the horrors of the battles of Peleliu and Okinawa. Sledge served with K Company, Fifth Marines, while my father had commanded C Company, First Marines. They had shared the intensity of the island fighting, especially on Peleliu. Before his book was recognized as one of the best from World War II, Sledge and I had corresponded on a number of subjects. He never mentioned that he had kept a diary from his time in China.

After Sledge died in 2001, another mutual friend, Colonel Joseph Alexander, arranged for Sledge's account of the Chinese occupation to be published, with the title *China Marine*. Sledge describes his time from the end of the fighting on Okinawa to the bombing of Hiroshima and Nagasaki, his deployment to Peiping (as Beijing was called), and his discharge from the Marines. He describes himself as a "fugitive from the law of averages," having survived unscathed so many Pacific encounters. When he inscribed his book to my father, he used the same expression, in saluting their mutual good fortune.

China Marine is written in the tradition of a number of memoirs of Marines who served in China between 1900 and 1948. They came to suppress the Boxer Rebellion and departed just before Mao's Communists routed the Nationalist army in Manchuria, to end the civil war that had its origins in the 1920s. The most poignant aspect of *China Marine* is the friendship that Sledge forms in what is now called Beijing with a local Chinese family. The bond allows him, by his account, to cross the difficult bridge that spans the gap between front-line combat and the rest of humanity.

Nominally there to disarm the Japanese army—which, until the Russians invaded Manchuria in August 1945, had remained undefeated in China during World War II—the Marines tried to maintain a disinterested equilibrium between the Nationalists and Communists, until they were lucky enough to be sent home to the United States.

Sledge's time in China had intimations of both hot and cold wars that were to follow. He writes: "In Northern China at this time were many different armed groups—Japanese, Japanese-trained and -equipped Chinese puppet-government soldiers, Chinese Communists, Chinese Nationalists, Chinese bandits, and U.S. Marines—all armed to the teeth and vying to fill the power vacuum resulting from Japan's surrender."

During his occupation duty Sledge found himself guarding or patrolling the track between Peiping and Tientsin. He writes of the skirmishes that often broke out with the Chinese Communists: "We had survived fierce combat in the Pacific and now none of us wanted to stretch his luck any further and get killed in a Chinese civil war. We felt a terribly lonely sensation of being abandoned and expendable."

Sledge is under no illusions that any of the rivals to control China are motivated by anything more than power or greed. He feels as distant from their power plays as he does from his home in Alabama, and wants nothing more than for his war to end, which it does in 1946. For him, not unlike my father's own time in Japan, China was a place to forget the horrors of Peleliu and Okinawa, not to choose sides in a civil war.[1]

At the end of World War II, the United States wanted to prevent the Soviet Union from dominating Manchuria, either directly or through the Chinese Communists. Toward that end, it was supplying the Nationalist armies. The First Marine Division, coming ashore near Tientsin, was there to keep the port and the rail line to Peiping "open," as if Marines were being sent yet again to China to do battle with Boxers. But neither General George Marshall nor the Marines on the ground had any desire to fight more war to see who, in the postwar world, would control Manchuria, and much of the Far East.

In the Boxer Rebellion, the United States sent Marines to recapture Tientsin and Peiping, in the name of an "Open Door" policy that preached the sermon of maintaining China's "territorial and administrative entity," not to mention the corner on some profitable markets. The irony of U.S. support for the European powers in suppressing the Boxers is that it was undertaken in the stated interest of protecting free trade and its share of the China market. Its motivations, those of protecting trade equality, were thought to be higher and more pure than the greedy colonialism of the European powers.

In *The Tragedy of American Diplomacy*, William Appleman Williams files the "Open Door Notes," under the category of "Imperial Anticolonialism," a phrase that later, to cite two examples, would explain other interventions across Asia. Williams writes: "When

---

1 Years later, Sledge reflected about the war, from the perspective of China: "World War II gave me a convenient measuring stick for duty, courage, terror, friendship, patience, horror, endurance, compassion, discomfort, grief, and pain that has remained with me daily. The English poet Robert Graves said World War I affected him in much the same way. Anyone who has not suffered the prolonged fear and limitless fatigue that was a combat infantryman's lot might find this difficult to comprehend."

combined with the ideology of an industrial Manifest Destiny, the history of the Open Door Notes became the history of American foreign relations from 1900 to 1958." He quotes a Boston newspaper: "The Americans regard, in a certain sense, all China as their sphere of influence."

Riding around Tianjin in my trishaw, I recalled my first trip to Asia in June 1983. It began with a long flight from New York to Tokyo, on which I read *Sentimental Imperialists: The American Experience in East Asia,* much of which is set around the city then called Tientsin, with many allusions to the Boxers. Written by several academics, the book describes the history of the United States from the Opium Wars to the Cold Wars and makes the point that the United States has never understood whether its role in Asia is that of conqueror or missionary. Evidence of both behaviors stretches from the liberation of the Philippines to Vietnam and now, perhaps, Afghanistan. In China, in the last two hundred years, the U.S. has saved and traded souls with equal dispatch. The authors quote the American poet Walt Whitman to capture the ambivalence about the U.S. empire in Asia that can be sensed from George Marshall down to Gene Sledge:

> *From Asia—from the north—from the God, the sage and the hero;*
> *From the south—from the flowery peninsulas, and the spice islands,*
> *Now I face the old home again—looking over to it,*
> *joyous, as after long travel, growth and sleep;*
> *But where is what I started for, so long ago?*
> *And why is it yet unfound?*

Port Arthur: *When you cross the tracks, you have gone too far*

TO GET TO PORT ARTHUR, on the peninsula that juts into the Yellow Sea between Tianjin and Korea, I had to take a night train to

Dalian, a large city on the Liaotung Peninsula, which in the last hundred years has been fought over as much as Flanders fields or the heights of Jerusalem.

The train left from the main Beijing Station, which I had scouted on several bike excursions. The main station is older than that in the south of the city, but equally enormous, on a scale that speaks to millions, not thousands of train travelers. Before leaving Beijing, I sadly returned my bike to George at Bicycle Kingdom and ate dinner from yet another street vendor, who, to my delight, was serving shrimp dumplings and beer. Back at the station, I found the cavernous waiting hall and the posting of my train's number. I boarded my sleeping car after rushing the train with hundreds of other night travelers, all of whom acted as if the engineer wanted to leave without them.

For less than $100, I had a berth in a first-class sleeping car, which was elegantly appointed and appeared brand new. Normally, Chinese sleepers separate men from women, and initially it looked as if my bunkmates were a father and his two university-aged boys. When they discovered that I was the fourth passenger in the compartment, they launched into an animated discussion, part of which they directed at me. I answered with a pleasant shrug, although there was nothing threatening about the loud conversation, which involved a conductor coming to inspect my presence on the train. Finally, the man's wife, an elegant woman in her forties, took the lower berth, opposite to mine, as if part of an arranged marriage. No one ever explained the reason for the switch. I worried, even though she was in the same compartment with her sons, that the woman would be embarrassed to share a bedroom with a foreigner. But space in China is not anything that concerns most Chinese, and I admired the dignity with which she handled the close quarters.

Although I had no trouble getting to Dalian and checking into the Bohai Pearl hotel near the station, I ran into problems trying to arrange a tour to the battlefields of the 1904 Russo-Japanese War. Not only was it the holiday week around the anniversary of the Chinese Communist Revolution of 1949, but Port Arthur, now called Lushun, is a "closed" city, because its downtown waterfront is a naval base. I knew this from the guidebooks and had written to a number of local tour companies to line up a travel permit and a guide. The answers had been negative, leaving me, upon arrival, to arrange a car from the hotel concierge.

That option proved futile, as the young woman at the front desk was dismissive when I mentioned wanting to visit Lushun. She said: "Maybe you come back next week? Today closed." I retreated to the sidewalk, where I found a taxi driver who, for $40, agreed to drive me for five hours. When I showed him on the map where I wanted to go, he gave a shrug that meant "Okay, let's go." We headed south along what the tourist literature calls China's Gold Coast. I expected something elegant, but the coast is awash with high-rise block apartments and hotels—the beach as an urban renewal project.

I wondered how the driver would deal with Lushun's closed-city status, as clearly I was a foreigner and had no permit to go there. (The guidebook states: "When you cross the tracks, you have gone too far." When I read that, we were on the wrong side of the tracks.) Most of the battlefields are outside the city, where no permits are needed. To reach them, the cabbie drove right through the downtown, with me ever-so-slightly leaning down in the back seat, as if I were in high school and trying to avoid an ex-girlfriend.

We drove past the naval station, with its many ships tied up to the town wharf, and through the business district, which echoes historic associations with Tokyo. A book I bought during the day shows the influence of Japanese architecture in Port Arthur, which after 1905 was in the Japanese sphere of influence until the end of World War II. The railroad station, one of the end points of the

Trans-Siberian Railway, however, has distinctly Russian architecture, as the czars laid the lines that stretched across Siberia to Port Arthur's lukewarm water. On those tracks are the origins of many wars.

The original line, from Lake Baikal to Vladivostok through Harbin, was the Russian-owned Chinese Eastern Railway. A second line, the South Manchurian Railway, went south from Harbin to Port Arthur. Both lines have caused their share of war during the twentieth century, as Russia, China, and Japan fought to decide who would throw the switches. In *To the Great Ocean: A History of the Trans-Siberian*, Harmon Tupper writes: "In the summer of 1897, work began on the Chinese Eastern Railway, a bold, dual-purpose undertaking by Russia to attain economic and political supremacy in China and to shortcut the long and difficult route to Vladivostok via the northern bank of the Amur [River]." Having won the 1895 conflict against China, Japan had lost the peace to the Russians, who ended up with Japan's spoils of war. To regain what it had lost at the bargaining tables, Japan launched its war against Russia, which it won, in 1904. To find the terminus of these disputes, I had come to Port Arthur.

203 Meter Hill: *parapets out of their dead and wounded*

IN THE HILLS ABOVE LUSHUN sits 203 Meter Hill, which overlooks Port Arthur from a distance of about four miles and away from the "closed" city. In many respects Russia can lay its 1905 and later revolutions to the events that took place on this hillside. The taxi parked near some souvenir shops at the base of the hill. I walked the last several hundred yards to a saddleback ridge, which connects the two small peaks that together are known as 203 Meter Hill. A few other tourists were lingering at the top and taking pictures of the harbor in the distance. Nearby was a long artillery shell, pointed to the sky, that the Japanese had erected to commemorate their victory here in 1904-05.

The Russian army had dug into the hillside to protect itself from a Japanese assault, as any artillery, placed on the summit, would control the strategic harbor below. Having marched troops south from the Yalu River, the Japanese army threw wave after wave of infantry up the steep hill, on the side that is away from the harbor. Suffering eight thousand casualties, the Japanese took the summit. The next day on the hilltop, after recommissioning abandoned Russian artillery, the Japanese army sank the remainder of the Russian fleet moored at Port Arthur. At that moment, Russia ceased to be a Pacific power.

The Russo-Japanese War has been called World War Zero, as it echoes the kind of warfare seen later in the two world wars. Both sides deployed industrial armies across broad fronts, dug trenches, engaged battleships, and suffered horrendous casualties.

The Japanese fleet attacked the Russians in 1904 because Japan remained furious that its 1895 victory over the Chinese had ended with the Russians controlling Port Arthur and the surrounding Manchurian peninsula. Not only was the Russian presence an affront to the Japanese army, but the government in Tokyo feared that the Russians would move on the Japanese sphere of influence on the Korean peninsula. To attack Port Arthur was to protect its flank.

Moving out silently from the Korean port of Inchon, the Japanese caught the Russian Pacific fleet at anchorage in Port Arthur. Although some ships survived, and others ran from the harbor, enough were sunk for the Russian czar to commit the bulk of his European army to the eastern front, which at first was drawn along the Yalu River, which now separates China from North Korea. There, where the Great Wall begins, the Japanese army outflanked and outmaneuvered the entrenched Russian army and turned south across the Liaotung Peninsula to attack Port Arthur from the land side. Once the Japanese were across the Yalu River, they had Port Arthur surrounded.

Below the summit of 203 Meter Hill, I walked on some paths that cut through the Russian trenches that were dug to keep the Japanese off the summit. They could well have been surrounding Ypres, that site of a deadly World War I fighting. In *Rising Sun and Tumbling Bear*, a history of the Russo-Japanese War, Richard Connaughton describes the carnage that ensued when Japanese banzai attacks were thrown against the Russian entrenchments: "The Russian machine guns scythed through the ranks while the attackers on the granite slopes built parapets out of their dead and wounded.... Rarely had the world seen such a concentration of slaughter over such a small area."

In about half an hour, I covered the area of the fighting, which reminded me of some of the knolls on Okinawa, such as Sugar Loaf, which claimed the lives of so many Marines in my father's and Sledge's companies. The ravines below the summit were rocky, steep, and, once the vegetation was blasted away, afforded little cover.

In *Soldiers of the Sun: The Rise and Fall of the Imperial Japanese Army*, Merion and Susie Harries write at length about the land fighting of the Russo-Japanese encounter: "The war that was to follow was, in the phrase of one contemporary observer, 'an encounter between such tactics as were employed by Agamemnon at Troy and those that might have been conceived by [Helmuth] Moltke.' The Japanese forces, near a peak of potency in 1894, were confronting an enemy in stagnant decay." The Harrieses quote from the London *Times*: "The story of the siege of Port Arthur is the story of a succession of Charges of the Light Brigade, made on foot by the same men over and over again, with the scientific destructiveness of modern weapons thrown into the scale."

Walking through the woods on the reverse slope of the hill, I came across a marker pointing me to "A Place Where Kitten Naikito Be Killed." It was a reference to the Japanese commander's son, who was killed in the frontal assaults on the Russian trenches. Sitting in the shade near the memorial, I found a passage in Connaughton that described the emotions of the Japanese commanding general, on learning of the loss of his son:

> ... a staff officer informed Nogi that his favorite son Yasukori, aged twenty-four, had been shot dead. Nogi responded with some facile questions as to whether his son had completed his duty, but the tears welling up in the old general's eyes told the real story. He saw in the death of his son a compensator for his own guilt feeling for the thousands of deaths already incurred in the Third Army.... There is a small memorial stone at the foot of the northern slope of 203 Meter Hill marking the spot where he died.

I was alone in the woods, thinking about the battle, when a young Chinese man approached the monument in the woods. He was well dressed and had a camera around his neck, but was obviously in a hurry. He paused a bit when he saw me, but then drew himself up and spat at the marker.

From 203 Meter Hill, I had the driver search for Dongjuichan, the remains of a Russian fortress that anchored another part of the perimeter in the Russian defense of Port Arthur. The driver wasn't keen to find it, and halfheartedly asked some residents where it might be. Finally he drove up a dirt lane. There we found a fortress as daunting as anything along World War I's Western Front—except that it barely held out against the Japanese attacks, given that supplies could not reach the Russian garrison from either land or sea.

Reminded of the French battlefields of Verdun, I walked around the entrenchments. The fortress had been built with coolie labor and was intended to protect Port Arthur from the Chinese hordes, not a mobile Japanese army, which took the fort after a brief siege, about the time that 203 Meter Hill fell. Reflecting on the battles, the Harrieses conclude: "In the natural amphitheater of Port Arthur, with the world's press and military observers looking on in fascination, the Japanese soldier was caught up in siege war that looked back to his country's middle ages and forward to the trenches of World War I."

Theodore Roosevelt's Peace Prize: *back-channel diplomacy*

ANOTHER REASON WHY I came to Port Arthur was to complete a circle that I began to draw when I went to Portsmouth, New Hampshire, to visit the museum that is dedicated to the peace treaty ending the Russo-Japanese War of 1904-05. The treaty was negotiated in and around the small New England coastal city, and a group of local residents has kept alive the diplomatic triumph, for which President Theodore Roosevelt won the Nobel Prize. Playing the role of "honest broker," he summoned delegates from Russia and Japan to the United States, greeted them at his home in Oyster Bay, New York, and then dispatched them to Portsmouth to work out a settlement to the terrible war.

The Portsmouth Peace Treaty Forum publishes monographs on negotiations, issues commemorative coins, holds seminars and lectures, gives out a prize, and distributes a map so that tourists can make their way around the contours of the settlement. When I was in Portsmouth, I met with the president of the Forum, Charles Doleac, whose law office was crammed with artifacts, paintings, murals, and maps, all showing aspects of the Russo-Japanese War. In many ways his walls reminded me of those that I found in the small Chinese museum, under the Dongjuichan walls, also dedicated to explaining the peace, although at Lushun what was on display was the Chinese perspective.

In his New Hampshire office, Doleac tells a compelling story of an American diplomatic triumph, which ended fighting that had become as gruesome as the Napoleonic wars, and on a similar scale. First, Roosevelt had to convince the warring parties that the U.S. could broker the peace. At the time, the United States was a Pacific power, although it had confined its imperial ambitions to the Philippines, taken from Spain in the 1898 Spanish-American War, and to fighting in the Boxer Rebellion.

In summer 1905, the United States and President Roosevelt were convincing in claiming to be neutral in the fighting between Russia and Japan. By contrast, the other European powers had conflicts of interest: France was an ally of the Russians, and the German kaiser was related to the czar. (Wilhelm had encouraged his cousin, Nicky, to go to war with Japan, which he regarded as a savage nation.) Britain was an ally of the Japanese and had trained the navy that had sunk the Russian fleet in the Strait of Tsushima. When Roosevelt extended the olive branch, the Russians and the Japanese agreed to the talks, provided that they were "direct" between the combatants and provided that Roosevelt personally stayed away from the negotiating table.

Portsmouth, New Hampshire, was chosen for the peace talks because a delegation from the local tourist industry had gone to Washington to promote the hotel infrastructure of nearby Lake Winnipesaukee as a place to hold the conference. Roosevelt, instead, wanted the U.S. Navy involved with the protocol. He moved the site of the peace conference to the coastal city, which also had a number of rambling seaside hotels, including the Wentworth, where the delegates stayed and which has become synonymous with the peace treaty. The actual talks were held at the Portsmouth

Naval Shipyard (technically across the river in Kittery, Maine) on the Piscataqua River. When Roosevelt had greeted the delegates in Oyster Bay, he urged them to skip deal-breaking points and to resolve all other issues.

True to his word, Roosevelt did not attend the talks for which he was awarded the Nobel Prize for Peace. He was kept informed of the discussions and the points outstanding. (Russia refused to pay an indemnity.) Through political and Harvard connections, Roosevelt had back-channel links to the Russian czar and the Japanese cabinet. He used this "multi-track diplomacy" to push the Japanese and the Russians toward a resolution of the conflict. Roosevelt found willing negotiating partners in Japan, because the army had taken the land that it sought, and in Russia, which had lost its Baltic fleet and was in a state of revolution. It did not hurt his chances that the spoils of war under negotiation belonged not to Russia or Japan, but were Chinese and Korean. In his history Tupper writes: "The Russo-Japanese War resulted from the competition of two nations for mastery over alien territories to which neither had the slightest shred of legal or moral right."

In fairly short order, the negotiating parties in Portsmouth had agreed to a number of peace-treaty terms. Japan would control the Korean peninsula and acquire the Russian leases to Port Arthur and the South Manchuria Railway. Both the Russians and the Japanese agreed that the rest of Manchuria would be returned to the Chinese. Where the negotiations faltered was on the subject of Sakhalin Island, which the Japanese wanted, and over an indemnity, which Japan thought it was owed by the Russians, as the losing party in the war. Indemnities were routinely paid after European wars.

Roosevelt's back-channel diplomacy persuaded the Russians to give up half of Sakhalin, along with the Kurile Islands, to the Japanese, and he persuaded the Japanese to drop the demand for an indemnity. According to Doleac, he made the point to the Japanese that it would look ruthless to continue fighting a war for the sake of money. Nevertheless, there were many moments, during the summer talks by the sea, when the negotiations could have ended. Several times the Russian czar recalled his lead negotiator, Sergius Witte, who gently ignored the orders and stayed at the table. He knew that the czar needed peace to deal with the growing revolution, and he was certain that Russia would go bankrupt before it drove the Japanese out of Manchuria. He was fortunate to find that his Japanese counterparts were also short on money to continue fighting and that English bankers had turned off the flow of funds to Japan.[2]

Ports Mouth Share Booty Peace Treaty: *bitter lessons*

WHAT NO ONE KNEW, when the improbable peace was announced—to world acclaim of Roosevelt and the United States, not to mention the hotel industry in Portsmouth—is that the peace treaty burned a generation of resentment into the Chinese, Japanese, and the Russians, all of whom spent the next fifty years trying to reverse the terms of the settlement.

A glimpse of Chinese anger at the Portsmouth Peace Treaty can be found in the small Dongjuichan Museum, which has a large relief model of Port Arthur, numerous pictures of the Rus-

---

2 In his self-serving, if engaging, *Memoirs*, Count Witte blames the march toward war with Japan on militarists within Nicholas' cabinet and credits himself for winning the peace. He writes: "I was aware that the conclusion of peace was imperative. Otherwise, I felt, we were threatened by a complete debacle, involving the overthrow of the dynasty, to which I was and am devoted with all my heart and soul," although later in the book he states: "The Emperor's character may be said to be essentially feminine." During the negotiations Witte describes a meal with President Roosevelt at Sagamore Hill: "The luncheon was more than simple and, for a European, almost indigestible. There was no tablecloth, and ice water instead of wine.... I should like to observe in this connection that, upon getting acquainted with President Roosevelt and other American statesmen, I was struck by their ignorance of international politics, generally, and European political matters, in particular."

sian czar sending off his Baltic fleet, and many storyboards, translated into English, that denounce the "Ports Mouth Share Booty Peace Treaty." The museum sums up the 1895 Sino-Japanese War as follows: "Lushunkou has important strategic position. Is a place contested by all strategists. It was invaded and occupied by Japanese army interfered on 'Return Liaodong Peninsula,' it was again invaded and occupied as naval base by tsarist Russia." Another storyboard reads: "After Russian army was defeated and surrendered, 'Ports Mouth Share Booty Peace Treaty' was signed by and between Japan and Russia under the control of America. Lushun became the colony of Japan again and was ruled for 40 years long." The English may be fractured, but the messages are clear.

On the lessons of the Russo-Japanese War, the museum captions conclude: "The age when Chinese people were partitioned by others at will has gone away forever. But we will remember the bitter lessons of lagging behind and being vulnerable to attacks in the past nearly one hundred year generation after generation. To rest invasion, make country strong and to invigorate the Chinese national are the aspiration of all Chinese people." Clearly, the Chinese were not among those voting for Roosevelt's Nobel Prize.

Equally, Russia burned with indignation about its military defeats in the Far East. Not only were the failures of the Russian army and navy laid to the czar, but the country literally and metaphorically went broke as the Japanese were battering against the defenses around Mukden. Although Russia could have kept the war going by retreating to Harbin and summoning more men and material from the West, the czarist government had lost its fleet, some of its best divisions, the South Manchuria Railway, Port Arthur's warm water, and its standing as an effective political force. Only repression and a world war kept the czar on the throne for another twelve years after the 1905 revolution.

Even the subsequent Soviet government in Russia burned with resentment over the terms of the Russo-Japanese War, so much so that at Yalta, in February 1945, much of the agreement that Stalin negotiated dealt with issues first covered in Portsmouth. Here are Articles Two and Three of the Yalta Agreement:

2. The former rights of Russia violated by the treacherous attack of Japan in 1904 shall be restored, viz.:

(a) The southern part of Sakhalin as well as the islands adjacent to it shall be returned to the Soviet Union;

(b) The commercial port of Dairen shall be internationalized, the pre-eminent interests of the Soviet Union in this port being safeguarded, and the lease of Port Arthur as a naval base of the U.S.S.R. restored;

(c) The Chinese-Eastern Railroad and the South Manchurian Railroad, which provide an outlet to Dairen, shall be jointly operated by the establishment of a joint Soviet-Chinese company, it being understood that the pre-eminent interests of the Soviet Union shall be safeguarded and that China shall retain sovereignty in Manchuria;

3. The Kurile Islands shall be handed over to the Soviet Union.

Nor did Japan easily accept the terms of the Portsmouth peace treaty. The Imperial Japanese Army had won what it set out to conquer, and the cabinet knew that the government, without support from Britain, was running out of money. But the Portsmouth treaty continued a string of postwar diplomatic defeats that weakened the government at the expense of army-dominated parties, which felt that they had been cheated of full victory.

This pattern continued in World War I, in which Japan sided with the Allies, in the hope that, yet again, it would be recognized as a player in the partition of China. For its alliance Japan had hoped to take over the German concessions on the Shandong peninsula (Tsingtao, where the beer is brewed) and its Pacific island colonies. Japan got only half of what it wanted, despite earlier Allied assurances, and walked out of the Paris Peace Conference, much as it would later depart in a huff from the League of Nations. In these examples, Japan learned not to trust Western negotiators. Not only was the attack on Pearl Harbor a rerun of the tactics used at Port Arthur, but it was also a clumsy attempt to redress the grievances that had built up since the Peace of Portsmouth. Some of the depth of Japanese resentment can be gleaned from the fact that the Japanese fleet that attacked Pearl Harbor flew the same pennants that had earlier flown from the ships that attacked Port Arthur.

Manchuria Gets Railroaded: *imperial branch lines*

To GET TO SHENYANG, formerly Mukden, where the Russo-Japanese War ended and where World War II may have began in 1931, I took a bus to Dandong and a train into the heart of Manchuria. Dandong is on the Yalu River, and a frontier town with North Korea, to which it is linked by a rail bridge. In Dandong I inspected the hostile shore from a tourist boat in the river, climbed the first section of the Great Wall, spent time in a Korean War museum ("The War Against U.S. Aggression"), and ate dinner in a North Korean restaurant ("Dear Leader soup"). Then I caught a local train that picked its way across the valleys and hill country of Manchuria through which the Japanese attacked to end the Russo-Japanese War. In their book the Harrieses describe the last phase of the fighting: "The final confrontation, which took place at Mukden in

March 1905, was the biggest battle in history before World War I. The front initially stretched for a hundred miles; along it 300,000 Japanese faced 350,000 Russians."

When I boarded the train at the expansive and elegant Dandong station, the coaches were packed and baking in the noonday sun. The window curtains were drawn, giving it the air of a funeral train. I sought refuge from the steamy crowds in the dining car, where I ordered the lunch special, a fat-fried fish (together with its head and tail) delivered on a bed of rice and some vegetables. Initially I had my doubts, but it turned out to be among the best train meals of the trip. Also I had the dining car to myself, until the train stopped in Fengcheng and the diner filled to capacity, with children wedged into the booths, and parents standing in the aisles. It reminded me of New Jersey Transit during the Christmas holidays.

Shenyang has two main stations, and I was confused about where my railroad hotel was located. I got off at the first station, a remnant of the South Manchuria Railway, itself a colonial legacy from the Russians and the Japanese. In an article published in 1930 about the Chinese Eastern Railway, Henry Kittredge Norton writes: "The South Manchuria Railway Company bore much the same relation to the Japanese Government as the Chinese Eastern Railway Company bore to the Russian Government; and Japan seemed to adopt the spirit as well as the form of Russian imperialism." All this explained why I was dragging my suitcase around the Shenyang station, but it did not help me find my hotel, which turned out to be located at the other station, about three miles to the north.

Other than the Berlin-to-Baghdad line, there is no railroad that figures in international politics or as a cause of war more than the Chinese Eastern or its branch line, the South Manchuria Railway. After World War I it remained a contentious flashpoint between the powers. In 1924, the Russians decided to return the railroad and the land around it to the Chinese government, despite its inability to control Manchuria. A year later, the Russians and the Chinese confirmed the terms of the Portsmouth Peace Treaty, which gave the South Manchuria Railway to Japan.

In 1929, upset that the Chinese were interfering with Russian management along the line, Stalin held an international conference on the question of the Chinese Eastern Railway, but decided against invading Manchuria to secure his rights. A year later, China asserted sovereignty over Manchuria, leading the Japanese to stage the incident at Mukden, to safeguard its control over the South Manchuria Railway, if not the entire province. During the 1930s, Stalin decided to get rid of the problem of the Chinese Eastern Railway, and he sold it to the Japanese in exchange for cash and influence in Mongolia. He then spent much of World War II plotting to regain control. Only in the 1950s did the Soviet Union cede the line to China, but not before the railway workers that helped the Japanese during the war were sent off to the gulag. As a flashpoint of twentieth century politics, the Chinese Eastern has to rank with Jerusalem, Alsace, Danzig, and Sarajevo.

Because I could not figure out how to rent a bike, I got around Shenyang by foot, buses, and taxis. Not only are there streets with a lingering Japanese influence, but Mukden also has an imperial quarter, like the Forbidden City in Beijing. This one, touristically speaking, is more manageable. The Manchu Dynasty came to power in Manchuria, and later these grounds became a summer palace for various Chinese emperors, whose rooms have been preserved. Some showed where the concubines lived while on their summer holidays; other houses were reserved for important generals and warriors. From the look of the palace interiors, Chinese emperors spent much of their time sitting on mats and sipping tea, although a few collected books and staged plays. No doubt the concubines provided some diversion. It is hard to imagine an existence more cloistered than that of many Chinese emperors, whose lives, at least until they were poisoned by a jealous wife, seem less dramatic than those of their porcelain dolls.

My reason for coming to Shenyang was to find the stretch of track where in 1931 the Japanese had staged its "Manchurian incident," which it used as the pretext to occupy the province, later renamed Manchukuo. In retrospect, the Japanese invasion of Manchuria is thought to be among the symbolic opening shots of World War II, a prelude to the fighting at the Marco Polo Bridge in Beijing and the shots fired on the blockhouse in Gdansk, Poland. In his history Fenby writes: "The puppet state was seen as an essential ingredient in recovery from the Great Depression, a valuable source of raw materials and an ideal theatre for heavy industrial growth in the cause of economic imperialism. Manchukuo became part of a yen bloc, and trade and Japan's investments soared."

Nothing was easy about finding the location where the Japanese had staged their cause of war against the local Chinese garrison. After World War I, like other Western powers, Japan had some troops stationed in China, to protect its commercial interests. On the night of September 18, 1931, the Japanese planted a bomb on the tracks just north of the Mukden station, to make it look as if the Chinese had attacked the Japanese garrison. The idea was to give the Japanese army a pretext to seize control of South Manchuria, in much the way that other foreign powers had expanded their treaty ports and spheres of influence around China. The Japanese *auto-da-fé* led to a military confrontation and the eventual annexation of Manchuria. With touches of cynicism, the Japanese appointed the deposed Chinese emperor, Puyi, to sit on the throne of their new kingdom, to preside over what they called a "Reign of Tranquility and Virtue."

Manchukuo: *the puppets play politics*

I RODE A CITY BUS out to the "9.18" Historical Museum, not sure exactly where the Japanese had planted their bombs. The museum, like so many in China, is a vast concourse of exhibitions, wax figures, maps, old weapons, and replicas of things such as the railroad carriages that the Japanese used to rush troops to the Manchuria front. I spoke at length with a curator to find where in the city the "Incident" had taken place in 1931. She explained to me that it was a short walk from the museum. I found it, but not before I went through the exhibits, which can best be understood as testimony to the hatred that the Chinese still feel toward the Japanese and their occupation of Manchuria.

Much is made in the museum of the fact that Puyi served from 1934 to 1945 as the puppet emperor of Manchukuo. The link between the former royal family and the Japanese atrocities gives the Chinese the perfect forum to equate the traitorous behavior of the Qing Dynasty with a rapacious foreign power. Perhaps the starkest exhibit at the museum shows two long lines of wax figures, each of whom represents a senior Japanese military officer who was put on trial for war crimes. The generals are dressed in simple black tunics. All are bowing, with their heads shown at an angle of deep regret. A few steps away is a large engraved inscription on marble that sums up the purpose of the museum: "Taking history as lesson anticipating peace and guarding against the rebirth of Japanese imperial militarism." Whenever I read in the newspaper that China and Japan are keen to improve relations, I think of the museum's humbled wax figures. The equivalent in American terms would be a wax museum devoted to the Nuremberg trials.

Beyond the museum I found a hole in a fence and from there walked to the side of the tracks, where I met a man working on the railway. He greeted me cheerfully, and I showed him a brochure from the museum. It was here, he explained, that the Japanese bombs had exploded on the night of September 18-19, 1931. He pointed to the location where the bomb had gone off. So slight was the damage from the first bomb that the subsequent train crossed over the site without derailing. Fenby describes what happened: "... a detachment from the Japanese army in the Kwantung Leased Territory... strapped forty-two packs of gun cotton on the railway line by a barracks on the way to the main station. The explosion caused little damage—the next train to pass jumped the break in the track and steamed on. But the Kwantung Army used it as a pretext to take over the city on the night of 18-19 September. When Japan's consul-general raised objections, an officer with a drawn sword told him to shut up. Reinforcements moved in from Korea."

It was the incident at Mukden that prompted the League of Nations to condemn Japanese aggression in Manchuria. Japan was incensed at such a condemnation in Geneva and walked out of the League—giving Italy and Germany confidence that the Western powers were powerless to act when faced with aggression. In emulation of Japan, Italy challenged the League of Nations in Ethiopia in 1935, and Hitler re-entered the Rhineland in 1936.

Is there a direct path from the Mukden crisis leading to World War II? I am uncomfortable with the argument that only Japanese aggression, ruthless as it was in Manchukuo, caused the war in the Pacific. In occupying Manchuria, cynical as this may sound, Japan was acting no differently than Britain, Russia, and Germany did in securing a sphere of influence on the Chinese mainland. Britain had her spheres in Hong Kong, Shanghai, and up the Yangtze River. Germany had extensive economic influence in Shandong. Even the Soviet Union, which had expressed anti-imperialistic sentiments about China shortly after the Russian Revolution, considered the network of the Chinese Eastern Railway to be synonymous with national interests, if not a colonial possession. The United States landed Marines in Shanghai all through the 1920s, to protect its citizens and economic interests.

The irony of the 1931 Manchurian affair is that neither the League of Nations nor the Great Powers thought Japan's moves were unjustified. All they objected to was the precipitate use of force, in the wake of the Mukden crisis. This argument is made in A.J.P. Taylor's *The Origins of the Second World War*, his revisionist interpretation that, in part, blames the Allies for failing to act to prevent the outbreak of war. He writes: "There were many precedents in China for independent action—the last being a British landing at Shanghai in 1927. Besides, the League had no means of action. No country, at the height of the economic crisis, welcomed the idea of cutting off its remaining fragment of international trade with Japan." By that point, Japan had left the League and had little use for negotiated solutions.

Taylor's point about the collective response to the occupation of Manchuria is that it was a success, not a failure, giving the League optimism that it could handle subsequent crises, like those in Ethiopia and the Rhineland. He writes:

In later years the Manchurian affair assumed a mythical importance. It was treated as a milestone on the road to war, the first decisive "betrayal" of the League, especially by the British government. In reality, the League, under British leadership, had done what the British thought it was designed to do: it had limited a conflict and brought it, however unsatisfactorily, to an end. [A year after the invasion, China and Japan restored diplomatic relations.] Moreover, the Manchurian affair, far from weakening the coercive powers of the League, had actually brought them into existence. It was thanks to this affair that the League—again on British prompting—set up the machinery, hitherto lacking, to organise economic sanctions. This machinery, to everyone's misfortune, made possible the League action over Abyssinia [Ethiopia] in 1935.

Another way to view Japan's Manchurian annexation is to place it in the context of Japan's diplomatic and military adventurism since the 1895 Sino-Japanese War, fought along the Yalu frontier. That war ended with Japan's military victory, but Western negotiators negated their successes on the battlefield, and China leased the Liaotung Peninsula to Russia. That betrayal led the Japanese to attack Port Arthur and capture Mukden, yet again in hopes of expanding their imperial reach, much as England, France, and Germany were doing in Africa and even China.

Russian losses at war were mitigated at the Portsmouth Peace Conference, which reined in Japan's colonial ambitions, limiting its spoils to Sakhalin and the South Manchuria Railway. Count Witte had come home a hero, for preserving so much of the czar's Far East empire. Nor did alliance with the Allies in World War I produce any material gains for Japan, and it walked out of Versailles in a huff, much in the same way it departed the League in 1931.

The Marco Polo Bridge: *Colonel Ichiki starts World War II*

FROM SHENYANG, I found a seat on the high-speed train to Beijing, which needs only four hours to cover what a regular train does overnight. I am aware of the arguments that China's high-speed rail network is an economic boondoggle and an environmental nightmare, but I loved having a window seat on a train streaking across Manchuria and then another day on my bike in Beijing. The train left me at the main Beijing station. Rather than trek back to my first hotel, I found another across from the station and went directly to George to reclaim my bicycle.

This time I wanted to visit the Marco Polo Bridge, on the western edge of the city, about ten miles from Tiananmen Square. Early the next morning I began the ride out to the bridge and the nearby village of Wanping, which survives as an example of early Chinese architecture, with quaint shops and small tearooms. On this ride, however, I got lost in the Beijing suburbs and ran into a stiff headwind. My maps that were accurate around the Forbidden City were vague on the location of the Marco Polo Bridge, except to indicate its general vicinity. Rather than lose more time, I locked my bike to a fence, memorized the location, and took a taxi the last miles to the bridge, which is yet another place where World War II began, this time in 1937.

The taxi dropped me at a museum that tells the story of the Second World War from the perspective of the Chinese Communists. Neither Chiang Kai-shek nor the Americans get much of a mention. There is a picture of the American journalist Edgar Snow, who wrote *Red Star Over China*, a book favorable toward Mao and his Long March, and a few dioramas of American aid being flown "over the hump" to Kunming. Otherwise, the museum maintains revolutionary discipline to make the point that Chinese partisans were the ones who drove the Japanese off the China mainland.

Wanping has charms as a tourist destination, although I wasn't interested to either linger over tea or buy a replica of a Ming vase. From the museum, I walked out onto the bridge, officially named Lugouqiao although associated with the Venetian explorer because he mentions it in his *Travels* ("the best and unique bridge in the world"). The bridge is distinctive because it is lined with elegantly carved granite lions, who guard the way into the walled village. I took a picture of a wall carving that shows the obviously decadent Polo getting carried around in a sedan chair, although he is sporting a wispy beard, as if Confucius had been one of his barbers.

The bridge incident that touched off the heavy World War II fighting between the Chinese and the Imperial Japanese Army took place in July 1937. Like the Americans in Shanghai, Japanese forces were stationed in Wanping according to the many agreements around the Boxer Protocol that had ended the Rebellion in 1901. That agreement had allowed foreign countries to station troops in China, and Japan had been among those powers. By 1937, it had almost a full division in the country, much more than other nations. The reason the Japanese had deployed almost a full regiment to the area around the Marco Polo Bridge is that near the bridge ran the only rail line that connected Beijing to Chiang Kai-shek's Kuomintang forces in the south, and it was this junction that it sought to control, as a way of maintaining its own Open Door.

On the night of July 7, 1937, Japanese forces were patrolling near the bridge when one of its soldiers went missing. Later accounts varied. Some said he had been abducted, was out drinking or had found romantic interests in the night. Nevertheless, before he returned in the morning the Japanese forces, led by Major Kiyonao Ichiki, responded to the disappearance by demanding entry into the town (to search for the missing soldier) and then by attacking a Chinese detachment of several hundred men, who were also stationed near Wanping. The next morning a firefight developed around the Marco Polo Bridge. One report of the fighting reads: "Other than attacking Wanping, Japanese, with armoured vehicles, mounted a fierce attack at Longwangmiao and the railway iron bridge to the southeast of Wanping. About two platoons of Chinese soldiers sacrificed their lives defending the eastern bridgehead."

Both the Japanese and the Chinese moved more men and artillery into the area of the bridge, with sporadic fighting breaking out through July and into August. Both sides made noises about defusing the situation, but the Japanese were not in a mood to be placated, yet again, by diplomacy. In August 1937, they launched a full-scale amphibious assault with their armies against Shanghai, sinking the rival Asian powers into a war that would consume some sixteen million lives.

Part of the reason I made such an effort to find the Marco Polo Bridge is that Major Ichiki, later a colonel, was to loom large in the battle of Guadalcanal, where in August 1942 my father commanded C Company, 1st Marines, which had a large hand in wiping out Ichiki's regiment at the Battle of the Tenaru, where my father led a bayonet charge into the Japanese lines.

Guadalcanal was the first offensive action by American forces in World War II, and the Battle of the Tenaru was the first American victory. In the 1980s, I went to Guadalcanal, one of the Solomon Islands, and hired a car and driver to take me to the Tenaru, which was actually the River Ilu, although before the battle a confused mapmaker had transposed the names. I found the coconut grove where my father's battalion, along with several others, had stopped Ichiki's regiment, which had landed on Guadalcanal with the mission to annihilate the Marine garrison. Along a beach spit of the Ilu, next to what became known as Ironbottom Sound (for all the American ships that were sunk there), Ichiki had launched wave after wave of banzai attacks against the Marine lines, which held.[3]

In the battle's last act, my father's battalion enveloped Ichiki's lines on the beach and wiped them out, almost to a man, as the Japanese refused to surrender. Ichiki had escaped the counterattack, including C Company's bayonet charge, and withdrew with

---

3   In the HBO mini-series *The Pacific*, this battle is shown in the first episode about Guadalcanal. Robert Leckie, whose story is told in the film, wrote about the Battle of the Tenaru in his memoir *Helmet for My Pillow*: "Here was cacophony; here was dissonance; here was wildness; here was the absence of rhythm, the loss of limit, for everyone fires what, when and where he chooses; here was booming, sounding, shrieking, wailing, hissing, crashing, shaking, gibbering noise. Here was hell."

the regimental colors to a nearby village, where he either committed hara-kiri or was shot. In a memoir of the battle written for *American Heritage* magazine, my father writes: "No quarter was asked or given as Marines and Japanese fought face-to-face in the swirling gunsmoke, lunging, stabbing, and smashing with bayonets and rifle butts. Horrible cries rose above the general tumult as cold steel tore through flesh and entrails and men died in agony." First Marine veteran and memoirist Robert Leckie recalls: "Our regiment had killed something like nine hundred of them. Most of them lay in clusters or heaps before the gun pits commanding the sandspit, as if they had not died singly but in groups."

The Harrieses describe the importance of the battle: "The defeat of the Ichiki detachment was not just the obliteration of a significant proportion of the Japanese troops allocated to Guadalcanal; it was the first American victory over the 'jungle supermen'—proof that 'spirit,' even a spirit as remarkable as Ichiki's, was not enough." After the battle, a Japanese officer, feigning a death that soon became real, threw a grenade at my father. In between Ichiki's action at the Marco Polo Bridge and his death near the Tenaru, war had come to all corners of the globe. After the battle ended in February 1943, the Japanese would call Guadalcanal the "Port Arthur of the Pacific," an allusion to the casualties sustained on 203 Meter Hill.

Shanghai: *a palisade of swords that answered the sun*

FROM THE MARCO POLO BRIDGE, the Imperial Japanese Army moved its theater of operations to Shanghai, where it spent several days, looking for the remnants of battle. Shanghai fell to the Japanese in late October 1937. The fighting took place in the estuaries that surround the city and in downtown Shanghai, along the

Bund that is now the Boardwalk and Park Place of the Chinese miracle.[4] From a Western perspective, the best description of the Japanese invasion of Shanghai is in J.G. Ballard's autobiographical novel *Empire of the Sun*, an account of an English boy losing his parents and trying to survive in a world turned upside down. He describes the Japanese invasion of downtown Shanghai: "Drawn up above them on the Bund were hundreds of Japanese soldiers. Their bayonets formed a palisade of swords that answered the sun."

I enjoyed Shanghai, even though the car has replaced the bicycle as the way to get around. At the art museum I went to an exhibit on Mao's Long March, which showed drawings of guerrillas fording mountain gorges on small rope bridges. I walked along the Bund, now overshadowed by a mix of colonial façades and the kind of modernistic office buildings that could be found in Las Vegas. I joined an excursion on the Huanpu River, which snakes through the downtown, one part the Hudson and the other a heart of darkness. Shanghai has Starbucks and Internet cafés, and lacks Beijing's socialist sentimentality. The French Concession district evokes the colonial era. Distasteful as it was to the Chinese, it left elegant architecture, and I enjoyed several long walks in its neighborhood.

On one of my walks I found the last house of Dr. Sun Yat-sen, the Chinese leader after the emperor abdicated in 1911, now preserved as a museum. On my first trip to mainland in China in 1983, I had joined a bus tour that went from Macau to the house where Dr. Sun had been born in 1866. I remembered seeing some of his

---

4   During the 1930s Shanghai had also played out the revolutionary struggle between Nationalists and Communists. At one point, when things were going poorly for the Communists, Chou En-lai and his wife had to disguise themselves as bourgeois capitalists and hide out in a hotel suite. Fenby writes: "Zhou and his wife hid in the Western Astor House hotel. To meld with the other guests, Zhou dressed in a three-piece suit and bought a pair of leather shoes, while his wife wore smart Chinese outfits with high heels. After two months in a room overlooking the river, they headed out of Shanghai."

books in the museum, and I associated him less with Communism and more with a path toward rational democratic discourse, a path that China has never taken. In 1983 I was surprised that his birthplace was on the show tour from Hong Kong, for foreigners willing to pay $50 for a visa and a bus ride. On this trip, I began to feel I could not go anywhere without visiting a Sun museum (there's also one in Hong Kong).

Sun's house in Shanghai on the rue Molière has the pleasant air of a suburban home. In what had been the living and dining rooms, there are cabinets with artifacts of his life, including a derringer, some clothes, pens and watches, and examples of his writing. He wrote for *The Atlantic Monthly* and G. P. Putnam, a New York publisher. (The book jacket identifies him as the president of "southern China." Northern provinces remained loyal to the Qing.) Sun had a lovely enclosed garden, with ample patio furniture. To relax he occasionally played croquet, something the Communists must have overlooked when elevating him to the ranks of socialist immortals. He was the only twentieth-century leader accepted both by Communists on the mainland and by Nationalists on Taiwan.

My favorite corner of the museum deals with Sun's time as the "Director for Construction of All Railways in China." According to Fenby, he declared that "transportation is the mother of industry, the railway is the mother of transportation," and then left "on a lengthy inspection tour of existing tracks, accompanied by several young women secretaries....On this trip, the 'Father of the Republic' drew 70,000 miles of track on a six-foot-square map. The lines were all completely straight, regardless of the terrain." A small copy of the map hangs in the museum, making China's rail network look as compact as the London Underground.

Trained as a medical doctor, Sun converted to Christianity and was a strong believer in the benefits of nutrition. One exhibit even plays up his friendship with Shokichi Umeya, a native of

Nagasaki, Japan, who at various times financed Sun's revolutionary activities, something that rarely gets a mention in the Little Red Book. At times he lived abroad in exile and was at home in Hawaii, San Francisco, New York, and London. After serving as China's first republican president, he went again into exile in 1913, this time to Japan, where he married Soong Ching-ling, one of the famous Soong sisters. Chiang Kai-shek, who followed him in the leadership of the Kuomintang or Nationalist Party was his brother-in-law, married to Soong May-ling (although only after Sun was dead).

Sun is best remembered for his "Three Principles of the People," a tract celebrating the virtues of nationalism, democracy, and "the people's livelihood" that he wrote partly while in office, having little else that he could do. The opposition called him "Sun the windbag." He was president for less than one year and died of liver cancer in 1925, at the age of 58.

What accounts for his dual legacy, embraced both by Nationalists and Communists, is that Chiang Kai-shek inherited the remains of Sun's Kuomintang Party while at the same time the Communists appreciated Sun's early embrace of socialism and the fact that he had a hand in the overthrow of the Qing Dynasty. Fenby writes: "In death, the doctor became a lay saint as he had never been in life, the basis of a new secular religion that rejected both warlords and imperialism." Sun's wife, Soong Ching-ling, lived in the Shanghai house until the Japanese invaded that city. Like her husband, she was a figure who during her long and tumultuous life embraced both Nationalists and Communists. In 1927, she fled China to Moscow, after the Kuomintang had purged the party of the Communists. During World War II in China (1937-45), she was reconciled with the Nationalists, but afterward sided again with the Communists in the Chinese civil war. While it lasted, she was head of the Sino-Soviet Friendship

Association. She was a presence in Beijing, where she lived in a mansion (there's no word whether it had croquet). Toward the end of her life she served as China's President (even though power remained with the party). She died in 1981 and is buried in a park in Shanghai. Sun is buried in Nanjing, formerly Nanking, on the grounds of a Buddhist monastery, near what are called the Purple Mountains.

Chou En-lai: *man's fate*

ALMOST ACROSS THE STREET from Sun's house in Shanghai, but tucked away on a side street and without any signs, is the Shanghai home of Chou En-lai. I saw it mentioned in a guidebook, but had to walk the block several times to find the entrance, which had a lonely sentry, stationed in a small hut. I didn't have change for the admission ticket, but he motioned for me to enter with a distracted wave of his arm. I walked around the house by myself, untroubled by guards, regulations, or gift shops. If Sun's house is taking on the air of a cultural center, Chou's house, equally grand, has the casual air of student housing during a term break.

Chou did not live full-time in the house, but it was his headquarters in Shanghai after 1946, whenever he was in the city. (Presumably he had lost interest in the Western Astor House hotel.) I walked through the house, taking pictures of his desk (which often doubled as the foreign ministry), his iron-frame bed, and his overnight suitcase (portrait of the revolutionary as traveling salesman). Like Sun, Chou had an enclosed garden, but only a few pieces of wicker patio furniture, as if they had been left behind by the previous tenants.

Before 1949, whenever Chou was in residence, Chiang's spies would watch the house from across the street. Probably all they saw was Chou typing letters at his desk or maybe climbing into his monastic single bed, no doubt to read Karl Marx's *Communist Manifesto*. It's hard to imagine Chou doing anything but work, and Mao's work at that. Because Chou spoke English and had an engaging manner with the likes of Nixon and Kissinger or the Western press, he generally avoids opprobrium in the Western press, despite all the rectification campaigns that he ordered during his lifetime. Chou was there to do Mao's bidding, and often that involved summary executions. (Three million are thought to have died during the Cultural Revolution from 1966 to 1976; countless millions died earlier.) In Andre Malraux's *Man's Fate*, a revolutionary tale largely set in Shanghai, there is a phrase that "the sons of torture victims make good terrorists," although Chou grew up in Tientsin and went to an elite preparatory school.

Chou's one bourgeois pleasure was his car, a 1949 Buick, which is parked in the garage. I found it while wandering in the basement and took a picture of the black roadster, the kind of car that Humphrey Bogart drives in *The Big Sleep*. Despite the Cold War, GM serviced the car every year. Seeing his Buick, with its polished chrome and whitewall tires, made me think about the opportunity that General Motors lost in the 1950s, for not giving their best Chinese customer a dealership. The last emperor was also a Buick man, and the model continues to do well in China. But GM's Shanghai plant opened only in 1997. GM now sells about a million cars a year in China, which overall produces thirteen million cars a year. Imagine what Chou could have done with GM sales if allowed to use the slogan "Not your emperor's Buick," or perhaps "The new class of the working class." He might have assuaged Mao's fears about "spontaneous tendencies towards capitalism" or met sooner with American politicians.

In *Nixon and Mao: The Week That Changed the World*, historian Margaret MacMillan tells the story of the president's February 1972 trip to China, during which Chou conducted most of the negotiations for the Chinese. Mao did meet Nixon and Kissinger, but for most of the visit he was confined to his house, if not bedridden (surrounded by pliant nurses and feel-good doctors). Nixon's goal was simply to show up in China; the protocol that emerged from the talks was of less importance, as it had to dodge such important issues as the Vietnam War or China's claim against Taiwan. The visit led to what MacMillan calls "mutual non-recognition" between the United States and China, whose international circle was previously limited to Albania. She says, "What is important about the visit is that it happened."

According to MacMillan, what was most on display during the weeklong visit was the extent to which Henry Kissinger viewed the summit as a chance to buff up his résumé and ingratiate himself with the revolutionary rich and famous. He described Chou as "one of the two or three most impressive men I have ever met," and liked to say later that had he "walked into a cocktail party, he would have known at once that Mao was the most important man in the room." He also described the chairman's terrific sense of humor. (How Kissinger deduced all this from a declining figure that his handlers had propped up for a few state photographs is anyone's guess.) Maybe Mao wasn't as far gone as his physicians later reported, as he described Kissinger as "Just a funny little man. He is shuddering all over with nerves every time he comes to see me." The national security advisor had an equally strange relationship with President Nixon, stroking his vanity when they were together, but when away from the throne rooms referring to him as "our drunken friend" or the "madman." Once Nixon resigned from office in disgrace, Kissinger rarely had any time for Nixon. As a State Department official remarked: "If Henry Kissinger is not the bride, there's going to be no other wedding anywhere else." In that sense, the China summit was his honeymoon, with any number of bridegrooms.

The Bullet Train to Nanking: *the Yangtze River ran red*

To get to the ancient capital of Nanking, I boarded an early morning high-speed train, which took two hours to make the 200 mile journey up the Yangtze River. Coach class was full, so I bought a ticket in business class or perhaps revisionist class. I enjoyed a hot coffee, my book, and leafing through the on-board magazine, with its delightful title *Fellow Traveller.* After capturing Shanghai in October-November 1937, the Japanese army traveled the same route as the train, to seize the Kuomintang capital of Nanking. The city fell in December 1937, after which followed what has come to be called "the Rape of Nanking," when for more than a month conquering Japanese soldiers brutally ran wild. Some 300,000 civilians may have died during this period, and the estimates on the number of women raped varies from 20,000 to 80,000. One witness said, "The Yangtze River ran red with blood for days."

The train to Nanking rushed through a number of smaller cities—Suzhou, Wuxi, and Jiangyin among them. Each was chock full of high-rise apartment buildings, as though all of modern China were a housing project, even if the roads leading up to them are dirt. In this part of China there are many canals and tributaries leading to the Yangtze, another reason why in 1937 Japanese troops had such a hard time taking Shanghai and then moving their armies inland toward Nanking. In *Soldiers of the Sun*, the Harrieses write: "The terrain given up by the Chinese was a mass of intersecting drainage and irrigation canals, paddy fields and swamps, and devoid of cover—at a time when the Japanese, who had initially only carrier-based planes, had not achieved local air superiority."

I wasn't sure how I would get from the station to the Nanking Massacre Memorial Museum. On the train I decided that I would try to join an organized tour of Nanking, of the kind that are often advertised in railway stations. I would see Sun Yat-sen's memorial tomb and then get off at the Massacre Museum, where I could spend the rest of the day. But Nanjing is one of those Chinese cities without a visitor center at the station, nor one in which much English is spoken. I would happily have engaged a guide, but none were forthcoming. I descended into the modern metro system, skipped Sun's memorial park, and headed straight for the museum, which is on the western edges of the city, near where many bodies of the victims were uncovered after the war.

To get into the museum I had to show my passport. The police asked that I sign a guest registry organized by nationality. On that day I was the only American to visit the museum. The Massacre Museum looks to have been built in the mid-1990s and has the layout and feel of a modern Holocaust museum. There are hints of "party formalism" here and there, but not many. From the setting, with large marble sculptures, I was reminded of the Vietnam Veterans Memorial in Washington, D.C., and the Holocaust Museum in Israel. Surrounding the museum is a memorial park, with eternal flames, and gardens laid out with walls of stark, somber black marble. Inside are the cabinets, storyboards, maps, and artifacts that tell the story of the massacres.

No plausible explanation has ever been given why Japanese officers tolerated the sacking of Nanking as if it were Troy. In *The Rape of Nanking*, American writer Iris Chang states: "No place was too sacred for rape. The Japanese attacked women in nunneries, churches, and Bible training schools." Senior Japanese commanders included Emperor Hirohito's uncle, Prince Asaka Yasuhiko, and General Iwane Matsui (he later captured Singapore and was known as the "Tiger of Malaya"). After World War II, Matsui was hanged for either ordering or not stopping the Rape of Nanking. The prince retired to the tranquility of the Imperial Palace in Tokyo, where he lived into his eighties and enjoyed afternoon rounds of golf.

The military explanation for the Rape of Nanking is that, after a long and costly campaign to take Shanghai, the Japanese marched to the gates of Nanking, only to find that the Chinese had retreated. With very little fighting, the Japanese entered the city, and there let loose all their demons from the three-month campaign. Other massacres—think of the Russian army raping its way into Berlin in 1945—have followed equally difficult battles that end with a sudden capitulation. Nor did the Japanese soldiers heed any restraint orders from their officers. Chang writes: "There seemed to be no limit to the Japanese capacity for human degradation and sexual perversion in Nanking. Just as some soldiers invented killing contests to break the monotony of murder, so did some invent games of recreational rape and torture when wearied by the glut of sex." She quotes an American anthropologist, Ruth Benedict, who writes that "because moral obligations in Japanese society were not universal but local and particularized, they could easily be broken on foreign soil."

In trying to estimate the numbers killed in the massacre at Nanking, Chang reviews the figures, which vary according to the source. She writes: "Officials at the Memorial Hall of the Victims of the Nanking Massacre by Japanese Invaders and the procurator of the District Court of Nanking in 1946 claimed at least 300,000 were killed. The IMTFE [International Military Tribunal for the Far East] judges concluded that more than 260,000 people were killed in Nanking. Fujiwara Akira, a Japanese historian, gives the figure of approximately 200,000. John Rabe [a German diplomat], who never conducted a systematic count and left Nanking in February, before the slaughter ended, estimated that only 50,000-

60,000 were killed. The Japanese author Hata Ikuhiko claims that the number was between 38,000 and 42,000. Still others in Japan place the number as low as 3,000."

The story of the Rape of Nanking is also a tale of power politics. The Chinese built the memorial to encourage its citizens in their "patriotic education." I followed long lines of school children on tour. Another goal of the memorial is to keep alive the "unharmonious relations" between China and Japan. In the displays Japan comes across as the evil empire, playing a starring role in the China that has suffered from "the capitulations," a series of humiliating treaties, invasions, and concessions made by the Chinese to foreign powers.

There is praise in the museum for the Boxer Rebellion and denunciations of the Versailles treaties, which awarded German concessions in China to the Japanese, especially in Shantung, in legitimizing Japan's presence on the mainland. Nor did any of the Western powers do much when Japan secured its presence in Manchuria, and the museum has large pictures of the sabotaged railway track in Mukden, where the Japanese army played out its lethal kabuki theater, to justify its occupation. The United States is less a part of this story, although it gets blame, later, for Chiang Kai-shek, Taiwan, and for re-arming the Japanese after World War II.

The official Japanese position is that the losses in Nanking were casualties of war, not the opening acts of an Asian genocide. Having endured the firestorms at Hiroshima and Nagasaki, Japan would like to think that all nations of World War II were victims, and that its losses were similar to those of the citizenry in Nanking. Even seventy years later, Japanese courts still hear testimony in cases about whether there actually was a Rape of Nanking. These cases recall the coverage in the Japanese press of the battle's after-

math, including one article that had the headline: "The Harmoni-
ous Atmosphere of Nanking City Develops Enjoyably."

Casualties of Nanking: *war guilt*

THE MUSEUM TELLS THE STORY of the German diplomat John
Rabe, whose diary of the tragedy Chang quotes at length. Although
briefly a Nazi, Rabe worked tirelessly for weeks to create a "Nanking Safety Zone," into which he herded women and children
of many nationalities to protect them from marauding Japanese
soldiers. He was the so-called "good Nazi," who, Chang writes,
"would flash his swastika in the face of miscreant Japanese soldiers,
as if invoking the Hitler deity." He was one of the few diplomats
to take decisive and humanitarian action.[5]

After the war, when he was back in Germany, his lifesaving
actions were forgotten, and he was branded a Nazi sympathizer.
He wrote in his diary:

> Yesterday my petition to get de-nazified was rejected. Though
> I saved the lives of 250,000 Chinese people as the head of the
> International Committee of the Nanking Safety Zone, my
> request was refused because I was for a short time the leader of
> the Ortsgruppenleiter district of the NSDAP in Nanking and
> a man of my intelligence must not have sought membership of
> this party. I am going to appeal...If they don't give me any pos-
> sibility to work at SSW [Siemens Schuckert & Werke, the name

5 Among those who did little in response to the Rape of Nanking was President Franklin
Roosevelt. During the attack on Nanking, the Japanese had strafed and sunk the U.S. Navy
gunboat *Panay*, which was then stationed on the Yangtze River at Nanking. Three were killed,
and forty injured. The Japanese tried to say that the attack was in error, that their pilots had
not seen the American flags flying on the ship. It was later established that the Japanese
had deliberately attacked the *Panay*. FDR, however, accepted the Japanese explanation
and, throughout the entire Rape of Nanking, limited American protests only to claims of
"reparations" for the damages inflicted on the *Panay*.

of Rabe's company] I don't know what to live on. So I must go on to fight—and I am so tired. At the moment I am questioned every day by the police.

In 1948 the people of Nanking sent him $2,000, but in 1950 he died a broken man. Chang writes: "Crowded into one tiny room with his family, fighting cold and hunger, Rabe was forced to sell, piece by piece, his beloved collection of Chinese artwork to the American army in order to buy beans, bread, and soap. Malnutrition and stress all but destroyed his health. In Nanking he was a legend, but in Germany he was a dying man."

By contrast, keeping alive memories of Nanking lets China maintain frosty relations with the Japanese, lay claim to Taiwan (seized by Japan in 1895), assert economic authority in its own Greater Economic Co-Prosperity Sphere, and make related points about the evils of foreign intervention—all part of the curriculum about the "century of humiliation" taught in grammar schools. China would prefer to have its "way" on the Korean peninsula, in the Pacific, and across Southeast Asia, something an expansionist (one could say "guilt-free") Japan might challenge. Who other than some Bismarckian diplomatist would take the side of a nun-raping nation, which is why, in modern statecraft, Holocaust museums are as valuable as battleships.

Another way to understand the Rape of Nanking is as a gate, like those that surround the ancient city. Before passing under its arches, the Japanese army had adhered to the norms of other Western forces in China. At the Marco Polo Bridge and even in Manchuria, how different were they from the Marines who suppressed the Boxer Rebellion, or the British troops in Shanghai? After Nanking, according to Margaret MacMillan, "The indictment against the Imperial Army stretched far beyond murder, rape, looting, and the wanton destruction of property. The war against insurgents in North

China assumed genocidal proportions; medical and biological-warfare experiments were carried out on civilians and prisoners of war."

In a city of sadness, nothing is more melancholy than the memories of the author Iris Chang, who found celebrity and perhaps clinical depression in her bestselling book about Nanking. As a Chinese-American born in 1968, she is celebrated for pursuing the truth about the Rape. In many ways Chang is the journalistic heir of the Western foreign correspondents who, immediately after the massacre, reported accurately on the casualties. The museum has pictures and news clippings by Frank Durdin of the *New York Times*, Archibald Steele of the *Chicago Daily News*, and C. Yates McDaniel of the Associated Press. The *Manchester Guardian* correspondent Harold John Timperley wrote the first book about the Rape of Nanking, entitled *Japanese Terror in China*; it was published in 1938. Each of these correspondents was faithful to an anonymous diarist who wrote: "Today marks the 6th day of modern Dante's Inferno, written in huge letters with blood and rape." But few in the West could comprehend the scale of destruction. Chang's book, however, became a bestseller, even though it is a compendium of earlier accounts.

The Massacre Museum has an exhibit of Chang's notebooks, 1990s computer mouse, blue jeans, T-shirt, and glasses—modern touches in what is otherwise a somber recollection of a barbaric underworld. Chang's research interests, after Nanking, moved to the Bataan Death March and the fall of the Philippines to Japanese forces in 1942. Like many on that deadly march, Chang did not make it to the end of her days—taking her own life in 2005. Did she die as an act of solidarity with the many victims that she wrote about in Nanking and Bataan? It's impossible to speculate, but it would track the tears of Greek tragedy if remotely true. The only hope remaining from her loss, like those lost in the ravished city, is that someday Nanking will stop claiming victims.

Night Train to Hong Kong: *past-due receivables*

To LEAVE CHINA, I took an overnight train from Shanghai to Hong Kong. It left Shanghai late in the afternoon, after all of the passengers cleared immigration and customs (although Hong Kong is part of China), and then rushed the train (by now, I was familiar with the platform scrum). Chinese sleeping cars have the weight and presence of old American Pullmans, on which, perhaps, they were designed. They are white with blue and red trim, have large windows, and give the impression that they will be on the lines for decades.

The train stopped in Hangzhou, where Mao insisted that Nixon and Kissinger go sightseeing in 1972, and then ran inland through the night, arriving in Guangzhou (formerly Canton) the next morning. I ate dinner in the dining car, but had to point blindly at the menu, as my efforts to order in Chinese were lost in translation. I got a line of small fish, marinated in a thick sauce, that were too big to eat whole and too small to fillet. The bones distracted me through the meal, and I washed them down with warm Budweiser beer. Occasionally the train stopped in a station where crews, manhandling rails in long slings, were working on the tracks. The trains in China might be high-speed, but the labor is closer to steam power.

After dinner, the dining car was largely empty and had the feel of a roadside diner at closing time. The train crew were seated in several booths and eating their dinner. Most of the other passengers had gone back to their compartments, although they reassembled the next morning for breakfast or to look out the window as the train crossed Guangzhou, a mega-city of high-rise apartment blocks. If Pearl Buck were still writing about China, her characters would live in apartment 37F, Tower Four. About one hundred million people, more than the population of Germany, live in the corridor around Guangzhou and Hong Kong. I liked waking up in my berth and looking out at the Chinese country-side, then swathed in early morning mist—as is so often shown in souvenir-shop landscape paintings.

Ironically, the area around Hong Kong was a sideshow in World War II and the Chinese Revolution, while across Man-churia the battles raged from the 1895 Sino-Japanese War until the Communists defeated the Nationalists in 1949. It is hard not to think that much of twentieth-century Asian history has been a protracted struggle for control of Manchuria, if not the Chinese Eastern Railway.

As I left the train in Kowloon, rolling my bag into the glare of the modern city, I carried with me the sense that the countries of the Far East have yet to deal fully with what China calls its "humiliations." Even though it is an emerging superpower, China still must look warily at its past, and its many partitions at the hands of foreign powers. Tientsin, Port Arthur, Portsmouth, Muk-den in 1931, Manchuria, the Marco Polo Bridge, Shanghai, and Nanking were a roll call of defeats that had led to the deaths of millions, but have their accounts ever been reconciled?

Russia had feared Japan's victories in 1895, leading to the construction of the South Manchuria rail line to Port Arthur. In turn, those leases prompted Japan to recapture militarily, in the Russo-Japanese War, what it felt had been taken away in the peace negotiations. Subsequently, the Russians and the Japanese divided the spoils of Manchuria, as if from a chapter of the Opium Wars. Despite their shared interests in dividing Manchuria, Russia and Japan harbored grievances for generations about their losses at Port Arthur: Russia mourned what it lost on the battlefield, and Japan remained angry about what was taken in the peace treaty. Fifty years later, at Yalta and Pearl Harbor, each power attempted to col-lect on its past-due receivables. Will similar notes ever get cashed for the attacks against Shanghai or Nanking? Who else might be tracking the legacies of Colonel Ichiki from the Marco Polo Bridge to the banks of the Tenaru?

Night Trains Around Malaysia

UNTIL I FLEW ON A DISCOUNT AIRLINE from Hong Kong to Kuala Lumpur, I had been to Malaysia only in my travel daydreams. Once on a trip to Singapore I had driven across the Johore Straits and poked around a rubber plantation. But an hour in a jungle hardly counts for a visit, especially to a country as spread out as Malaysia, which is a crescent stretching along the South China Sea.

On this occasion I had business meetings in Kuala Lumpur and later Singapore. A long weekend came in between, and I decided to spend the time riding Malaysian trains and looking for the battlefields of the ill-fated Singapore campaign in World War II, during which the British lost their colonial fortress to an invading Japanese army that swept down the Malay peninsula. When Singapore fell, so did Britain's Asian empire.

That first night in the country, I found the modern central railroad station and lined up at a ticket window, assuming that I had to trade my Internet confirmation for real tickets. At the window the clerk waved me away, saying I was good to go with my online tickets. How convenient to buy a rail ticket from Kuala Lumpur to Alor Setar (in northern Malaysia) on a personal computer in Switzerland.

Malaysia's brand of Islam is secular and relaxed. Although the women in the station had their heads covered, the air of the waiting room had the feel of a Western mall. With time to kill, I bought a local chip for my cell phone, ate a rice dish from a vendor, and, seated in a plastic waiting room chair, read a history of the Singapore campaign.

On the day the Japanese bombed Pearl Harbor, they also launched an amphibious landing at Kota Bahru on the northeastern coast of Malaya. As at Pearl Harbor, the invasion fleet sailed in under the radar, and the landing forces attacked down both coasts of the Malayan peninsula, traveling largely on bicycles.

Peter Thompson writes in *The Battle for Singapore*: "With an Arisaka rifle slung over his shoulder, a ration of fish and rice-balls in his pack and rubber-soled boots on his feet, the Japanese infantryman mounted a bicycle and pedaled furiously southward, while artillery and tanks followed along the bituminized roads, mending blown-up bridges, as they went."

At many key road junctions, British imperial forces, including Australian battalions, attempted to put up roadblocks, only to find that the Japanese would encircle them by going through the jungle. The campaign ended in February 1942, with a frontal assault across the Johore Straits and into the colonial fortresses.

When the night train to the Thai border was called, a scrum swarmed down the platform stairs and began an assault on the train. The stainless steel cars of the Malaysian railways reminded me of SEPTA, the commuter rail network around Philadelphia. Many cars looked like bunk rooms, with curtains partitioning the berths. I was fortunate that not only did my $35 ticket get me into first class, but also that I had the sleeping compartment to myself.

Dinner was another matter. In the station the ticket agent had promised me that the night train had a dining car. I had imagined lingering over a meal as the narrow-gauge train worked its way up the west coast. But the diner was virtual. To find food I was told to walk up four cars, where two men with a picnic cooler in the vestibule were selling take-out rice, meat, and warm soda.

I was doubtful about the meal, which I ate back in my compartment, but it was surprisingly good. After collecting my ticket and giving me bottled water, the rail staff left me alone and, between reading and listening to my iPod, I stared at the bright lights that occasionally broke the otherwise dark jungle. Around Slim River, the scene of one of the many roadblock battles, I fell asleep, happy both to be on a night train and traveling across the chapters in the book I was reading.

I should have, as they say in English novels, alighted at Butterworth, on the mainland near the island of Penang. But the train stopped there about 5:30 a.m., and I didn't want to face the early wake-up call. So I devised a late-sleeping option, which had me getting off the train at Alor Setar, and then taking a succession of island ferries to Langkawi and then Penang. Not only would I get to sleep until 7:30 a.m., but I would get two ferry rides and cross Langkawi, an island celebrated in tourist literature.

The British had an airfield at Alor Setar, then called Alor Star. Early in the 1941 campaign, the Japanese overran it. Stepping from the train, I found a tropical fish tank on the station platform, and a taxi driver ready and eager to drive me to the ferry, fifteen minutes away.

The ferry to Langkawi was a sorry affair. The seats down below looked like they were on loan from an Iron Curtain airline, circa 1975. The chop in the Malacca Straits made the ride feel like an abortive landing in bad weather, and the boat offered neither coffee nor tea. When we arrived in Langkawi, rain was slanting across the docks, reminding me that the better season to visit these islands is autumn and winter, not in the rain-soaked springtime.

The weather made it hard to explore Langkawi, which has jungle at its core and a necklace of hotels and resorts on its sandy fringe. Instead, I had brunch at the Frangipani Resort and Hotel and talked to its environment manager, Nurul Fatanah Zahari, who deserves international recognition for operating one of the most environmentally friendly hotels in the world.

On the surface, the resort has the typical palm-shaded beach and bungalows for the guests. On closer inspection, however, I found recycled water, endless vegetable gardens, free-range ducks, solar panels, mulch piles, and even an artificial lake stocked with fish. Coming from Switzerland, where recycling is a national passion, I was traveling with my old batteries and the plastic from my train dinner, which Zahari happily dropped in the appropriate bins.

The afternoon ferry to Penang wasn't much different than that from Alor Setar, except that this seaborne equivalent of an Aeroflot jet was overbooked, and chock full of luggage (of the wrapped-with-string variety). Penang is several hours' passage from Langkawi, and I had thought I would idle on an open deck during the crossing. Instead, I had an aisle seat on what felt like a seaplane to nowhere.

I imagine when Penang was a British colony, rickshaws would have been thick on the ground at the ferry landing. Instead, I dragged my suitcase out to a main street and started walking toward my hotel, the Eastern & Oriental, until a trishaw, those pedaled rickshaws, found me at a busy intersection and agreed to my idea of a tour of historic Penang, where are some of the most appealing and evocative buildings in Asia.

Penang is the place to go to change your money, faith, or identity. The old quarter has Anglican churches, Indian dress shops, Thai marriage brokers, Indonesian faith healers, Arab traders, Armenian moneychangers, Chinese silk merchants, and Malaysian food stands. It covers about twenty square blocks of two-story buildings, many with wooden shutters and second-floor balconies, and I rode silently along the historic streets, as if on a Venetian gondola.

The British established a colonial presence on Penang in the late 18th century, and named the town after King George III and the fortress for Lord Cornwallis, who revived his career, after defeat in the American Revolution, with a governorship in India.

The sense of George Town, and Penang, as a colonial outpost is felt most strongly in the lobby of the Eastern & Oriental Hotel, one of the grand dames of Asian accommodation. It was there that the British rode out various world crises with tea dances, not to mention gin and tonic. Before checking into my room, named after the writer Somerset Maugham (the poet laureate of colonial hotels), I sipped Earl Grey tea on a plush sofa and flipped through a history of the Eastern & Oriental Hotel, entitled "Pearl of Penang."

The hotel dates to 1885 and was founded by the Sarkies brothers, Armenians who found their way east from Persia and India. Penang was then part of the Straits Settlements, together with Singapore, and just developing a tourist trade off the ocean liners drifting, in Rudyard Kipling's verse, "somewhere east of Suez."

Travelers in those days were encouraged to pack, among other items, "24 calico night dresses," a riding habit, and a sewing machine. Over the years the hotel attracted the likes of Hermann Hesse, Douglas Fairbanks, Mary Pickford, and Noël Coward. Standing at the front desk, in the elegant lobby, I wished that I had packed a white linen suit, not to mention "24 pairs cambric trousers (plain)."

Like Singapore, Penang fell to the Japanese with a minimum of shots fired in anger. At the southern end of the island, the British had an artillery garrison, there to protect shipping in the Malacca Strait, and the island from invasion.

The fortified hillside feels like an Asian Gibraltar, but the turrets and large guns did little to stop the Japanese from crossing the channel from the mainland and capturing the island. What softened up the island was deadly air attacks on December 11, 1941, that killed several thousand civilians. Initially civilians had waved at the incoming aircraft.

It did not help morale that steamships evacuated British women and children to Singapore, and left behind the subjects of other colonial nations. The evacuation policies of the British later hurt the cause of re-colonization. Thompson writes: "Many Chinese families who had gathered at the station expecting to find relatives on the train were shocked to discover that only Europeans had been evacuated.... The preferential treatment of Europeans in the evacuation of Penang soured relations between the British *tuans* and many of their Asian subjects."

Together with a guide, I drove down to the fortress, now being converted to a World War II museum. Had it been properly garrisoned and supplied, the British would have had a fortified position in the flank of the Japanese invasion, and thus might have prevented the imperial army from advancing on Singapore. General Tomoyuki Yamashita, the so-called "Tiger of Malaya," said Penang could have been "a dagger in our flank." Only 500 Commonwealth troops were on station in Penang, and they quickly surrendered.

I liked the museum, especially as Asia has few devoted to the history of World War II. Along with turrets and big guns, the displays include Japanese bicycles, cots, birdcages, wicker chairs, shelves with books (including James Boswell's *Tour of the Hebrides*), and a chrestomathy of soldier slang from the war. For example, a "rooky" was a new recruit; "punk" meant to feel unwell; a "godwallah" was a chaplain; and a "poodle faker" was someone who cultivated female companionship at a tea dance.

To catch the night train back to Kuala Lumpur, I first had to cross to Butterworth on a car ferry and then spend several hours on the steamy platform (this one without fish tanks), waiting for a train that was hopelessly late. This time I was assigned the upper berth in a shared compartment, and for whatever reason my room-mate had to sleep with the lights on. I was too tired to care, and woke up only when the train braked to an abrupt halt at KL's main station.

Kuala Lumpur is more modern than many Asian cities, and, despite the equatorial heat, has parks and wide boulevards, and many new high-rise towers. In sections it feels like Canberra or Brasilia, or other invented capitals. There is a colonial core to the city, with a cricket ground and barracks that have been converted to a shopping mall. The twin towers of the Petronas Center dominate the skyline, but no one that I met proposed that I go up to the top. Instead, when I had some free moments I spent them down by the old railroad station.

The British left Malaya with a good railroad infrastructure, not to mention a glorious station hotel, which on the outside looks like an Islamic palace. Inside, alas, it's a flophouse, with tired carpeting, suspect plumbing, and ceiling fans that sound like low-flying aircraft. I would rather stay in a bad station hotel—with the sound of shunting engines coming through the walls—than a modern, non-railroad hotel, and this one even has a railway museum off the lobby.

Across the street from the old station is the headquarters of the KTM, or Malaysia railway, where I wangled an appointment with the head of strategic planning. Having spent several nights on the railway, I wanted to hear what its plans for the future were, and my meeting did not disappoint. Several railroad officials, with large maps and timetables, met me in a conference room, and for more than an hour they explained how someday it might be possible to connect by rail from Malaysia to China. One option is to complete the line across the River Kwai (remember that movie?) to Myanmar, although I would prefer to push through eastern Cambodia to Vietnam.

When not riding the rails around KL, I went to the National Museum, and another devoted to Islam, which has a number of exquisite models of mosques in cities such as Cairo, Istanbul, Damascus, and Tashkent. I lingered over the models, surprised at how many I had seen in my travels. I also wandered through displays of bejeweled daggers, and inspected a *firman* (an Islamic pronouncement) encrusted with gold. There is an elegance to Islam that rarely gets into the newspapers.

The National Museum tells the story of Malaysia's growth from the East India Company leasehold and the various federated states—complete with sultans and rajahs—to the independence of the modern country in 1957. East met West in the colonial entrepôt of Malacca, which the Portuguese, Dutch, and British fought over for more than 400 years. Joseph Conrad writes in *Lord Jim*: "Where wouldn't they go for pepper!"

I spent my last night on the train from Kuala Lumpur to Singapore, which in the timetable is an overnight ride. What I had not figured into the equation was that the border between Malaysia and Singapore took more than three hours to cross, and that we would start the formalities around 6 a.m. I loved lying in my berth and watching the full moon rise over the outline of rubber plantations, but it was a short night followed by the early wake-up call. At Woodlands station, I joined the sunrise service before Singapore's dour immigration officials.

I spent my time in Singapore trying to figure out how the British had allowed the Japanese army to capture its colonial fortress. During December 1941 and January 1942, the Japanese had swept down both Malayan coasts and then forded the Johore

Straits on inflatable boats that presumably they had carried on their handlebars.

The British and Commonwealth forces attempted a last stand on the northern shores of Singapore—mangrove swamps that were visible from my train window. The Japanese were not to be denied, and General Arthur Percival surrendered the city-state on February 15, 1942. General Yamashita asked the British commander: "All I want to know is: Do you surrender unconditionally, or do you not?"

British Prime Minister Winston Churchill had exhorted his forces in Singapore to fight to the last man (them, not him). But much of the defeat can be laid at the doorstep of Churchill, who for years had dismissed the possibility that the Japanese might someday attack Singapore by land. He wrote in January 1941: "The political situation in the Far East does not seem to require, and the strength of our Air Force by no means warrants, the maintenance of such large forces in the Far East at this time."

Although the British lost the capital ships HMS *Repulse* and *Prince of Wales* in the air and sea battles around Malaya, Churchill never did order the British fleet to make a stand around Singapore, and his commanders never fortified the island's northern shore, fearing, as Percival admitted, to demoralize the local colonial population. He said, "Defenses are bad for morale—for both troops and civilians."

The Japanese turned occupied Singapore into a prison camp. Australian forces, in particular, were marched off into the jungle to work on the rail line around Kanchanaburi, the so-called "death railway" that crossed the River Kwai. Even today the few surviving Australian veterans are bitter at their treatment by the Japanese, pointing out that a soldier perished from starvation and brutality for each foot of track laid. In Singapore, the famed Raffles Hotel became a brothel for Japanese officers, who, by one account, "disported themselves in loincloths, drinking bottles of Tiger beer and twirling samurai swords."

Modern Singapore reminds me of a shopping mall with a national flag. I had coffee at Raffles Hotel, bought a few books about Malaysian history, and met the writer, motorcyclist and former Quantum Fund founder Jim Rogers. A friend of a friend had his email, and I petitioned him for an interview, having enjoyed his books, which, if you don't know them, are a blend of gonzo, motorcycle journalism, and contrarian investment analysis.

In his late sixties, Rogers lives with his wife and young daughters in a house near the Botanical Garden. He chose to settle in Singapore so that his girls could learn Mandarin. (Children used to be evaluated by obedience; now we judge them on the number of languages they can speak.) We spoke overlooking the swimming pool, and the conversation ranged over the one hundred fifty countries (and economies) that he has come across on his bike.

Rogers grew up in rural Alabama, made his fortune in New York, and headed out of town on a motorcycle in the 1980s. On one of his first epics, he rode from the west coast of Ireland to the Pacific Ocean, through the new markets of Eastern Europe, Central Asia, and China, to which he remains devoted. His latest book, *A Bull in China*, is a revival hymn to the Chinese economic miracle.

For Rogers, a great investment is one made in a country just coming out of a crisis or a war. While the rest of the world is looking on in horror, for example, at Sri Lanka, Burma, and North Korea, Rogers has them on his bottom-fishing, investing radar. He believes that a reunited Korea, with the South's capital and the North's manpower, could rival Japan or even China for economic growth. He loves Botswana, but not the countries of the former Soviet Union. Of the United States, he asks flatly: "What debtor nation ever remained great?"

Singapore declared its independence from Britain only in 1963, wanting neither an affiliation with British colonialism nor Muslim Malaysia. It has since grown into an Asian economic power, based on its capital surpluses and the merchant mentality of the local population.

I had my farewell dinner at Raffles Hotel, founded by one of the Sarkies brothers, which retains its colonial air, although the escalators and gift shops give it some of the feel of an airport departure lounge. With some time to kill before my flight, I read my book on a wicker sofa and bought a railroad poster in the hotel store.

On my travels I was sorry to have missed the colonial museums at Malacca and not to have taken the so-called jungle train to Kota Bahru. I felt lucky to have spent time in Langkawi and Penang, and to have taken so many overnight trains for a cost of less than $200. Before setting off, I had no idea that Penang was the Jerusalem of Southeast Asia, a warren of so many histories and religions. Nor did I understand that Britain's defeat in Singapore could have been so easily avoided (a reinforced Penang would have held out for years).

I loved the museums in Kuala Lumpur, a city of subtle charm compared with the chaos of Bangkok or the density of Hong Kong. I admired Jim Rogers' stubborn contrarianism. What's there not to like about a writer and hedge fund manager who has traveled 150,000 miles on a motorcycle? I wish I could have stayed longer in my room at the Eastern & Oriental, which had a writing table and a pot of hot tea, not to mention a view of the container ships on the line of the Malacca Straits. Next time I might even learn to use the sewing machine.

Crusading Across Syria

MANY EVENINGS AFTER DINNER at my home in Switzerland, when I would slip away to study train schedules (who doesn't have similar pastimes?), I have wondered if it would be possible to take the train from Istanbul to Damascus. For decades there has been a *Taurus Express* across the mountains of southern Turkey to Aleppo, but in the last several years that train has been withdrawn from service. Periodically I would consult the *Thomas Cook Overseas Timetable* or railway websites for an update. The news always came back that the Turkish trains now stopped in southern Turkey at Adana, except for some locals that meandered toward the provincial cities of Gaziantep and Iskenderum.

To add to my speculations, in spring 2010 I did not know if it was safe or even possible to travel around Syria, which every so often shows up on the U.S. State Department's no-go list.[1] I knew that Syria supported Hezbollah in southern Lebanon, and had cozied up to Iran in the great game over Iraq. I had also heard from other travelers that the old city of Damascus was a delight, and I dreamed about taking my fourteen-year-old son, Charles, who

---

1   This was written a year before Syria erupted into civil war.

was studying Latin in school, to the ruins of the Roman Empire at Palmyra and Apamea. He had also studied Islam. Maybe, after all, this was the right time to take the train across Turkey, and then another from Aleppo to Damascus? At the very least, I decided to apply for a Syrian visa and see what happened.

The Syrian consulate in Geneva is a casual affair, with desks pushed together in one room to handle visa applications. I filled out the forms, went to the post office to pay the fee, and returned in three weeks to pick up the stamped passports. To judge by the stacks of passports on the consulate's desks, I calculated that Damascus was popular as a "destination," although the only guidebook I had on the subject was published before the word "website" was in circulation. It suggests writing letters to hotels, like the Baron in Aleppo, and "allowing time for a response." As we were on the trail of Crusaders and Roman centurions, I saw no reason to update my library. (My Swiss guidebook came out in 1928 and still travels well.) I booked a discount airline to Istanbul, dusted off the backpacks from the luggage closet, and told my son that we would be traveling to the Levant for Easter vacation.

To phrase it diplomatically, my wife "passed" on the travel opportunity, even though we told her about the Turkish night trains and showed her online pictures of the dining room at the Orient Palace Hotel in Damascus, which looks like it is getting ready to host a family dinner for Bashir Assad. On the Saturday before Easter, Charles and I flew from Zurich to Istanbul's Sabiha Gökçen International Airport (it's on the Asian side of the city), caught a bus to Kadikoy, and then devoured the skyline of Istanbul from the deck of a Bosphorus ferry, as we crossed to the Golden Horn. On deck a waiter served us tea, orange juice, and grilled cheese sandwiches. We took night pictures of Haydarpasha Station, once a terminus for the Berlin-to-Baghdad Railway, which faces toward the Bosphorus, as if Grand Central Terminal were located on New York Harbor. The following evening we would leave from there on the night train, heading toward Syria.

Easter Sunday in Istanbul: *an Ottoman harem*

HAVING BOUGHT THE RAIL TICKETS to Adana through the train website, The Man in Seat Sixty-One, I also booked a hotel room by a similar link. This hotel website had offered up the Hotel Esen, at what my father would call "modest prices." I had wanted something near the Blue Mosque, Topkapi Palace, and the ferry landing, and for that it worked. When Charles and I finally tracked down the Hotel Esen, we found that it had given away our room. Rather than admit that, "We have given away your room," the desk clerk handed us a key to a room that, after we had climbed four flights of stairs, had only a single bed, as if we would be sleeping in shifts.

To find another hotel, at 9 p.m. on the night before Easter, was difficult, and we wandered around the neighborhood without finding a vacancy. Reduced to taking "anything," we paid $40 in cash to a hotel manager, who then gave us a room that looked like it was last used during the filming of "Midnight Express." The window faced a minaret that, had it gone off at 5 a.m., might have lifted us and the bed to the rafters. I made the point that bad hotel rooms have a way of improving in the morning, although Charles was doubtful. We had better luck with dinner, in an elegant restaurant on the main avenue, and went to bed, expecting shortly to hear the cries of the muezzin. Mercifully, he slept in.

On Easter morning, we walked in the direction of the travel agency that had booked our overnight train tickets to Adana. Along the way we passed the Sublime Porte, the gate between a main Istanbul street and the inner sanctum of what was once the sultan's government. The Porte has an Asiatic look, as if maybe Genghis Khan were waiting on the other side. I stuck my head through the gate, only to be waved away by a security guard. At the travel agency, there was an involved conversation about the return train tickets from Adana to Gebe, which I had figured was closer to the airport than Haydarpasha. The friendly agent, who had no trouble finding the sleeper tickets to Adana, kept saying that the return train had yet to be posted in the railway's computer.

We had a long walk through Hagia Sophia, trying to imagine the national historic place as a mosque and, before that, as the center of Byzantine orthodoxy. Turkey's famed leader, Kemal Atatürk turned it over to the forces of historic preservation in the 1920s, although he left on the walls enough Arabic script to give it the look of a mosque that has been grafted onto a cathedral. We admired the arches, which seemingly hang in midair, and ascended to the second level, which looked down on where the altar had once been, in the years before 1453 and the fall of Constantinople. I explained to Charles how the Fourth Crusade had caused more damage to Hagia Sophia than had the Turkish conquerors.

Inside the Blue Mosque, sitting on the lush Oriental carpets and looking up at the mosaics that glitter in blue, Charles explained things I had never known about a mosque, such as: it is possible to eat and work inside one; talking is fine; informality is tolerated; and many Arabs come to mosques the way that Western families go to open spaces. He described the mosque as a sanctuary from the pressures of daily life, not a redoubt of fundamentalism. He said, "You can work here, you can rest here, you can read, you can sleep."

As a cheerful travel companion, Charles was game for anything. He was never moody or angry, loved plotting over maps and timetables, could amuse himself for hours with books and solitaire, and, like his older brother and sisters, warmed to the souvenir hunt. On our way to the Topkapi museum, the sultan's royal palaces, however, we had a moment of low travel energy. We retreated to our hotel for lunch, bag-packing, water, and a power nap of about ten minutes. On our final look around the hotel room, we were sad to be leaving. To be sure, the walls were dingy, and the elevator creaked. But the shower water had been abundant and hot. When the fog had parted, we found that the room had a harbor view. The shed that we wondered about in the darkness turned out to be the contours of Sirkeci Station, terminus of the *Orient Express*, and the muezzin had stayed silent through our stay.

We were refreshed to tackle the throngs at Topkapi, which can be overwhelming, even though we had headsets and guided recordings. ("On entering the Tulip Garden, if you look to your left, you will see the place where Mehmet IV used the head of King Boris as a footstool.") Paying a little extra, we loved getting into the sultans' harem, which has tiled baths and small nooks, ideal for, well, a concubine. The sultan had the choice of dozens, all of whom were raised for a few imperial moments and then discarded to the dustbin of history. Concubines solved the problem, now confronting the Japanese royal family, that arranged marriages will not always produce a male heir. There was a separate exhibition of Kremlin jewels, odd because of the intense rivalry over the centuries between the czar and sultan to control the Bosphorus strait. We were amused by the screen that overlooked the meeting room of the Council of Ministers. Here sat the eavesdropping sultan, who formally pretended to absent himself from the affairs of state, but who heard every word of his ministers, as if using one of Richard Nixon's White House tape recorders.

Late that afternoon we had been invited to meet a Turkish writer in the Istanbul suburb of Bebek, which faces onto the Straits. The meeting would have worked fine, if he had explained that Bebek, on a spring Sunday afternoon, is a two-hour cab ride. We almost could have walked. To be on time, we had jumped in a taxi in front of the Doblabahe Palace, and it sat in stalled traffic on the edge of the Bosphorus. The only consolation for missing our meeting was watching the procession of ships, tankers, barges, and sailboats work their way north and south on the busiest stretch of warm water in the world—that which so engaged the senses of the bejeweled czars, not to mention the Crusaders, Winston Churchill, and Ottoman Turks.

Our host had long since fled the café in Bebek where we had arranged to meet. Charles and I decided to linger on the waterfront and play backgammon, in which, as part of my introductory lessons, I lost all five games. He comforted me with words couched in parental praise: "You're doing very well… for someone at your level." Shunning both taxis and buses, we walked back to Istanbul, stopping in a quaint seaside village to eat a tourist dinner, which was served under lamplighter heaters and in front of a medieval wall that reflected the image of that night's football match. On the walk along the Straits, we talked about the 1915 campaign for Gallipoli, and its chances of success. (I still think it could have worked.) Long after dark we boarded a ferry that picked its way down the Bosphorus to Uskadar, and got to the train station about two hours before the 11:50 p.m. train to Adana was scheduled to leave.

The Midnight Express to Adana: *the Anatolian plain*

HAYDARPASHA IS UNUSUAL, as an Asian railroad station, for its absence of activity. Late in the evening, the platforms were forlorn, although elegant, with polished marble and palm trees and plantings where, in Calcutta, there would be ghosts of the Third World. Off the waterfront, Istanbul is a sprawling city of sixteen million, and perhaps half live on the Asian side, although clearly not with the idea of taking trains. We were early enough to walk around what had once been the waiting rooms, which looked out on the Bosphorus, and to withdraw Turkish pounds from a cash machine. We then found a table in the station restaurant.

Despite the few trains arriving or departing after 10 p.m., the restaurant was lively, with a number of local clients, the television switched to a football match, and large tanks full of seafood, which looked like tropic fish on steroids. All around were pictures of Istanbul and Atatürk, looking like stern stationmaster, as if maybe the trains were not running on time. The waiter took our order—ice cream for Charles; raki, the national drink, for me. In Turkish he asked me if I wanted a "double." Not understanding the question, I nodded cheerfully and received a full glass, which, over ice and with some water, went down smoothly. When we walked to our sleeping compartment, I went with a raki buzz.

The *Içanadolu Mavi Treni* was about eight cars, consisting of day coaches, several sleepers, and a dining car, and it left on time at 11:50 p.m. The beds in Turkish railway compartments fold easily from the wall, and we had no trouble changing into our pajamas, brushing our teeth using bottled water, and going to sleep, although I lay there for a long time, craning my neck to see those empty platforms that were bathed in the half-light of station lamps, so reminiscent of Edward Hopper's paintings.

In the morning we lay in bed for a while, then went into the dining car, where we ordered breakfast by pointing at the plates of other diners. Throughout the day we loved sitting in the dining car, and after a while the chef took to making us whatever we fancied.

We were surprised to see the broad Anatolian plain, imagining from relief maps that it would be a maze of mountains and valleys. Instead, it looks a cross between the Russian steppe and the valleys of Wyoming, as there were mountain peaks in the distance. Some of the fields near the tracks were cultivated, but mostly what we saw was prairie, closely cropped grassland, and dried riverbanks, snaking through the landscape like the fault lines of global warming. To make the time pass, I lost about nine hands of gin rummy. We read from our books and took pictures out of the window.

The afternoon passed much as did the morning, with cards, books, meals, and tea. Late in the day the train started to snake its way through the Taurus Mountains, which look more like Western buttes than the Swiss Alps. It was in the Taurus that many Armenians perished on their genocidal exodus from Turkey in 1915. The "caravan of death" was trying to reach Aleppo, but crossing the Taurus Mountains proved too much for most Armenians, and only the hardiest made it out of Turkey. It was a holocaust of exhaustion.

Night Comes to Iskenderum: *Gallipoli and backgammon*

WE HAD HOPED TO GET INTO ADANA, a Turkish city near Tsarus, the early home of St. Paul, around 6:30 p.m. It was after 8 p.m. when we arrived. The guidebooks pan Adana as a functional Turkish city. Without a reason to stay, and hoping to spend as much time as we could in Aleppo, we cut a $60 deal with a taxi driver to take us to Iskenderum, which under the Ottomans was known as Alexandretta. It lies on the bay at the northeast corner of the Mediterranean, and was part of the French mandate for Syria until 1939, when the French traded the port and the surrounding province to Turkey in exchange for Turkish neutrality in World War II. Turkey did not ally itself with the Axis powers, but the Syrian loss of Hatay province has remained a sore point in relations between Turkey and Syria. The border between Hatay and Aleppo can involve hours of waiting, and otherwise looks like a Cold War frontier, with barbed wire and long lines of parked trucks. It is one of the few overland ways to cross from Turkey into Syria, and recently trade has boomed between the two countries, as Turkey's relations with Israel have soured and it has moved closer to the Arab world.

Iskenderum, in the language of Michelin, is probably not "worth a detour," but still we loved it. The taxi dropped us in the main square and sped away. We walked across the street to the only hotel we saw. If the clerk was surprised to see two backpackers at 10:30 p.m. on a quiet Monday in April, he didn't say so, and gave us a room with twin beds. Restless from the long train ride, we walked to the seafront—a modern collection of foot paths and concrete benches overlooking the harbor—and found an open café, where we ordered cold drinks and a backgammon set. The day had been warm, and late in the evening the café still had a number of players. A few drifted close to our game and offered Charles strategic advice, which only made it worse for my slim chances.

The next morning we played more backgammon on the terrace of the hotel restaurant. Maybe I thought my game would get better overnight, but I resumed my losing streak, along now I had the comfort of a Mediterranean view. We drifted away from breakfast and the hotel, and walked again to the seafront, to see the Bay of Iskenderum in daylight. We found the bus station and a minivan heading to Hatay, where other buses, we were told, would take us to Aleppo. It sounded involved, but the morning was warm and sunny, and we happily climbed aboard the minivan for the first leg of the journey.

During World War I, after Britain was disgraced at Gallipoli, Winston Churchill resigned from the war cabinet and served a time in the trenches, and then rejoined the government, to which he proposed another amphibious landing—this time at Alexandretta, with the goal of cutting off the Ottoman armies fighting around Jerusalem and Damascus. Both Churchill's plan for Gallipoli and this later one for Alexandretta, to my mind anyway, were strategically sound. For want of a few minesweepers and more nerve by his admirals, the British navy failed to breach the Dardanelles on March 18, 1915, the day that a loose line of mines sank a number of Allied cruisers and made the Turkish defenses look more sturdy than they were. Churchill alone realized that with one more push

Constantinople was his. Failure to achieve it became, according to one historian, "the torment of a lifetime." It was only six weeks later that ground forces landed at Gallipoli, hoping to capture the surrounding hills. By then the Turks, along with their commanding German officers, had blocked the land path to Constantinople, and Britain was committed to the destruction of the Ottoman Empire.

After the loss of some 250,000 Allied casualties at the Dardanelles, few in the British government in 1917 wanted to hear another plan from Churchill for an amphibious landing at what is now Iskenderum, although once the troops had passed over the surrounding hills they could have cut off the Ottoman forces to the south on the rail line from Aleppo to Damascus. Such a landing, if successful, would have spared the Allies a long campaign for Jerusalem and Damascus, and knocked Turkey out of the war sooner—the original goal for the Gallipoli landings. The British cabinet, however, wanted no part of the scheme.

St. Paul's Antioch: *not even Jesus could find a taxi*

As a CENTER OF CHRISTIANITY, Antioch, now the Turkish city of Hatay, to which we headed in a small bus, is hard to beat. On the edge of town is the cave where it is said that St. Paul first articulated the meaning of the life of Jesus. Around the town are many signs indicating "the way," either to the cave or to Jesus in general. In his travels up and down the coast of Asia Minor (to preach his sermons and write his letters, to the likes of Corinthians), Paul often made Antioch his home, although to be historically accurate he lived more for the road than a sanctuary. Given the choice between more time in Hatay (I imagined the cave surrounded with souvenir touts and icons of the saints) or Aleppo (one of the great caravan cities in history), we went with Aleppo and only gazed from a distance at the early hills of Christianity.

I am not sure that Jesus would have had more luck than we did finding a taxi to make the border crossing. At first we had thought a bus would take us, but the taxi drivers lingering near the *otogar*, Turkish for bus station, all said that the only way go was in a shared taxi. We might have felt better about the journey were the drivers not pushing and shouting at each other, each desperate to be the ones to drive us to Aleppo. The marketing strategy of the drivers was to take me by the arm, lead me toward an old beat-up car, and then say, "Okay, okay, no problem, no problem, you come with me."

We decided on the taxi of the driver who looked the least threatening, a man with a droopy walrus mustache. While he vanished with our passports, we climbed into his back seat, to be joined by several more passengers, men wearing leather jackets, even though the temperature was heading to 90 degrees. The driver and our passports returned, and we drove toward the border, listening to Arab music, the kind that pulses more than plays. At least the windows were down, we had some air circulating, and the scenery was lush farmland, not what I had expected in *Felix Arabia*.

Border Crossing into Syria: *the wrong week to quit smoking*

FOR FUN AT AN INTERNATIONAL BORDER, nothing matches the formalities, not to mention the informalities, of the Reyhanli crossing. Leaving Turkey wasn't much of an issue, as we presented our passports at what looked like a toll booth, got them stamped, and returned to the car, which then drove to a duty free shop in the no-man's land between Turkey and Syria. Everyone in the car headed inside for shopping.

We browsed, but had no intention of buying whiskey, until the driver approached us, speaking broken English. He started with the familiar refrain of "no problem, no problem," and that led to a request that we carry a few cartons of cigarettes into Syria. I didn't feel much like becoming a smoker on the Turkish–Syrian border, but figured the driver was our only ride in Dodge City. Besides, how could it hurt to carry in some duty-free cigarettes? Back at the car, all sorts of cigarettes came out of plastic bags and were stuffed into our backpacks and my briefcase. To Charles, I whispered the line from the movie *Airplane*, "I picked the wrong week to quit smoking."

All around the customs bays at Reyhanli were lines and lines of trucks, clearly on runs from Iran to Bulgaria, or Italy to Iraq. I could only imagine all the side dealings that went on to clear a long-haul truck through Syrian and Turkish customs. While we were at the border, the truck lines hardly moved and stretched well back into both countries. When our turn came to clear customs, the guard showed no interest in our backpacks, my briefcase, or why a fourteen-year-old boy had several cartons of cigarettes, and he waved us through. Our traveling companions, however, had to pay duty on some Italian sport shirts. As the taxi pulled away from the customs shed, the driver stopped, and all the cigarette cartons were reunited with their rightful owners, as plastic bags were hurled onto the littered roadside.

On the far side of the border, the driver stopped the taxi in the parking area of a Syrian desert strip mall, now largely abandoned except for a few stalls. An Arab man came out of one of them, and there followed a heated and unpleasant conversation with the driver. Clearly, a transaction larger than a cigarette deal had not gone down well. There was gesturing and strong language. Everyone in the taxi shrugged (I translated it to mean "Fuck him"), and the drive to Aleppo resumed, with everyone in the front seat now relaxed and cheerful. The music was turned to louder decibels.

The lush farmland of Hatay had given way to a landscape of dry, rocky hills, and closer to Aleppo the traffic got heavier, as we picked our way through the outskirts, which were a hodgepodge of high-rise apartment buildings and dusty back roads. Rather than take us into the center of Aleppo, the driver left us near a park, and we celebrated the journey with pictures and handshakes. His son had gotten into the car along the way, and he was now giving us his business card, hoping to be able to drive us elsewhere in Syria (*"inshallah, inshallah..."*). We found the last of the Winstons in my backpack, handed them over, and headed off on foot to the Hotel Baron.

Haggling in Aleppo: *squeeze yourself*

ACCORDING TO ONE OF MY MAPS—I had four of Syria and its cities—we should have been able to walk through the bus station and find the hotel. But it was hot, we were tired, and after a fruitless walk down creepy-looking side streets, we decided to take a taxi to the hotel. Although Aleppo has a modern Sheraton Hotel, near the old city and the souk, Baron is the most famous hotel in the city, as it dates to the days of T.E. Lawrence (of Arabia), and guests have included all sorts of celebrities, such as Agatha Christie, Theodore Roosevelt, Atatürk, Charles Lindbergh, and Yuri Gagarin. I assumed that the driver would have no trouble finding it, but he turned out not to have a clue, and left us on the other side of the city, near the citadel that overlooks Aleppo. At other moments we might have wanted to see the citadel, but we were hot from the taxi ride, worn out from cigarette customs, and just wanted to check into the hotel, which we now figured was an even longer walk across the city. We found it, and were given the room in which Agatha Christie had stayed, no doubt while researching a novel about the mysterious death of an Aleppo taxi driver who took two backpacking tourists on a joy ride around the city and then left them far from their hotel.

The best meal of the trip was our late lunch in the Baron dining room, where we ate a spread of grilled chicken, hummus, salad, and tomatoes. The irony was that we had ordered only one meal, not two. The meal for one was more than we could finish, and we lingered over the plates, hoping that our appetite might revive. After lunch, although it was by then late in the day, we walked to the Sheraton Hotel and rented our car for the next day.

As I was planning the trip, I had, by chance, met in Berlin the chairman of Europcar Syria, who had me convinced that driving on my own across Syria would not be crazy. I was doubtful, but as I researched how to get around Syria, I found the only way to visit remote Crusader castles or Roman ruins would be with a tour bus or taxi, and both had little appeal. I agreed to a three-day car rental with Europcar, and in exchange received a number of grateful emails from the Damascus manager, assuring me that everything would go well. But renting a car in Aleppo is not like picking one up at the Dallas-Fort Worth Airport.

For the better part of an hour I sat with the manager, who was wearing a dark business suit, while he filled out forms in triplicate, copied my license and passport, took a credit card deposit, and asked me the same kind of questions that admitting doctors go through in emergency rooms. Finally the rental car was ours, although for the last step the manager and I sat in the front seat, while he explained the finer points of the air conditioning, and the gas cap. I imagine that corporate mergers have taken less time.

Leaving the car in the Sheraton garage, Charles and I headed to the Aleppo mosque, a great oasis of polished marble near the souk and the citadel. The actual interior of the mosque was small by comparison to the courtyard, which felt like a city park, with families having picnics and small boys chasing soccer balls. Charles was asked to wear a monk's cowl, to cover up his shorts and bare arms. He looked like a character from Harry Potter, about to descend into the Chamber of Secrets. We watched the sun set through the mosque's Romanesque arches, and then tried our luck in the souk, where we were set upon by hawkers, all of whom had rugs, silver, soap, leather goods, and pottery that was unrivaled on the Silk Road.

I wasn't in what I would call "a buying mood." The day had been too long, with the bus and taxi rides across the border, and the futile hotel search in Aleppo. But it seemed sacrilegious to have come to Aleppo and not to haggle in the market. We ended up in a stall that sold cloth goods and silver earrings. I bargained with the owner for what seemed liked hours, hoping that I was only paying double the local rates, instead of the normal markup, which must be four or five times the going price. (In Tunisia, my wife came close to buying a pair of leather sandals for $30, believing the price "fair." In the end, I got her two pairs for $5, and the merchant thanked me for the business.) In Aleppo the shop owner had only one bargaining phrase, which was "squeeze yourself." It meant "offer me a little more." I refused to budge, but still think I overpaid. Charles thought that it was magic that we bought for $200 items that had first listed at over $1,000. After that, "squeeze yourself" entered our travel lexicon, and we used it to describe every situation.

We were out of sync for dinner. We strolled under the illuminated citadel rather than eat in a restaurant. In 1911, reflecting on the same magnificent castle, T.E. Lawrence wrote a letter to the editor of the London *Times*, satirizing the cultural barbarism of the Turks, who were considering tearing it down. Whether he knew it or not, he was echoing the nineteenth-century sentiments of Prime Minister William Gladstone, who said the Ottoman Empire was "a bottomless pit of fraud and falsehood." The Arabist Gertrude Bell called it "a land of make-believe." Lawrence wrote to the newspaper:

Sir, Everyone who has watched the wonderful strides that civilization is making in the hands of the Young Turks will know of their continued efforts to clear from the country all signs of the evil of the past. They may not know, however, that this spirit is gaining ground in the provinces. All visitors to Aleppo will have seen the great castle that rules it from every part, with its ring of battlements and its memories of prehistoric, Hittite, Assyrian, and Roman domination. The great mass is now to be cleared away and leveled, and one of the prominent Levantine financiers of the town has the project of constructing there a new quarter for the poorest of the inhabitants on the lines of the London East End. The property will soon be put up to auction, and there are strong hopes that the end will be achieved.

We also walked around the Armenian Quarter. In 1915, for many Armenians, Aleppo was the promised land, and it's where many families hoped to find loved ones who had disappeared in the Taurus Mountains. At the front desk of the Baron, I had spoken with Lucine Sanjioghlu Soghikian, known to all as Lucy. She had worked in the hotel for forty-five years. As we talked across the front desk, most of her memories were on the relatives of her father. Of the large family that had tried to walk away from the horrors of the Ottoman Empire, only her father, who was then ten years old, survived. He had grown up in the neighborhood where were walking that evening. Lucy talked to me at length about what her father had endured to get to Aleppo, and her eyes watered as she recounted the stories of the Armenian genocide. She said: "I am pleased you are asking about my family, but now I will be sad for the rest of the day." I told her about the Armenian Quarter in Jerusalem, where she had never been, and Yerevan, the capital of Armenia, even though it bears little resemblance to the world that her father had departed.

When Lucy heard that my own father, now ninety-one, enjoys getting envelopes from hotels around the world, she opened a leather portfolio and rummaged around to find two original pieces of Baron stationery and matching envelopes, which are embossed with the citadel above Aleppo. Later, when I went to New York around the time of my father's birthday, I made a collage of the envelopes and some Syrian stamps that had been issued in 1925. On one stamp Aleppo is written as "Alep," and it shows the imposing portico of the castle, over which Lawrence had despaired at Ottoman barbarism and under which Lucy's father grew up.

The British Middle East: *'worse than the old Turkish system'*

BREAKFAST AT THE BARON was disappointing—stale bread rolls and tea. I did take a chair out onto the balcony of the hotel, and read David Fromkin's *A Peace to End All Peace*. It would be wrong to say that I went to Syria only to read this book, but the trip was the occasion to start it, something that had eluded me for years, even as friends promised me that I would love Fromkin's accounts of T.E. Lawrence, the desert war, the Sykes-Picot Agreement, and the way the borders of the modern Middle East emerged from the diplomacy of Versailles and the Cairo Conference of 1921. One reason I had never read Fromkin is that his book covers the same ground as many others that I have read, and I wasn't sure I wanted to read yet another account of the diplomacy that carved the Near East into a collection of ungovernable, artificial states. Like our journey, Fromkin starts his book on the Bosphorus and ends it in Damascus. His point is that "British policy-makers imposed a settlement upon the Middle East in 1922 in which, for the most part, they themselves no longer believed."

To read Fromkin is to embrace the possibility that World War I is best understood as the struggle over the Ottoman Succession.

Between the Congress of Vienna in 1815 and the guns of August in 1914, a cornerstone of the British Empire was the wobbly existence of the Ottoman Empire. The Crimean War was fought, in part, to keep the Russians away from the Bosphorus, and the later 1878 Treaty of Berlin was another attempt, by the "concert of Europe," to keep Constantinople in business, even if it was under reduced circumstances. To be sure, British support for the Ottomans was a sometime notion, and Gladstone, among others, challenged the support of a nation so prone to atrocities and pogroms against the Bulgarians and the Armenians. To the geopoliticians at Whitehall, even a dysfunctional Ottoman Empire kept the Austrians and the Russians away from the Dardanelles and the Bosphorus strait. In exchange for protections from predator powers, Britain could continue to rule in Egypt, which was nominally a Turkish colony. That gave the British control over the Suez Canal, its lifeline to India and the colonial riches of the East.

It was Winston Churchill who broke the umbilical cord between the British and Ottoman empires. At the time, he was First Sea Lord, and at the outbreak of war he "nationalized" two warships, *Osman* and *Reshadieh*, that the Turks had ordered from British yards but which as of August 1914 had yet to be delivered. Turkish school children had contributed money for their construction, and the ships were meant to solidify, not threaten, the neutrality of the Dardanelles and the Bosphorus. Churchill could not bear to part with two warships, especially after Turkey had tilted toward Germany and, later, gave safe harbor to two German dreadnoughts that the British had chased unsuccessfully after the outbreak of war. Churchill might have acquired, on the cheap, two near-ready warships. He also set in motion the events that made the dissolution of the Ottoman Empire one of Britain's many war aims. Fromkin writes about Churchill: "... there are frontier lines now running across the face of the Middle East that are scar-lines from those encounters with him."

By his own account, Churchill's career was devoted to the preservation of the British Empire. He spoke often about not wanting to preside over its dissolution. After the British government's seizure of the Turkish warships, Churchill had the idea to seize Constantinople, although a column of warships failed to clear the Dardanelles. Through most of 1915 the Allies waged the campaign at Gallipoli to secure the Dardanelles and take Constantinople. The strategic hope was to bolster the wobbly Russian front, knock Turkey out of the war, and advance against the Central Powers through the Balkans, breaking the stalemate of the Western Front. The Gallipoli invasion, however, never got off the beaches and cost the Allies 250,000 casualties.

The loss of so many men in the war against Turkey fueled the British war aim to bring down the Ottoman Empire. Communities and tribes from Mount Lebanon to the Hejaz (on the Arabian peninsula, near the Red Sea) were promised independence if they sided with the Allies against the Turks. In the postwar betrayal that drew the subsequent fault lines around the modern Middle East, Britain and France reneged on the promises of Arab independence (not to mention that of a Jewish homeland) and divided the Ottoman Empire among themselves. New, and artificial borders were drawn around Greater Syria, Palestine, and Trans-Jordan, which became British and French mandates, leaving everyone unhappy. Even T. E. Lawrence was heard to say: "Our government is worse than the old Turkish system."

One of the features of the Syrian mandate that emerged from the Peace of Paris was that it grouped together, under French control, the line of cities stretching from Aleppo to Damascus. In between were Hama and Homs, not to mention the railway that connected Constantinople to Damascus, known formally as the Société Ottomane du Chemin de Fer Damas-Hama et Prolongements. Usually railroads take the names of the countries that they cross. Here the country followed the meandering course of the tracks, much as we did in our rental car, as I steered through the morning Aleppo traffic and followed signs on the autoroute for Hama, made famous by the 1982 massacre. The government of Syrian President Hafez Assad (another famous guest at the Hotel Baron) killed thousands of Islamic militants, who, he believed, were opposed to his Socialist Ba'ath Party, dominated by Alawites, who the more conservative Sunni Muslim Brotherhood considered infidels. Bystanders were also killed in the army attacks, which may have claimed as many as 25,000 casualties in the street fighting around the old city.

Crusading Across Syria in a Rental Car: *many lost cities*

BEFORE GETTING TO HAMA, we turned off the highway near Ariha, and wandered—sometimes lost—on small back roads until we found the Byzantine ruins of al-Bara, a "lost" city that was abandoned in the twelfth century C.E. for reasons that scholars cannot ascertain. Now it looks like the ruins of a Greek city, as the tumbled stones and fallen columns stretch across dry, rocky hills. Although a site of considerable archaeological importance, there was neither a sign, a front gate, nor a kiosk selling entrance tickets or cold drinks. We parked the car near what we judged to be an ancient temple—I could imagine a similar building in Pompeii—and then climbed over and through the broken walls of the many surrounding buildings, which looked as they would have after the last earthquake shook the city apart. As we were leapfrogging around the fallen blocks of stone, a small bus drove up. A guide spoke for a few minutes to the group of travelers, who nodded reverentially about the importance of the Byzantine Empire, and then vanished down the road, leaving us to contemplate the end of civilization in solitude.

I am not sure that I would recommend to everyone the experience of driving a rental car around the central hilly spine of Syria. We later marked X's on our road map at all the places where we had gotten lost, and now the map looks like a geometry textbook, with X's everywhere. We had come to Syria with four road maps, including one in Arabic, and two guidebooks. The problems were apparent after we left the highway. First, many smaller roads in Syria are unmarked. Nor are there signs indicating the names of the towns and villages. Second, most of the maps that we had were wrong. For example, al-Bara was about ten miles from the spot where it was shown on a map.

At least on the road we had the constant companionship of Hafez and Bashir Assad, the father-and-son team that has run Syria, as if it were a Mafia family business, since 1970. Their portraits adorn trucks, factory gates, shopping centers, and store windows, as though they were the management and shareholders. Although Syria is often depicted as a front-line state in opposition to Israel, from the road that posturing looks secondary to the cause of local economic and political ascendancy. The people get to denounce Israel, while the Assads and their crowd get a cut of everything. My sense is that Syrians enjoy relative freedom— we met many villagers, who were endlessly cheerful in providing directions—so long as they don't get involved in any proxy fights with the board. Those turn deadly.

As I was driving, Charles had the unpleasant task of trying to "triangulate" where we were from the guides and the maps, while I used the sun to navigate and called out the names of passing villages. It led to some strains during the day, and we spent a good hour lost on the roads to Apamea, site of some of the most imposing Roman ruins in the Middle East. It didn't help, I suppose, that signs for "Famia" were haphazardly placed in town squares. When everything failed, as it often did on that long afternoon, we would park the car, and I would head into a shop with the Arab map. In turn, that drew happy crowds of well-wishers, all of whom had clear, and usually conflicting, ideas on the best way to Apamea, which we finally found around 3 p.m., in time to discover that the only restaurant in the area served only orange soda for lunch.

Apamea was worth the wrong turns. It sits on a bluff, near the fortress town of Afamia, and commands a view of the broad surrounding Ghab Valley, which feels like an extension of the fertile Bekaa Valley, which runs through Jordan and Lebanon. Apamea had a few more tourists than al-Bara, but not many. Perhaps two buses were parked near the entrance. My guess is that it is a draw for the cruise ships that stop in the Syrian port of Latakia. What everyone does at Apamea is walk along the mile-long colonnaded main street or cardo, which, unlike many Roman city ruins in Europe, has many sections that are largely intact.

Because I think a lot about trains, I was reminded of the imposing columns that used to greet travelers entering New York's Pennsylvania Station, which was torn down in the 1960s, to make way for the nihilistic Madison Square Garden. In the case of Apamea's destruction, a twelfth-century earthquake, more than "progress," brought down the interior walls of the buildings, although the columns survived and the Crusaders incorporated the city and the nearby fortress into their lines of fortifications. We loved Apamea—to find sweeping Roman columns after a harried drive through claustrophobic Arab villages was magic. We might have enjoyed it more had we found lunch or had we not been stalked along the main Roman way by touts, who dig up figurines (or buy them in China) and try to sell them to tourists. Maybe those annoyances explain why Pompey sacked the city in 64 B.C. or why later both Julius Caesar and Cassius took aim at the city walls?

Our hotel reservation that night was near the magnificent Crusader fortress, Krak des Chevaliers, which should have been a two-hour drive south from Apamea. Instead of heading straight there, we fueled up on roadside bananas and turned the rental car east across the mountains to find the Crusader fortress at al-Marqab. The guidebooks spoke of its imposing setting, overlooking the Mediterranean Sea, and we convinced ourselves that the highway along the water would be an easier drive to Krak than to continue our meandering ways on the back roads of Syria.

Only at 7 p.m. did we drive up the steep mountainside and park under the imposing castle walls. Why we even bothered to get close to the fortress remains a mystery, as it was off-season (a cold and blustery Tuesday afternoon in April), and in Syria many tourist attractions close at 5 p.m., if not earlier. We thought that at least we would see the castle up close from the outside, and maybe look down on the sun setting across the Mediterranean. As we got out of the car, a guard—his uniform was a bit makeshift—waved to us from the portcullis, encouraging us to come up the stairs. We followed his directions, handed over $10, and then spent a delightful half hour, as it grew dark and the rains started, wandering through the remains of the fortress, which feels like a Camelot stronghold that has washed ashore in the Levant.

Lawrence of Syria: *a foreigner and a Christian*

My reason for pushing on to the fortress of al-Marqab is that I associate Crusader castles with my readings around the life and times of T.E. Lawrence. Fromkin's view of Colonel Lawrence is that he was something of a poseur, yet another war memoirist prone to exaggeration. ("Lawrence possessed many virtues but honesty was not among them; he passed off his fantasies as the truth.") Much as Fromkin blames the British for mindlessly attacking the Ottoman Empire, and saddling modern politics with the legacy of its subdivision, he also takes issue with Lawrence for promising the Arab world an independence that his colonial overlords had no intention of delivering. Nor does Fromkin buy much of the Lowell Thomas and Hollywood myth that "Lawrence of Arabia" was an effective instrument of war against the Turks along the lines of the Hejaz Railway.

Whatever Lawrence's legacy as a soldier and diplomatist, he understood the geography of the Middle East better than almost any European since the time of the Crusades. He began his education with a walk across Syria in 1909, to research his Oxford thesis on Crusader fortifications, and I was thinking about the iconography of Lawrence when I drove the car up those twisting roads to al-Marqab.

I first heard about the Lawrence legends around 1964, when I was ten, and had to have four recalcitrant baby teeth pulled from my mouth. During my recovery, my mother took me to see the movie *Lawrence of Arabia*, with its many scenes of exploding track. For my first trip to the Middle East in 1985, I read Lawrence's *Revolt in the Desert*, a condensed version of *Seven Pillars of Wisdom*, and my wife and I had plans to walk around his encampment at Wadi Rum (where in the movie he has to shoot his faithful servant) and the battlefield around the Red Sea, about which Lawrence later reflected: "Later I rode for Akaba… and a home-sickness came over me, stressing vividly my outcast life among these Arabs, while I exploited their highest ideals and made their love of freedom one more tool to help England win."

Because of 1980s Jordanian travel logistics (our rental car died on the highway), my wife and I made it only to Petra, on the road to Wadi Rum. The travels, however, left intact my impression of

Lawrence from the images in the movie, and I followed up the trip by reading several biographies that are also favorable to Lawrence: Lowell Thomas's *With Lawrence in Arabia*, which spawned the "of Arabia" hagiography; and Jeremy Wilson's *Lawrence: The Authorized Biography of T. E. Lawrence*, which digs deeper into Lawrence's emotional struggles after the war, when he enlisted in the armed forces as a private, under such aliases as John Hume Ross and T.E. Shaw.

Both books make the point that Thomas first advanced when he covered the Arab revolt in the field. He writes: "Lawrence overcame the two greatest prejudices of the Bedouin, namely, that he was a foreigner and a Christian…. In this, the most brilliant and spectacular military operation in the world's history, Allenby and Lawrence lost only four hundred and fifty men, captured over one hundred miles in less than a month, and broke the backbone of the Turkish Empire." Thomas ends with the encomium: "Little did young Lawrence dream, when he was studying Hittite ruins, that it was his destiny to play a major role in building a new empire, instead of piecing together, for a scholar's thesis, the fragments of a dead-and-buried kingdom."

From al-Marqab, Charles and I drove in the darkness along the Syrian coast to Krak des Chevaliers. The road was a variation on an autoroute, although there were no painted lanes, and trucks barreling south from Latakia weaved like suicide bombers. I thought about the passages in Wilson's authorized biography that described Lawrence's early trips to the Levant. When we got home, I looked up the passages, and discovered that in 1909 Lawrence had walked much of the route that Charles and I were undertaking, in the opposite direction, in a rental car.

Lawrence started his tramp in Beirut, wandered down through what is now southern Lebanon and northern Israel, had a look at Lake Tiberias, and then turned around and went north along the coast to the city of Tripoli, and into what is now Syria near Krak des Chevaliers. He arrived there on his twenty-first birthday, describing it as "the finest castle in the world: certainly the most picturesque I have seen—quite marvelous: I stayed three days there." Wilson continues: "From Latakia he struck inland once again to Sahyun: 'perhaps the finest castle I have seen in Syria: a splendid keep, of Semi-Norman style, perfect in all respect: towers galore.'" Lawrence noted in his letters home that it would take three weeks to walk from Tripoli to Aleppo, as there were, writes Wilson, "fifteen castles in the first 125 miles." He ended his walk at the Euphrates River, at Carchemish, where he spent several summers on an archaeological dig, at one point showing the ruins to the travel writer and Arabist Gertrude Bell, who served with Lawrence at the 1921 Cairo Conference that so disastrously partitioned the remnants of the Ottoman Empire. Charles and I missed Carchemish, which is northeast of Aleppo, but when we drove up the lonely hillside toward Krak des Chevaliers, I am sure it was to pay homage to Lawrence's early wanderings.

We had little luck in the darkness in finding the Hotel Francis, which was folded into the lee of some sharp hills. Signs occasionally spoke of its presence, but then the trail would go blank. More than once I turned the car around on the mountainous road. Finally we found the Francis and a sign over the front door, "Please, no enter." Early the next morning, despite the rain and low swirling clouds that encased the fortress, we parked near the entrance and wandered through the main gate, which had neither a ticket agent nor any signs indicating the way around.

Spectacular as is Krak des Chevaliers, it feels like the Crusaders left in 1959, not in the twelfth century. The Syrians have made some effort to block off some dungeons, and a movie about Cleopatra was improbably being filmed in one of the inner halls, made to look like a pharaoh's boudoir.

To escape the gusts of rain and wind, and to understand what we were seeing, I tried reading aloud passages from a history of the Crusades ("*The Crusaders found shelter in a tomb that was also a dream*"), which said that Krak had belonged to the Hospitallers and told how it had never fallen to Saladin, the Arab liberator. It is still not clear from my reading whether Krak fell in the late thirteenth century to siege guns of the Mamelukes or whether the Hospitallers simply withdrew over time from the lines of fortified castles and melted away into desert heat. As for the cause of the Crusaders' defeat, I attribute it to their failure to make common cause with the governments of Byzantium, their natural protector and regional ally.

Many Crusaders, especially the Venetians, treated Constantinople as another treasure chest to pry open and loot, in the name of the kings of France and England, the pope, and God, all of whom presumably got a cut. The Byzantine Empire looked suspiciously like what they were trying to crack in the Levant, and this schism in the church left the Christian communities, in places such as Syria, cut off from the protections of the Orthodox world. Robert Payne writes of the Fourth Crusade: "The inexhaustible rapacity of the Venetians harmed the Crusaders as nothing else had harmed them. The Muslims saw once more that the Crusaders were treacherous and never more treacherous than when they fought among themselves." Without a protector in Constantinople, the Christian communities, like the Maronites in Lebanon, were isolated from their origins, a cause of unrest now for a thousand years.

From Homs to Palmyra: *memoirs of Hadrian*

LEAVING KRAK DES CHEVALIERS after lunch in a tourist hotel, I pointed the car in the direction of Palmyra, the ruins of the Roman Empire that are in the Syrian desert, about a hundred miles east of

Homs, a city on Syria's north-south axis between Aleppo and the capital. Thinking it might be interesting to see something of Homs, we drove through the town center, which put us in the middle of the old market and its narrow lanes. After a while, we were driving at the speed of a donkey cart, through crowds of Arabs, the kind of setting that in a James Bond movie usually precedes a chase scene through the market. Instead of taking out half the town, as Bond often does, we found an alley that led to a bigger road, and finally the highway east to Palmyra, an oasis that the Romans fortified with the splendor of the Forum.

After winding through the hills of the Ghab Valley, it was a pleasure to drive the car on an open road, even if the only scenery was the brown scrub of the desert and the occasional dusty town. It interested me to find train tracks and a small station at Ayn al-Baridah, which looked to be part of the line into a phosphate mine in the desert. That was also where we found the Baghdad Café, run by an exile Iraqi, who, when I asked how things were at home, gave me a long, dark shake of the head and whispered, "Very bad." More by luck than by planning, we got to Palmyra after the heat of the day, and we strolled the columned main street of the ruins in the glory of a late spring afternoon.

The ruined city of Palmyra is an odd mixture of scattered marble blocks and intact columns, as though the earthquakes could selectively spare certain sections of the Roman way. Strolling along the main street of Palmyra, I thought of the Roman emperor Hadrian. He came to the city in 217 C.E., during one of his imperial excursions, and so loved the setting that he decided to rename it Palmyra Hadriana. In her book about his travels, Elizabeth Speller writes: "No man ever loved Greece more who was not a Greek." In Marguerite Yourcenar's fictional *Memoirs of Hadrian*, she imagines him saying: "I could see possibilities of Hellenizing the barbarians and Atticizing Rome, thus imposing upon the world by degrees the only culture which has once for all separated itself from the monstrous, the shapeless, and the inert, the only one to have invented a definition of method, a system of politics, and a theory of beauty."

The small town of Tadmur is on the edge of the Roman ruins, and there we spent the night in a bare-bones hotel—although it had photographs of Alexandretta in the lobby—and checked our email at an Internet café that had waiters as slow as the computer's server. During the night motorbikes gunned up and down the main street, under our hotel room, and breakfast the next morning was tea and hard rolls. The reason Tadmur is a sad tourist backwater is because most visitors to Palmyra come from Damascus on the daily tour buses, although it is almost a four-hour drive in each direction.

We set off in the rental car after another look at Palmyra and a hillside fortification, and drove toward Damascus on a two-lane road that crosses nothing but rolling desert—the Middle East as a New Mexico butte. There were signs along the way for Baghdad, seven hours to the east. Sometimes on the long drive, when Charles and I were lost in the middle of crowded Syrian villages, when everyone around us wore headscarves, I would say: "Imagine you're a soldier in Iraq, and you come into a town just like this one, and in a split second you have to decide who's on your side and who's not."

Footloose in Damascus: *a breeding place for future war*

In *Revolt in the Desert*, Lawrence describes his own entrance into Damascus in 1917: "When dawn came we drove to the head of the ridge, which stood over the oasis of the city, afraid to look north for the ruins we expected: but, instead of ruins, the silent gardens stood blurred with river mist, in whose setting shimmered the city, beautiful as ever, like pearl in the morning sun." This description did not match my first impressions (few would call

Damascus "green"), but then I was behind the wheel of a rental car, and none of the maps or guidebooks could pinpoint our location on the outskirts. We asked people on the street for directions to downtown, and their answers suggested that they had not been there since the Ottoman retreat. By chance, we passed through one of the old city gates and found our hotel, the Orient Palace, which I had chosen because it promised a room overlooking the old Hejaz Railway main station.

State-owned and-run, and distant from its glory in the 1930s, the Orient Palace may have been slightly disappointing—when I ordered a beer, the bellhop went across the street and came back with it in a brown paper bag—but the view was not. Our room, with cavernous ceilings, looked directly at the imposing façade of the station, now a museum, although tracks still led from its platforms. Until recently it was possible to take a remnant of the railway between Damascus and Amman, Jordan. The service was dropped several years ago, even though the Hejaz Railway has an active fan base, museum, and historical society.

Lawrence got to know the railway as well as anyone: "Our ideal was to keep his railway just working, but only just, with the maximum of loss and discomfort. The factor of food would confine him [the Turks] to the railways, but he was welcome to the Hejaz Railway, and the Trans-Jordan railway, and the Palestine and Syrian railways for the duration of the war, so long as he gave us the other nine hundred and ninety-nine thousands of the Arab world."

I was happy to return the rental car, having logged about six hundred miles in three days across the backbone of Syria. As navigator, Charles had struggled with the inaccurate maps and the deceiving signposts, and did remarkably well for a fourteen-year-old boy in a strange land. From the car rental agency, we took a taxi to the old city of Damascus, which, like Dubrovnik or parts of Venice, can be seen only on foot. Charles had to borrow another hooded smock to enter the Umayyad Mosque, and it took us a long time to get our bearings in the market, which was clogged with shoppers and tourists.

In the headlines, Damascus is the antechamber of the Axis of Evil, but on the ground it feels like a village square in Provence, chock full of art galleries, rug stores, and tourist souvenirs.

In Damascus I didn't have many political discussions, except one with a businessman, who spoke about all the flight capital from Iraq that was driving the price of one-bedroom apartments past $1 million. Apparently exiles paid with suitcases of American dollars, which would indicate that the Damascus real estate market is one of the few winners in the war on terror.

To the eyes of a teenager, the old city and its many shops looked like the reward for his hours of navigating across the Syrian hinterland. I set him loose with $50 and directions to the café where I would be waiting in several hours. There in the shadow of the Umayyad Mosque, instead of concentrating on Fromkin's *A Peace to End All Peace*, I fretted about what I would tell my wife if, like Kipling's Kim, Charles had vanished into the Damascus market and became a boy of the road.

When my son showed up at the rooftop café, I carried on with my book, in which Fromkin describes the war aims of Britain and its commander, Lord Kitchener: "They were intrigued by the notion that whoever controlled the person of the Calliph—Mohammed's successor—controlled Islam." In the end, the British hoped that by the end of the war "Turkey must cease to be. Smyrna shall be Greek. Adalia Italian, South Taurus and North Syria French, Filistin [Palestine] British, Mesopotamia British and everything else Russian—including Constantinople... "

After General Allenby took Damascus in 1918 and the war ended, the Ottoman armies in the Near East drifted away. There is a scene in *Lawrence of Arabia* in which the British-led forces massacre a wagon train of Turkish soldiers. The Arabs hoped that peace and the dissolution of the Ottoman Empire would allow for the creation of an independent Arab nation, with its capital in Damascus, and encompassing the lands from Aleppo to Saudi Arabia and then east across Mesopotamia, now Iraq.

Lawrence had promised as much when he was recruiting volunteers to cut the tracks of the Hejaz Railway. Lowell Thomas describes one negotiation: "Emir Feisal, backed up by Lawrence's advice, insisted that the new Arabian state should include, not only the Hejaz, but all Mesopotamia, Syria, and Palestine as well. Feisal would not listen to any proposal that Palestine should ever become a Jewish state. From his point of view, and in this he represented the opinion of the whole Arab world, Palestine could not be looked upon as a separate country, but as a province which should remain part and parcel of Syria." Whatever Lawrence implied, or the Arabs inferred, the many peace conferences on the Ottoman succession between 1919 and 1923, at places such as Sèvres, Cairo and Lausanne, partitioned Arabia into the fragmented states that everyone recognizes from today's violent headlines.

The British had spoken of Arabia for the Arabs, although they had also promised some of Palestine (in the Balfour Declaration) to the Jews, and the French (thanks to Sykes-Picot) were to get the majority of Greater Syria, including the Christian canton of Lebanon and the surrounding Shia and Sunni cities of Tyre, Sidon, and Tripoli. For themselves, the British decided to keep Mesopotamia, largely for its oilfields, and from the remnants they decided to reward various Allies with a claim to Trans-Jordan and Saudi Arabia. Instead of the self-determination at Versailles that minted so many independent nations from the ruins of European empires, the Middle East (a phrase coined by the American naval strategist Alfred Thayer Mahan) became the last preserve of colonial privilege. Fromkin writes: "It was the Liberal dream of triumphant Hellenism and Christianity, promoted by Gladstone's political heir, David Lloyd George."

Even the French prime minister Georges Clemenceau thought little of foreign possessions; he agreed with the partition as a spoil of war and perhaps out of distant loyalty to the heirs of Frankish Crusaders. In the question of Palestine, Fromkin describes British ambivalence: "In 1922 Britain had accepted a League of Nations mandate to carry out a Zionist program that she had vigorously espoused in 1917—but for which she had lost all enthusiasm in the early 1920s."

Nearly all the Near East "countries" stamped from the many peace conferences—between 1919 and 1922, Lloyd George attended thirty-nine—might well have been conjured from a genie's lamp. Palestine and Syria were vague terms, not used before this time. The same can be said of the states that became Israel, Jordan, and Lebanon. Only President Wilson's senior advisor, Colonel House, saw the region for what it was, remarking, "They are making it a breeding place for future war." Even though she had a hand in the fateful 1921 Cairo Conference, which advanced the cause of Arab partition, Gertrude Bell said: "You are flying in the face of four millenniums of history if you try to draw a line around Iraq and call it a political entity!"

Although he was minister of colonial affairs after World War I, and pressed on with the terms of the settlements, Winston Churchill realized that the consequence of British policy was that everyone would hate the colonial overlords. He said, "The unfortunate course of affairs has led to our being simultaneously out of sympathy with all the four Powers exercising local influence in the Middle East: Russians, Greeks, Turks, and Arabs." After World War II the United States took up the cause of the White Man's Burden in the Middle East, with the same results.

The Night Train to Aleppo: *shadowing the Hejaz Railway*

CHARLES AND I HAD less weighty issues on our minds toward
the end of our stay in Damascus. We had toured and shopped,
but we still did not know exactly how we would get home. Our
plane reservations were from Istanbul, but I had not been able
to find a one-way flight to that city at an affordable price. I had
thought maybe I could find a travel agency in Damascus with signs
advertising "Istanbul $200." All the quotes I could find routed us
through Cairo, and would have cost almost $1,000 for the two of
us. In the end, despite the uncertainty with the railroad tickets,
we decided to retrace our steps on the overnight train from Adana
to Istanbul. Not only would we enjoy another twenty hours in our
Anatolian stateroom, but in Damascus Charles had put together a
portable backgammon set from the market (where one shopkeeper
was considerate, while another tried to cheat him).

Getting to Adana from Damascus is not as easy as it looks on
a Syrian map. We decided to try the overnight Syrian Railways
sleeper to Aleppo, and then retrace our steps across the border in
a taxi. To buy tickets, we took a taxi to Kadem station—the one
that Lawrence saw in smoke. In less than ten minutes, and for $6,
we had berths on the midnight train. The station to the southwest
of the old city was quiet, and we asked at the ticket counter for
directions to the Hejaz Railway Museum. The agent made a call.
In a minute another railway clerk was walking us to a freight yard
across the tracks from the main station.

There we found to our delight about twenty narrow-gauge
steam engines, all in excellent condition and some even made
in Switzerland, that had once been the workhorses of the desert
railway. Nearby were some restored passenger cars, with freshly
painted wood, that perhaps until recently had taken rail buffs down
to Amman. We found the museum inside a modern building, with

all sorts of memorabilia about the line. We were the only visitors, and the director, Ahmad Kheir Aboura, warmed to the story of our train trip from Istanbul and started to show us some of the 17,000 pictures he claimed to have of what's left of the Hejaz Railway.

From one of the cabinets, I had the director show me an early map of the railway. Along with the line south across Jordan to Medina, the network indicated a line that connected Der'a, in southern Syria, to Haifa, now in Israel, and a second branch line from Damascus to Beirut. In my mind, these track beds formed the outline of my own Middle East peace plan, although it is probably not one that will get discussed at the conferences.

Would it not be a step forward for the troubled region if steam service were restored between Beirut, Damascus, and Haifa? Nor would I consign the railroad simply to tourists, but use it for freight and local cultural exchanges. I suppose there would be some risk that latter-day Lawrences might try to blow it up. At the same, time it's one of the few existing physical links between Amman, Damascus, Beirut, and Israel. Who could resist the elegant sight of a narrow-gauge steam engine sweeping around Lake Tiberias, near where Jesus lived, or stopping at Zahle, in Lebanon, so that passengers could buy Ksara wines? Hoping for an elusive peace, the U.S. gives millions each year in weapons to Arabs and Israelis. Why not earmark a little for a cross-border peace train? At the least it would honor the promises of Lawrence, who confessed: "It was hard, anyway, for a stranger to influence another people's national movement, and doubly hard for a Christian and a sedentary person to sway Moslem nomads."

Our $6 Syrian sleeper to Aleppo was rundown, but the sheets on the berths were clean, and the train arrived on time at 6 a.m., giving us plenty of time to catch a taxi to Hatay. We had telephoned our inbound, cigarette-laden taxi driver, now known to us as Mr. Inshallah, and he had promised to meet us on the platform.

279

He was nowhere to be seen, so we took another taxi to Hatay. Because it was early morning, the border crossing between Syria and Turkey was uneventful, although, yet again, it involved cigarettes and gasoline in Pepsi bottles.

In Adana, we were disappointed to find that the Turkish railways had canceled our night train to Istanbul. That explained why none of the clerks could find it in the computer. No reason was given, although I suspect track work south of Ankara, where they are introducing some high-speed service. We sought refuge in a nearby Adana travel agency, but the clerk said, as it was last-minute and on Sunday night, that all the Istanbul flights were booked.

Out of options and out of luck, we took a thirteen-hour bus ride from Adana to Istanbul by way of Ankara. It sounds worse than it was. Turkish buses have drinks and TV, and I spent a long portion of the ride watching local soap operas. (Hadrian reflected: "If I have learned one thing on this journey it is that we are an empire held together by entertainment.") On the night ride, I also got to finish Fromkin and see Ankara, admittedly at 2 a.m.

Back in Istanbul, getting from the bus terminal to the airport meant recrossing the Bosphorus, which Charles and I did on a sunrise ferry, again drinking orange juice and sipping tea. In my mind that's where the trip ended, as we were looking back at Topkapi Palace and the Blue Mosque, on a clear, cool morning. Although we had traveled the lengths of Turkey and Syria, and traced the ruins of several vanished empires, I thought of our travels more as a journey involving a father and a son.

I had learned to lose gracefully at backgammon, and Charles had learned never to rely on the accuracy of a Syrian road map. The high point was our terraced breakfast in Iskenderum, and the low points were any of those wrong turns on the twisted road to Apamea, not to mention its many aliases. Charles had loved climbing around the strange Byzantine ruins of al-Bara while I was still savoring lunch at the Hotel Baron. As I finished my 600-page Ottoman history, my son rolled a Syrian carpet into his backpack. Together across the silk roads, we had squeezed ourselves.

AMTRAKS ACROSS AMERICA

"A man who has never gone to school may steal from a freight car, but if he has a university education, he may steal the whole railroad."

—THEODORE ROOSEVELT

Private Car to Pittsburgh

THE FIRST TIME I WENT TO PITTSBURGH, in spring 1972, I came up the Ohio Valley on a series of buses that stopped in such places as Moundsville, Wheeling, and Weirton, West Virginia, and Steubenville, Ohio. Pittsburgh was still a steel city, although the London fog of soot no longer hung over the downtown. Still, it looked more like the past than the future, with the riverbanks lined with rusting barges and empty steel mills as forlorn as an Edward Hopper painting.

My visit to Pittsburgh came after two weeks in Appalachia, studying coal mining. In the spring of my senior year in high school, everyone graduating had to complete an independent study project. If only to ride the trains around West Virginia, I had chosen to study coal, and enlisted a classmate, Kevin Glynn, to make the journey.

After leaving New York, we started by taking the Baltimore & Ohio Railroad from Washington, D.C., to Harpers Ferry. Over the next ten days or so, we picked our way west on passenger trains to Clarksburg, West Virginia, and, occasionally, by bus and hitchhiking.

In springtime, surrounded by flowering dogwoods, even the rough edges of Appalachia had a soft feel. We spent our days and nights talking to miners, either at the coal pits or in nearby bars. Mostly I read Harry M. Caudill's *Night Comes to the Cumberlands* and improved my game at pool.

Approached from the south, Pittsburgh felt like the coal and iron ore capital, where train, road, and river traffic came together to form the crossroads of the carbon revolution. Opposition to cap-and-trade explains why Pennsylvania has considered voting Republican, for the first time in recent memory.

As we made our way up the Ohio Valley, we went by car plants, rail yards, smelters, and gas flares, which, had I known more in 1972 about economics, I might have recognized as the eternal flame of industrial America.

Even then, heavy industry was moving to places such as Japan and Korea, which left downtown Pittsburgh with the air of a frontier settlement in which the saloon and the company store had closed. Kevin and I stayed in a shabby hotel, went to a baseball game, and caught a night train home to New York, having liked Pittsburgh more than we expected.

After the narrow valleys of West Virginia and the claustrophobia of the fading mines, Pittsburgh had felt expansive, and the rivers that converged off Fort Pitt suggested that the city had currents to wider worlds, as Abraham Lincoln found when he drifted from Kentucky to New Orleans.

Thirty-eight years later I came back to Pittsburgh, this time on the aft, open deck of a private railroad car, as if whistle-stopping in a political campaign. A friend who owns the car invited me to join an excursion. I made the trip largely on a folding chair that gave me a box seat as the train crossed the Alleghenies and moved toward Pittsburgh through the historically drenched valleys around the towns of Conemaugh and Johnstown.

According to a history of the 1889 Johnstown flood that I was reading, the dam of the South Fork Fishing and Hunting Club "contained 20,000,000 tons of water before it broke—equivalent to the volume of water that goes over Niagara Falls in 36 minutes." A wind tunnel preceded the wall of water that killed 2,000.

Although the rail car offered excellent food, wine tasting, and good company, what interested me most was to see how Pittsburgh had changed since Kevin and I had left in spring 1972. My guide this time was Kevin Horner, a friend who drove me to such landmarks as the departed Forbes Field, where Bill Mazeroski and the Pirates beat the Yankees in the last at-bat of the 1960 World Series, ruining my childhood.

Together we looped the city, poking into the historical museum and an out-of-the-way bar where Kevin needed to buy cole slaw and where I discovered on a local "Wall of Fame" (much to my satisfaction) that the wrestler Bruno Sammartino has a higher local standing, thirteenth, than Andrew Carnegie, eighteenth.

Along the banks of the Monongahela and Allegheny rivers, the steel mills that belched fire are gone, replaced by highways, empty spaces, apartment blocks, and hotels. As in the New York of civic planner Robert Moses, elevated highways choke off much access to the rivers. Kevin said that much of the local steel production had been outsourced to Eastern Europe, reminding me that I had seen a train emblazoned "US Steel Serbia" on a trip to the Balkans. From our city drives, what was clear is the extent to which Pittsburgh has shifted into the service economy, with universities, hospitals, government office buildings, and sports complexes accounting for the local growth industries.

Because Kevin and I are sports fans, we spent a lot of time talking about the football industry, which has its factory lines across the river from downtown Pittsburgh. A joint venture among the Pittsburgh Steelers, the University of Pittsburgh, and local government accounted for the financial package that replaced Three Rivers Stadium with Heinz Field, a hulking monolith that instead of producing steel by night hosts football games on about twenty days a year. At the same time, the city replaced the baseball stadium and added on to the convention center, for a total expenditure of $809 million. Costs allocated to Heinz Field are estimated to be $281 million, although the accounting is more impenetrable than the Pittsburgh Steelers' "Steel Curtain."

The Pittsburgh Steelers are the emotional heart of the city. In season on Sundays, the faithful wear their jerseys to church, and the city takes a reverential pause during the games. Why would a city struggling to replace jobs lost to Asia put millions into two stadiums that are little more productive than Crusader fortresses in the Levant?

Some answers might be found in the Obama appointment of the Steelers' owner, Dan Rooney, as U.S. ambassador to Ireland. Presumably Rooney and some local unions had delivered Pennsylvania to the Democrats over the course of many elections, and their reward was a contract to build a football stadium, and an ambassadorship. The arrangement casts professional football in the light of another protected industry, although perhaps one as vulnerable as steel tubing to competitive destruction. Were professional football not to enjoy an antitrust exemption, the Koreans and the Serbs might be supplying games for costs far less than those requiring a publicly funded stadium ($158 million directly) in which the Rooneys keep the $125,000 per year from each of the high-end sky boxes.

At the Western Pennsylvania Sports Museum, I collected more notes on the extent to which football is among the region's thriving industries. A wall map shows the location of the many local quarterbacks exported to the professional ranks. I marveled at finding such names as Dan Marino, George Blanda, Joe Montana, and Jim

Kelly in places that once produced things like barbed wire. When will the U.S. Labor Department come up with a statistic (GEP, or Gross Entertainment Product) to measure to extent to which the economy is dependent on fun?

Kevin and I ended our Pittsburgh touring in nearby Beaver Falls, Pennsylvania, in homage to another quarterback, Joe Namath (one of my heroes), who grew up on its gritty streets. A steel-product company once operated in the town, but the mill looks closed. Beaver Falls lives on the fumes of a community college and its sporting legends (the county hall of fame has more than 300 inductees). We found the houses where Joe lived growing up, including rooms over a bar and grill then called the 1223 Club, which may explain Joe's remark that he liked "his women blonde and his Johnny Walker Red." Both options are available inside the bar.

On the way home, Kevin drove me past the location of Fort Pitt, the battles for which, as Fort Duquesne, had ignited the global Seven Years War (1756–63) between the English and the French. Of George Washington's blundering campaign against the fort in 1754, the French governor, Duquesne, wrote: "He lies a great deal in order to justify the assassination of Sieur de Jumonville, which has recoiled upon him and which he was stupid enough to admit in his capitulation…. There is nothing more unworthy, lower, or even blacker than the opinions and way of thinking of this Washington." Then Pittsburgh was near the geographic center of the New World, as it was later the capital of an industrial nation. The only wars now being fought around the Ohio Valley relate to foreign trade and the Super Bowl.

Amtrak Runs Off the Rails

WHEN THE UNITED STATES was in the money during the 1990s and 2000s, the Congress grudgingly voted Amtrak a $1 billion subsidy every year, and then engaged in histrionics about how it might be cheaper to send most passengers to their destinations on private jets. Then oil went to $140 a barrel, the United States dropped into recession, and one of the answers was to vote $12.9 billion in stimulus money, over the next five years, to Amtrak, the railroads, and state-supported transportation agencies.

Even though the American freight-train business has enjoyed a renaissance in the last twenty years—companies such as the Burlington Northern Santa Fe and CSX are admirable for their competitive spirit and financial results—I am skeptical that Amtrak is the company that can lead the way to the rebirth of U.S. passenger service. Freight, let's remember, flourished only when Conrail was privatized and the industry deregulated.

To be clear, the $8 billion appropriated for high-speed corridor service has yet to be earmarked, and is best understood as discretionary funding that can be doled out to the states, if not to loyal unions. For his part, Senate Majority Leader Harry Reid hopes to open a drawbridge to fund high-speed rail service between Anaheim and Las Vegas. Somehow, it is hard to imagine that the U.S. can restore its economic prosperity by rushing high rollers to the blackjack tables in Vegas.

Now in its thirty-ninth year of operation, the government-controlled Amtrak provides good service between Boston, New York and Washington, and Los Angeles and San Diego. Elsewhere, it's a land-cruise company. Beyond the corridors, Amtrak plies routes that were hastily drawn in 1971 to ensure that they touch as many congressional interests as possible. That means meandering sleepers from New Orleans to Los Angeles, or Chicago to Seattle, which are a delight to vacationers (myself included), but inconsequential to the business of America, which drives or flies to get somewhere. Amtrak handles less than 1 percent of America's intercity travel.

To defend Amtrak for a moment, it has been chronically underfunded, owns little of the track on which it operates, defers its schedule to freight interests, and is hostage to union rules, Congress, and microwavable food. European trains get more subsidies in a year than Amtrak has received in its lifetime. So will the $12.9 billion give the United States a passenger railroad network comparable to those that are now flourishing in Europe?

Before answering the question, let's take a look what European railroads have to offer:

—In Switzerland, where I live, the trains or a bus connect every village, town and city in the country. Geneva has more than 100 trains daily. Austin, Texas, a comparable city in terms of size, has two. But the railway is expensive for foreigners who visit the country. Round trip from Geneva to Zermatt for a family of four is about $600. Nonetheless, the rail network is a national asset.

—The German passenger railway, Deutsche Bahn, is incomparable. Nothing matches its speed, comfort, and service. Its Inter-City Express trains (ICEs) are the best in the world for the cost, not to mention the beer that's served.

—The United Kingdom, which has privatized much of what was BritRail, is a mixed bag of passenger service. Private companies are now competing for passengers, which means lovely new carriages, and better pork pies on the tea trolleys. But neither the private companies nor the government are spending what is needed on Britain's roadbed and infrastructure, which explains some of the horrible accidents in the system.

—France has its Train à Grande Vitesse (TGV), which operates on segregated, elevated high-speed track, and makes the runs from Lyon and Avignon to Paris not much longer than local commuter service. I find its seats cramped in second class (too airlinerish), and French stations are dingy, but otherwise the TGV is a model train. A comparable system in the U.S. could reduce the trip from New York to Washington or Boston to less than two hours. But it would mean building a new interstate for trains.

—Italy has some excellent trains, and fast ones too. I know this because I have seen them speed by as I have stood on platforms in Italy. But I never seem to catch any of them. The trains I ride have dirty seats, broken air conditioning, and inexplicable delays in places such as Domodossola.

—Eastern European night trains—I am partial to these, I confess—include heavy sleepers that go from Ljubljana to Belgrade, or Iasi to Bucharest, with reasonable fares, starched sheets on the berths, brandy at breakfast, and the chance to visit such exotic places as Debrecen, Lviv, and Chisinau.

—The Russian Railways has, remarkably, become an excellent company, with improved passenger and freight services, including trans-Siberian container shipping that can get boxes from the Pacific to Berlin in less time than cargo ships can.

How does Amtrak compare, and how is it likely to improve with stimulus funds? Amtrak already looks good on one account: Europe's international reservation system is medieval. Amtrak is miles ahead of Europe here. This summer I tried, in person and on the web, to book a sleeper from Geneva to Sevastopol, and failed. In Europe, international travel usually requires a trip to the ticket window at the station. Even simpler journeys, when they cross borders, are either prohibitively expensive or impossible to book. Geneva to London comes in at about $400; EasyJet does it in an hour for $60.

While I am all for spending stimulus money, or any money, on American passenger service, I have yet to see anything remotely like a good strategic plan for its restoration. The glossy maps projecting new corridor services depend on the states, not Amtrak, to realize the dreams. Nor am I sure that throwing money at the Amtrak model will do much more than refurbish some Amfleet coaches and make members of Congress look good in midterm elections. The railroad, like many in American history, strikes me as better at delivering pork than passengers. The current chairperson is a former small-town Illinois mayor, and Joe Biden's son was a board member until February 2009.

Perhaps equally important, where is Amtrak's passion for railroading? Why hasn't the route map changed in forty years? Where are the car-carrying trains, the elegant stations, the sleepers that cater to business people with showers and wi-fi, or even the special tourist trains that would take travelers across America to Civil War battlefields, major league baseball games, rock concerts, or national parks? Why do cities such as Phoenix or Louisville have no trains at all? Where are the creative railroad financiers, selling sleeping cars as time shares or condos? If it's truly a government-run corporation, why aren't there more investment-grade Amtrak bonds in world markets?

Here's another irony of the railroad stimulus package: Freight companies are prospering with deregulation and private capital, but Amtrak is running late while on the dole. Right now we're in a golden age of railroads, much of it funded with investor capital. The common stock of large American railroads is attracting serious money, including that of Warren Buffett.

Around the world, private luxury trains are crossing Russia, India, China, Tibet, the Silk Road, the Alps, and the Andes. In Asia, investors are plotting to complete the line from Singapore over the Burma Road to China. A company in Africa charges about $30,000—and gets it—for a deluxe train trip from Cape Town to Cairo. Bureaucratic protectionism keeps these dynamic groups from operating in the United States.

After World War II, America traded in the greatest railroad system in the world for interstate highways, sleazy rest stops, and now-crowded airports. Today, General Motors is emerging from bankruptcy, gas is close to four dollars a gallon, and politicians have to kowtow to Saudi princes. I would love to think that for $8 billion, corridor service would flourish and German-style trains would pop up around the country. Heck, I would love to ride a Romanian-style sleeper between New York and Bangor, Maine. Despite my hopes, my fear is that the transportation stimulus money is probably going to end up on a roulette wheel in Vegas.

New England Ramble

To escape the elegant summer crowds in New York's Hamptons, I rode the S92 bus (fare $1.50) for almost three hours as it cruised the south and north forks of Long Island, before leaving me at the ferry that connects Orient Point to New London, Connecticut.

Not many Hampton People leave on a local bus, which in my case was filled with Latino day laborers, giving it the air of a John Steinbeck novel. I was headed to New England, and I wanted to see if I could make a circuit to Providence, Boston, Amherst, and Keene entirely with public transportation. I might end up late to some meetings, but this way I could monitor the progress of the American Recovery and Reinvestment Act of 2009, at least as it pertains to the more than $8 billion earmarked for trains, buses, and ferries. Conclusion: Mass transit works better as a White House sound bite than as a way to get around New England.

The S92 rolled through the Hamptons to Riverhead, the county seat, where the Latinos got off, leaving me with the driver (from Masuria in Poland) to pass by the North Fork vineyards, which are vast and sophisticated. When I was young, only winos drank Long Island vintages; now some of it costs $40 a bottle.

The ferry to New London made the crossing in local fog banks, which obscured Plum Gut, but parted for the run into New London, the American Gibraltar. I saw a surfacing submarine and, in the harbor, a sculpture of the playwright Eugene O'Neill, shown as a boy gazing out to sea—even if he spent most of his adult life looking at bad marriages rather than the waves.

The train to Providence ran along the snug harbors around Mystic and Stonington, although inexplicably it arrived forty-five minutes late. Brown University and some local technology companies are the reason that the Rhode Island capital does not feel like a failed mill town. My friend on the local newspaper whispered that the university was long on celebrity children and short on academic excellence.

I switched to the Massachusetts Bay Transportation Authority (MBTA) for the hour run into Boston's Back Bay Station. Like much of summer America, it ran with air conditioning on full blast, as if it were a rolling meat locker. The rail car had wi-fi, a train first for me and much appreciated.

I like Boston, to a point. It's not one of the cities where I am at home, but I appreciate the glimpses of the Freedom Trail and thinking I might have to make way for ducklings. The $15 billion Big Dig, to bury the city's interstates, not to mention the U.S. Treasury, is largely done. Even so, much of downtown feels like an exit ramp, usually named after one of the Kennedys.

After my Boston meetings, I headed for Amherst in central Massachusetts. The bus would have meant changing in Springfield, and so would Amtrak (estimated travel time, about four hours). Instead, I took a MBTA commuter train to North Leominster, a gritty mill town now given over to Jiffy Lube and doughnuts, and had my friends pick me up.

The Amherst area has thousand of students from eastern Massachusetts, but few plans to improve its bus or train connections.

Nor is possible to take public transportation from Amherst an hour north to Keene, New Hampshire. Had I done so, I would first have gone south to Springfield, then back up to Bellows Falls, Vermont, spent the night, and connected the following morning to Keene on Greyhound ("safe, reliable, courteous, and slow").

I surrendered, and rented a car. Before leaving Amherst, I visited the Emily Dickinson House, where I had the good luck to join Ms. Casey Clark's tour. She made the reclusive Emily come to life by quoting from her poems ("Forever is composed of nows"), showing us her white dress, and pointing to the solitary window table where Dickinson wrote many of her 1,800 poems, the passionate Tweets of the nineteenth century.

I had not been to Amherst College since October 1963, when as a nine-year old boy I was taken to see President John F. Kennedy dedicate the new Robert Frost Library. Back on campus, I recalled seeing JFK's helicopter land on the football field and then the motorcade along the main street. He sat on the back of an open car—the president as prom queen. His bright red hair and toothy smile are etched in memory. Even to a rapturous boy he looked vulnerable. Less than a month later, he died in the same convertible.

For the benefit of my university-bound children, I gave it the old college try, and joined a campus tour led by the Amherst admissions office. After exhaustive inspections of laundry rooms, showers, dorms, lounges, and food courts—why are colleges marketed as subdivisions?—I gave up and drove to Brattleboro, Vermont, another mill town that is trying make a go of the industrial revolution in cappuccino.

My New England ramble ended on Amtrak's *Vermonter*, a train that goes from northern Vermont to Washington, D.C., in about the same time that Indians probably made the journey in canoes. The train poked across Massachusetts, idled in Springfield, and picked up speed south of Hartford, where we crossed the Connecticut River.

The biggest problem with American public transportation is that it lacks a critical mass. The infrequent service is more of a problem than the slow speeds, which could be padded over with comfortable seats, wi-fi, and better coffee. Massachusetts has only one train a day north of Springfield, which in turn has one train to Boston and spotty bus service. Little wonder that everyone drives.

Why throw money at high-speed rail when Amtrak runs to such dilatory schedules? Spend the money, instead, on more traditional rail cars and engines, which are in short supply, or hire some Swiss conductors and engineers to keep to the schedules.

Amherst to Princeton, New Jersey, where I was headed, is a five–hour car ride. I did it on the train in a leisurely eight hours, although I had the proximity of an AmCafé and a power outlet for my computer. I appreciated not having to drive on the interstate or sit on a cramped bus, although the station waits were maddening. The train crew changes were frequent, suggesting a company that is hostage to union rules and featherbedding. If you had $8 billion, would you let Amtrak manage it?

What I liked about my ramble is that I saw lot of places that stirred the mind: the North Fork, Long Island Sound, a General Ambrose Burnside statue in Providence, Boston's Public Garden, and the rolling hills of Vermont. I spoke with all sorts of people I would never have met in a car. On my leisurely way south I also thought of some American writers—Hawthorne, Melville, Dickinson, and Twain—who did their best work near the Connecticut River. For example, in a great feat of American imagination, Melville described Moby-Dick from a farmhouse in Pittsfield, Massachusetts.

From Emily Dickinson's bedroom window, it was possible for her to hear the arrival of the New York trains, which brought her letters and newspapers from the outside world that she longed to engage—at least from the vantage of her Amherst bedroom. To my knowledge, she never wrote a poem about Amtrak. If she had, it might read:

> *I cast my Fate upon the Rails—*
> *As if a spirit on Indian trails—*
> *We stopped, and shuddered, and watched our steps—*
> *And sweated during A/C fails.*

Enjoying the Journey

MY TRAIN TO RALEIGH, NORTH CAROLINA, is four hours late. At least I am stranded in Fredericksburg, Virginia, and I can console myself with a view of the Rappahannock River and the Fredericksburg Heights that broke the Civil War attacks of Union General Ambrose Burnside.

Why do I persist in riding Amtrak, the short name for the National Passenger Railroad Corporation, a company owned by the freight railways but subsidized by Congress and run like a Russian bureaucracy, complete with late trains, sullen employees, a myriad petty regulations, budget deficits, cold coffee, featherbedding, broken seats, clogged toilets, rail cars that feel like buses, and a schedule that serves the interests of congressmen, lobbyists, unions, budget stimulators, and small-town mayors, but rarely passengers?

Isn't it time to let Amtrak go the way of such defunct roads as the Nickel Plate, Erie-Lackawanna, Chicago & Alton, Rock Island, Maine Central, Wabash, Missouri Pacific, or New York Central, lines that outlived their corporate incarnation and were either shut down or merged into larger entities? It's hard to imagine Leland Stanford or E.H. Harriman buying into the Amtrak business model.

Set up in 1971 to replace the passenger rail network that government regulations, the Interstate Commerce Commission, subsidized air and road travel, and urban blight killed off, Amtrak went to work hauling passengers on a route system better adapted to 1921 than 1971. The earlier trains were faster.

Forty years after Amtrak's creation, little has changed in the business plan that offers corridor services on the East and West coasts and, in between, a meandering schedule of trains that account for less than 1 percent of all intercity travel. Buyers can be found for the Northeast Corridor service between Boston and Washington. Better yet, allow competition on the line, and auction off the franchise rights, using the proceeds to pay down the national debt.

England had the dreadful network that operated as BritRail. After it was privatized, Britain's rail service became competitive, passenger-friendly, faster, and more comfortable. Compare the new English trains with the Amtrak experience ("Enjoy the journey") in New York's Pennsylvania Station, a subterranean strip mall with dank corners, uncomfortable chairs in cheerless waiting rooms, confusing destination boards, and dreary platforms that are unchanged since I first used them in the 1960s.

Passengers buying Amtrak tickets in Penn Station meander along a line that feels like Ceaușescu's Romania, only to find that only one or two agents are on duty, the tickets are expensive, you need your passport to buy one, and getting on the train has the feel of descending into a Chilean coal mine. For the cost of billions, there's a plan for a new "Moynihan Station" across the street, although much of what's wrong with Penn Station could be fixed if Amtrak outsourced the operation to Hyatt.

Such shoddy service explains the rise of discount bus lines that are now digging into core Amtrak passenger revenue between Boston, New York, and Washington. Companies such as Bolt Bus or Fung Wah charge $15 or $20 to get from New York to Boston. (Amtrak costs from $67 to $95.) Bolt leaves punctually on the hour, from West 34th Street. The seats are cramped, but the buses are clean and have wi-fi. The trip takes less time than many trains, when you add in inevitable Amtrak delays. Nor is there a surly Amtrak conductor reading the riot act at each station.

As a flavor of Amtrak's attitude toward its passengers, listen to the cheerful words that its CEO writes in the on-board magazine: "Our identification policy, random screenings in stations, random on-board ticket verification process and more interactive police efforts—including our K-9 teams—are some of the visible activities we have been working on." The Chesapeake & Ohio used to advertise comfortable berths with sleeping kittens.

Killing off Amtrak would mean the end of long-haul passenger service, the sleepers that are the heirs to trains such as the *Twentieth Century Limited*. As much as I would regret the absence of long-distance train travel in the United States, my feeling is that what would replace Amtrak's overpriced and indifferent service is a network of private operators that would compete to take Americans around a glorious country that longs to be seen by rail.

Already there are nascent private companies and sleeping-car owners that offer rail trips to national parks, art museums, jazz festivals, baseball games, and the homes of famous writers. Deregulate the passenger industry, and it will flourish. Recently, for $325, less than the cost of a cramped night in an Amtrak "Slumberette" (emphasis on the "ette"), I rode round-trip in a private rail car, *New York Central 3* (owned by my friend Lovett Smith III), from New York to Pittsburgh.

If you want to find similar excursions, go to the AAPRCO website. If Amtrak were a service company, not a protection racket set up to bleed government money into padded contracts, it would have the imagination to operate similar excursions. Instead, Amtrak wants to position itself as the paymaster for a national rail plan. The U.S. Department of Transportation recently issued a strategic plan called "Moving Forward: A Progress Report," although if the report were an Amtrak passenger, it would be entitled, "Sorry for the Inconvenience: Due to a Track Incident, We're Being Held in Baltimore."

Currying favor with its overlords in the Obama administration, Amtrak imagines itself as the federal agency that should be hired to spend $117 billion, over thirty years, to build a segregated high-speed rail system between Boston and Washington, and for additional billions to operate Core Express Corridors between cities less than 500 miles apart. Such visions of grandeur come from a company that needs nine hours and fifteen minutes to run a train the 444 miles from New York to Pittsburgh (an average speed of 48 m.p.h.)

To be fair, not all Amtrak's failings are its fault. Most of the tracks on which it operates are owned by freight companies that find passengers a nuisance and think nothing of shunting aside "the varnish" (rail slang for a passenger train) to send through more coal and containers. Amtrak, however, is responsible for a corporate culture that makes a mockery of customer service. In many ways it is the perfect metaphor for everything that is wrong with letting Congress have a heavy hand in the economy or to imagine that an economic revival can be built around companies with federal guarantees.

Amtrak lacks direction, lives off subsidies and stimulus money, and now wants $117 billion to operate high-speed rail that, for the cost differential, would be only marginally better than the private bus companies now competing up and down the East Coast, with fares of $20 or so. Maybe it would help its cause if Amtrak reached out to passengers, even adopted some of the slogans of the passenger railroads incorporated into its route system ("Count on

Katy," "Santa Fe All the Way," or "Water Level Route—You Can Sleep"). For the transcontinental service, I would suggest: "Give up a week for your country." At the moment, however, Amtrak is four hours behind schedule into Rocky Mount, North Carolina, and to use a phrase from railroading legend, I would not pay a "plated nickel" for its services.

Boondoggle Express

GIVEN THAT WARREN BUFFETT ponied up $44 billion in cash and stock to take private the Burlington Northern Santa Fe Railroad, I wonder why President Obama is betting that the way to lift the country out of stagnant growth is to invest another $50 billion, in public funds, to swing aboard the dream of high-speed intercity rail.

According to the administration, new money needs to be allocated to such high-speed rail projects as those between San Diego and Sacramento, Orlando and Tampa, and—my personal boondoggle favorite—the DesertXpress between Los Angeles and Las Vegas, a $4 billion bet that getting high-rollers to the blackjack tables will lift the U.S. economy out of its doldrums.

To establish some track credibility, I spend much of my life dreaming about trains, consulting timetables on how to catch them, and plotting trips that might end up on night trains to Butterworth (the station for Penang) or Iasi (change in Ungheni, on the Moldovan border).

More to the point, I have ridden nearly all the high-speed trains—in China, Japan, and France—that are being held as speeding examples of what the United States could build if Congress would fork over another $50 billion, and if the President could appoint a railroad czar with the acumen of E. H. Harriman. Painful as it is for me to admit, the $50 billion high-speed stimulus package is a way to lay track to nowhere.

Take the rail link between Tampa and Orlando that imagineers hope will shuttle theme-parkers at speeds reaching 186 m.p.h. President Obama has already thrown $1.25 billion at the line. Presumably the named expresses will be *The Absentee Balloter* and *The Recount*.

Local officials have been busy buying rights-of-way and planning stations in their home districts, although, oddly, downtown Orlando is given a miss. When the stimulating project is finished, for close to $3 billion, a family visiting Walt Disney World can drive to the station, catch a high-speed train to Lakeland, pay a cab driver to take them to the Detroit Tigers spring training facility, and watch a game. After the game, to get back to their hotel, they would do the trip in reverse. Or they could drive to Lakeland in the hour projected on MapQuest. What would you do?

The reason high-speed rail has more allure in Europe is that people live in or near cities. Nor do they like driving their cars on the cobblestones of historic quarters. In China, cities are megalopolises, and few Chinese own cars or want to drive them across the vast country. France is essentially a one-city country, so all rail lines lead quickly to Paris, as Louis XIV would have wanted.

In Targeted America, everyone has a car, lives out of town ("we like it here"), and, except for a few New Yorkers, drives everywhere, except when they fly. Orlando might be the most car-centric suburban cluster in the country. Not long ago I had to drive from my Orlando motel just to find dinner. Is it remotely possible that Floridians will hop a high-speed train to rush them into downtown Tampa, which after 6 p.m., when I was last there, looked like Death Valley?

I can imagine Chicagoans taking a fast train to St. Louis, as opposed to flying out of O'Hare. Normal trains, and lots more of them, that reached the 100 m.p.h. speeds of the 1930s would suffice in most corridors.

What logic explains betting public billions on a concept—intercity rail transportation—that the same government has devoted countless resources to destroying? Through most of the twentieth century, the American government used public money to lay down roads and interstates, and to subsidize airports, that choked off demand for passenger rail service.

Federal bodies such as the Interstate Commerce Commission, which regulated the profits out of the industry, killed off the national jewel that was the railroad network, with its 250,000 miles of track in the 1920s. It is doubtful that the combined forces of the Texas Railroad Commission, Jay Gould, railroad baron Daniel Drew, and Leland Stanford could have kept passenger service alive when confronted by a government that lived by the rail credo of William Vanderbilt, who said: "The public be damned."

Between the 1970 collapse of the Penn Central and the 1980 passage of the Staggers Act—President Carter's successful deregulation of the industry—most Class I railroads flirted with bankruptcy, earning less than 1 percent on their capital, and were unable to set rates competitively.

The Staggers Act got the government off the freight rails; since then, the vital signs of the business have flourished to the point of attracting Warren Buffett's capital. Trackage has been downsized from 270,623 to 160,734 miles. Container traffic has grown from three to twelve million boxes a year. Productivity has more than doubled, and, adjusted for inflation, prices are down (although the big coal companies hate deregulation, and they are 45 percent of the business).

I mourn the loss of such evocative railroad names as the Grand Trunk, Boston & Maine, Nickel Plate, and Chicago & Alton (for which my grandfather worked). Nonetheless, from more than thirty failing companies, mergers have produced five thriving Class I railroads. The industry employs 164,439 workers at an average annual wage of $72,836. Even the government made a profit by spinning off Conrail.

Despite such a success story, renewed federal intervention threatens the freight revival. A George W. Bushism called Positive Train Control, a computer system to reduce accidents and allow tighter spacing between trains, will cost the industry an expenditure of $15 billion, although there's little proof that it will work better than what Casey Jones would have known as the "dead man's hand" (a device that stops the train if the engineer dies and releases his grip).

The new stimulus package represents the government belief that it understands the passenger business better than either the industry or the capital markets, neither of which wants in on any high-speed rail action. (You would think the *Vegas Highball* would tempt Wall Street.)

More to the point, the government's record with Amtrak ought to disqualify it from any say in how to run a railroad. Freight companies are leery of high-speed rail because of what it might do to their rights-of-way. Many plans project high-speed rail running on freight lines, which are notorious for "putting the varnish in the hole." Meaning: Let the passengers wait on a siding while a freight train goes through.

I love trains, so I take Amtrak often and everywhere, and it's an endless disappointment, with late trains, cold food, clogged toilets, and indifferent "customer service representatives." Even though I collect its schedules and prowl its website, Amtrak reminds me of Russia's Aeroflot airline. Nor is Amtrak's meandering route system anything more than the arteries of a patronage network that would warm the heart of E.H. Harriman, who knew all about railroad patronage. Remember Mark Twain's aside: "I think I can say, and say with pride, that we have some legislatures that bring higher prices than any in the world."

Before the United States rushes further into high-speed rail, it needs first to decide whether passenger rail service should be a public or private business. I like the English model, flawed as it may be, in which BritRail (the U.K. equivalent of Amtrak, but with cold pork pies) was privatized, and routes around the country were sold to private railways. A government corporation, albeit one starved for capital, held on to the track and infrastructure.

On the surface, anyway, British trains are now shiny, clean, faster, and a pleasure to ride. The airline Virgin has some trains, and newer lines, like Eurostar, have come into business. It used to take BritRail ninety minutes to chug out to Cambridge from central London. Now two companies compete on the line, and the trip takes forty-five minutes.

I doubt that Warren Buffett wants to get the Burlington Northern back into the passenger business. His bet is that he can monopolize container traffic from Asia to Chicago and maybe, some day, with another acquisition, to New York—although I still think he should have a look at acquiring the Trans-Siberian Railway or the Chinese Eastern.

With proper incentives, why wouldn't a private company bid for the line between Boston and Washington, or San Diego to Los Angeles? Maybe Disney could integrate the Orlando-Tampa train into its monorail? At least it could fill the seats without stimulus money.

In Praise of Slow Rail

EVER SINCE JAY GOULD, Leland Stanford, and Cornelius Vanderbilt acquired their first legislatures, railroads have been best understood as political networks, rather than as transportation lines. The Obama administration is hyping high-speed rail with a $53 billion proposal not because the president is a trainspotter or because he collects back copies of the *Official Guide of the Railways* (like I do). Rather, it's because politicians understand that the states blew their money on generous pension plans, pretentious sports stadiums, and bridges to nowhere, and now need billions to plug their budget deficits. It's easier to funnel money into tapped-out state capitals under the smoke and mirrors of a feel-good rail project than it is to announce that the federal government stands behind states' subprime debts. The Government Accounting Office estimates unfunded state liabilities at $405 billion, which is probably what high-speed rail would, in the end, cost. Think of it as the *Stimulus Express*.

The high-speed scheme is a dream of superfast trains, traveling at 150 m.p.h., linking Portland, Maine, with Charlotte, North Carolina; Chicago with St. Louis and Kansas City; the Orlando corridor in Florida (which the governor there has recently rejected); and express trains in Texas and California. Another way to look at the proposed high-speed rail network is to imagine it connecting the cities and states with high-speed cash that Obama needs to carry if he is to have a chance of winning the 2012 election.

Along the high-speed tracks-to-be are stops in Michigan, Ohio, North Carolina, Florida, and Pennsylvania, key states in the 2012 electoral contest. Red states west of the Mississippi, by contrast, will have to wait for Amtrak's *Southwest Chief* to arrive three hours late in Dodge City, Kansas.

Before the U.S. goes into hock over high-speed, it might consider making a virtue of low-speed rail. Slow food has its followers. Why not the same for slow trains, since that's the best that Amtrak can offer? Herewith are ten ideas that will get more (fare-paying) Americans back on the (less-than-perfect) rails. Implementing them wouldn't cost anywhere near $53 billion. Done right, they would even make money.

—Privatize the corridor services between Boston and Washington, Chicago and St. Louis, and San Diego and Los Angeles. Mandate that at least two competing companies operate passenger service on the lines. If American railroads are not interested in the job, French or German national rail companies might bid on the service.

—Sell off the franchise rights to Amtrak passenger cars to mall stores, restaurants, and bars. A movie car could run between Philadelphia and Pittsburgh, and a discotheque (Pullman 54) could operate, for example, on the night train from New Orleans to Atlanta. I am sure the Outback restaurant chain would want some cars in the West. Who cares about speed if you are having fun or can use the time productively? I would happily ride the Barnes & Noble to Charlotte or the L.L. Bean to see my family in Maine. Why can't Amtrak add a few FedEx Kinko cars? Auction off Amtrak's sleeping car services to Hyatt, Holiday Inn, Embassy Suites, or Motel 6? They know more than Amtrak does about making beds.

—Instead of catering to the gun lobby (Amtrak now allows passengers to pack heat), work with the car rental agencies to create a car-sharing alliance at Amtrak stations to solve the problem of getting anywhere from far-flung places such as the Richmond station, which is located miles from downtown.

—Spin off Amtrak Vacations to Outward Bound, the American Youth Hostel Association, Carnival Cruises, the Boy Scouts, or the Green Tortoise (a hippie bus tour company), and let them offer rail cruises to national parks, jazz festivals, fall foliage, major league stadiums, and jamborees.

—Create Amtrak University, and outfit trains to take high school and college students to places such as Gettysburg, Little Bighorn, Bunker Hill, Dallas's Grassy Knoll, Mark Twain's museum in Hannibal, Missouri, and Marion, Ohio (where Warren Harding owned, and at one time, ran the local newspaper).

—Invent a clean steam engine that runs on scrubbed American coal, and market passenger railroads as green travel, locally grown. Retrofit some baggage cars to carry bicycles easily and cheaply, and develop a national network of "Rails and Trails," so that passengers can have a seamless connection between the train and their bikes. At the moment, it's easier to ship a gun on Amtrak than it is to take a bike.

—Deregulate passenger service, to encourage the flourishing short-line rail industry to carry passengers on some of their freight lines, as the Housatonic Railroad is proposing to do on its own line to Pittsfield, Massachusetts.

—Invest surplus funds in commuter rail projects, including the proposed Hudson River tunnels that New Jersey Governor Chris Christie turned down. Commuter rail is a proven, if dreary, commodity. High-speed rail dreams are the stuff of State of the Union addresses, but the top ten commuter systems together transport about 1.63 million passengers daily (Amtrak has 74,000 a day). Most commuter systems need nicer stations, easier links to other lines and buses, and to provide comfort zones with better coffee (not a federal budget concern), clean restrooms, and wi-fi. I love the coming Long Island Rail Road link to Grand Central and the new BikePorts of the Massachusetts Bay Transportation Authority.

Had the United States integrated high-speed rail into the interstate highway system—imagine tracks in the median strips—the idea might have worked. Imposed on a society addled with cars and planes, it has the risk of becoming a cost-overrun nightmare of $82 million per mile versus $2.4 million for traditional rails.

Much of the infrastructure is already in place to develop a national revival of low-speed rail, at a fraction of the costs of subsidized high-speed rail. The trains we have can be privatized, franchised, hot-spotted, double-bedded, and showered, and no one will care about the engine speed. To save billions, if not to make money, why can't the U.S. subscribe to what author Paul Theroux said: "Better to go first class than to arrive."

Playing with Trains

Night from a railroad car window
In a great, dark, soft thing
Broken across with slashes of light.

—CARL SANDBURG, "WINDOW"

PART OF MY FASCINATION WITH RAILROADS comes from the model trains that whistled and steamed their way through my childhood, circling Christmas trees and later sweeping around the basement in Port Washington, New York. My first train was a set of Army cars, pulled by an olive-green steam engine as though conveying the American Expeditionary Force to the front lines of World War I. Later came a number of diesel engines—running with the colors of the Great Northern, Wabash, Pennsylvania, and Rock Island—and a train set of stainless steel passenger cars with names such as *Betsy Ross* and *Molly Pitcher*.

Nominally, the set was what Lionel called O-gauge, the largest of the model train sizes. In reality, the railway, which we called Sands Point Southern, was mixed and matched from purchases that my father made on his trips around the world, during which he had an eye out for replicas of English stations or French semaphores. Over the years the railway acquired a Swiss dining car, numerous freight cars including one for German hams and another for fresh fish, many hopper cars, a rolling post office, and a parlor car that would have graced the tail end of the *Phoebe Snow*.

315

By right of gifts, the trains were legally mine, but emotionally they belonged to my father, who had played with trains as a boy, when a wind-up key powered a London, Midlands & Scottish steam engine which pulled freight carriages across the landscapes of his childhood. During the heyday of the Sands Point Southern, my father and I spent many happy afternoons playing with trains, which included the company of Art Milk, a real-life railroad man for the Long Island Rail Road who liked to come by the house in his free time and wire up the transformers and signals that were constantly being added to the system. Art even cut a hole into a basement closet and installed what was called Union Station, a replica of a Chicago terminal that had classical columns and soft lighting.

The system was laid out on a plywood table, and it conformed to my father's railroad dreams. Trains had been a constant in his life since an early age, and I am sure the Sands Point Southern evoked many happy hours spent on the rails. His grandfather had been the comptroller of the Central Railway of New Jersey (Jersey Central) and later the Rock Island. One of his assistants, a Mr. McManus, would save timetables for my father, then about ten years old. When dropping them off, he would question the young boy on possible connections. For example, he might ask: "Nick, how would you go from Kansas City to Dallas?" As my father now recalls, he would offer Mr. McManus a connection on the Santa Fe or the Frisco, but then the older man would say, reflectively, "I think you might find the schedule more attractive on the MK&T"—the Missouri, Kansas & Texas, often called "the Katy."

As a boy of eleven, my father traveled to Europe with his mother and rode steam trains around France and Switzerland. In a notable story from this journey, his mother found him near the engine of their train just before it was to depart the Paris'

Gare de Lyon for Geneva. He had planned to wait until the train started moving before jumping on, and his mother was furious with him for imagining that he could attempt such a stunt. Little did she know that later, while at Columbia University, he would travel the country "riding the blind," which involved boarding a moving steam engine and riding between the coal tender and the first or "blind" baggage car. After college graduation in 1940, and before five years on the front lines of World War II, he and his friend Bob Lubar rode the blind from New York to Los Angeles, another family train legend that gets discussed after dinner in what the children call fireside chats—long evenings of father-child conversation.

After the war, which involved many troop trains across the country and several rides in occupied Japan, my father began a career in sugar, which in the early days involved day coaches around his sales territories in West Virginia, Virginia, and Pennsylvania. Later, until the passenger system collapsed in 1970, he would criss-cross America on the trains that he could find in the *Official Guide to the Railways*, a national timetable that arrived every month at our house. He wasn't opposed to planes and flew often but I now suspect that the flights were bridges to a train. No doubt the inventive spirit of Mr. McManus never left him, and he would endlessly weigh the choices of the Erie or the New York Central to Chicago, or the best way to get to Clifton Forge, Virginia (probably the Chesapeake & Ohio).

When I went with my father to the Midwest in the summer of 1962, we started on the Baltimore & Ohio, switched to the Illinois Central, and came back on the Pennsylvania, with some side trips on the Chicago & Northwestern. Inevitably, on these trips, there would be changes in the dead of night (I am reminded of the empty platforms, with baggage carts bathed in the soft light of hanging lamps) and long hours in parlor cars, where I discovered a love of reading on trains. As many nights as possible were spent in sleeping cars, where I would lie in the upper bunk, but at such an angle that I would not miss any of the landscape that rolled by like spools of film, spaced by telephone poles. My two favorite morning scenes were the farms of Ohio and the scrubland of northern Florida. For sunsets, I loved the pale light on the Capitol dome in Washington and the wheat fields of Nebraska, waving their amber waves of grain.

IN RECENT YEARS, when my father and I could no longer could play with trains, we discovered that it was just as much fun to remember and talk about them. On my trips back to the U.S. from Switzerland, I would stay in the guest room at my parents' house, and during the long conversations that the visits became, the topic was often trains. We had always casually discussed railroads—his trips and mine—although we got more serious when I suggested that together we write a magazine article about his riding of the blind.

Sitting at the kitchen table, my father dictated, I typed, and he recalled the adventure west in summer 1940, when he and Bob Lubar left from Newark, climbing aboard a Pennsylvania Railroad express heading to Pittsburgh. They were chased off the coal tender in Altoona, Pennsylvania, but later made it to Chicago, where they caught the Chicago & Alton to Kansas City. During that long night, the fireman on the steam engine found them huddled on the coal tender. He put my father and Bob to work shoveling coal, to make up for some lost time. The next morning in Kansas City the engineer stopped the train near a railway hostel, so they could shower and sleep. He said something like "Don't you boys worry. We'll take care of you."

The next day they rode as far as Clovis, New Mexico, where railway detectives discovered them and hauled them in front of a local magistrate, who said famously, at least in our family lore: "I don't want ever to see you boys in Clovis again. And whatever you do with the rest of your lives, I don't want it to happen here in Clovis." They rode a freight to Roswell, New Mexico, and a combination of freights and passenger trains across Arizona to Los Angeles, sometimes in the company of hoboes and other drifters of the Depression. In California they stayed with my father's grandfather, who had spent his career working on the railroads. He asked many technical questions about the trains they had been on, and then bought them each a coach ticket back to New York. In all, the trip west cost less than $40.

In writing the article, almost seventy years after my father had made the trip, he confused the town of Bowie, Arizona, with that of Needles, California. He was sure they had gone through Needles on the Southern Pacific. As I checked the railroad maps on the Internet, the route made no sense, as it would have involved an odd dogleg north from Yuma. We discussed the Needles question for weeks, as the article went through various drafts, until finally I had the idea to search out an old copy of the *Official Guide to the Railways*, which I found online. It arrived a few days later. Inside we found many detailed maps of American railroads. One of them showed the Southern Pacific mainline going through Bowie, not Needles, and the factually correct version of the story was sent to *Trains* magazine, where it was published.

Neither of us had seen a copy of the *Guide* in years. I had never used it, as the Amtrak schedule—a flimsy brochure by comparison—was all I ever needed for American trains. The presence of the *Guide* back in our lives has sparked many hours of railroad conversation, in its way as pleasant as model trains. Because my father can no longer read the small type, I thumb through the pages and read him aloud the name of a railroad and give a brief summary of the route map.

No sooner will I say the words "Louisville & Nashville" or "Illinois Central" than he recalls where it went or why he had used it. Sometimes I read out the intermediate stops on a particular line—say, the Bristol branch on the Norfolk & Western, which the photographer Winston Link celebrated in black-and-white pictures—and the conversation stops while he recalls a sugar buyer in Abington or a hotel in Roanoke. In no particular order, during the course of an evening, we talk about the parlor cars that went from Pittsburgh to Montauk, Long Island, the merits of the Erie versus those of the Lackawanna and why they later merged, the railroads of Maine, including the Bangor & Aroostook, or the history of the Delaware & Hudson, which my grandmother rode to her college in Oneonta, New York.

In front of the gas fireplace in Princeton, we are trainmen, moving at will across the map of American railroads, endlessly changing in the night from the Chesapeake & Ohio to the Monon, and finally the Union Pacific. Sometimes we retrace trips that we have made together (on the Reading to Tamaqua, Pennsylvania, or the Missouri Pacific to Harlingen, Texas). At other moments we reconstruct all the railroads that have been merged to form the Burlington Northern Santa Fe (the Rock Island and the Great Northern are but two lines from the Sands Point Southern that Warren Buffett now owns). Amtrak, with its cheesy interior designs and sluggish service, is impossible to contemplate. The red carpet is still rolling into the *Twentieth Century*.

BACK HOME IN SWITZERLAND, I am sometimes asked why I continue to live abroad. Usually I mumble something about good public schools or the fact that I can bike to work. The truth is more closely related to the trains that span the continent, making it possible to ride overnight from Basel to Berlin or take the Balkan local that takes all day to go from Zagreb to Sarajevo. But the trains from Switzerland to the rest of Europe are not as easy or as affordable as I like to imagine. Getting deeper into France, for example, involves a two-hour slow train to Lyon. Nor are European trains cheap. On many days EasyJet flies to London for $60; the train to Paris and the Eurostar to London can cost $300 one-way. In Europe's perverse logic, flights are cheap and trains are expensive.

Nevertheless, I take comfort in living close to the rails, and spend many evenings at home, charting my passages across Europe. In one of my standby daydreams, I try to get from Laconnex, where we live, to the Crimea. One option involves a Swiss train to Basel, a night train to Berlin, and then a two-day ride across Ukraine to Simferopol in the Crimea, although I just read in a timetable that the direct service from Germany to the Crimea has been canceled, which means rerouting my daydream through Kiev.

Another way to get there is to take the train from Geneva to Milan, Venice, Zagreb, and Budapest, where it is possible to connect to Lviv in western Ukraine. From there, other connections are possible to Odessa and the Crimea. I have thought of a cheap flight to Riga and an overnight train to Kiev and the Crimea. That would mean applying for a Belarus transit visa, which is time-consuming and costly, just to see Minsk and Pinsk. There's also a way to Yalta through Istanbul and with a Black Sea ferry, although the boat's website does not inspire much confidence. ("Please, your pleasures is our services.")

Another journey that has kept me up at night involves the three-day trip across eastern Turkey to Tehran and Esfahan. The train leaves Istanbul's Haydarpasha station just before midnight, arrives the next morning in Ankara and the following day on the shores of Lake Van, where it is necessary to change to a ferry. The Iranian cars are waiting on the eastern end of the lake, and they go overnight to Tabriz and Tehran. Esfahan is served with another train that leaves Tehran at midnight, and on the Internet I have found a small hotel in Esfahan, which sounds like an ideal place to read the histories that I have collected about the Iranian revolution. Although my plan is a good one, the problem with Iranian travel is that the mullahs, or whoever issues the letters of transit, are not keen to give out visas to Americans arriving on the Stamboul train. I have applied twice for a visa, through an online service. After each application, the Middle East has erupted in the paroxysms of the Arab Spring, and the clerk writes back: "Now is not a good time to make our request."

As an alternative, I have looked at the Berlin-to-Baghdad Express, at least what's left of it, as I am convinced that someday a good train will run from Iskenderum, Turkey, to Baghdad and Basra. Why ship container boxes from the Persian Gulf to Europe, if in three days they can be hauled across Mesopotamia (now Iraq) to the Mediterranean? Plans for such a project get written up in railroad magazines, and I have followed them with interest online. In my railroad conversations with my father, when we're imagining new lines, I include this one in the mix. Naturally he's all for it, although that's an easy endorsement, as he has also blessed my notion to complete the line over the River Kwai, so that trains can finally run from London to Singapore.

More recently I went to the website of the Indian Railways, wondering what had become of that second-class sleeper that I took in the summer of 1983 from Calcutta to Bombay. There I found a picture that looked exactly like my compartment, with hard bunks and bars on the windows. Instantly I was looking out the window in Mughal Sarai or buying food on the platform in Allahabad. It reminded me that one of the remarkable things about trains—which I know from fireside evenings with my father as well as the *Bombay Mail*—is that they provide direct service to the stations of our past.

Acknowledgements

I HAVE HAD MUCH HELP with the preparation of this manuscript and book. Michael Martin, Zina Klapper, Martin Daly, and Robert Juran labored over the syntax and my seventh-grade spelling. Mary Nicklanovich Hart, the editor of *Serb World U.S.A.*, made invaluable suggestions to my chapter on Macedonia and Greece. My sister Nanette brought order and elegance to the jacket and the design, and my other sister, Julie, kept me supplied—over many birthdays and Christmases—with books that I often stuffed into my traveling briefcase.

Lovett and Barbara Smith kindly invited me to join their excursion on *New York Central 3* to Pittsburgh, and many people—impossible to list here—picked me or drove me to railroad stations across these landscapes. Although my father, Nick Stevenson, died in October 2012, he was very much alive during all of these trips, and the writing here echoes the conversations that we had in front of his gas fireplace in Princeton, New Jersey, which on many nights had the look and feel of a dispatcher's tower, with maps, timetables, and histories scattered around the floor.

Many of these trips would not have been possible without the assistance The Man in Seat Sixty-One, whose creator, Mark Smith, has explained why he picked the name of his website that describes worldwide passenger train services and how to buy their tickets:

> Zaharoff, the notorious arms dealer, would always book compartment 7 on the Orient Express to or from Istanbul. When treating myself to Eurostar's first class, I would always request seat 61 (in cars 7, 8, 11 or 12) to make sure my seat lined up with the window, one of a cosy pair of seats facing each other across a table complete with table lamp, rather like those in an old Pullman car. It became something of a tradition, and I've left London in seat 61 en route to destinations as diverse as Italy, Greece, Malta, Albania, Tunisia (via Lille & Marseille), Marrakech (via Paris, Madrid & Algeciras), Istanbul (via Vienna, Budapest & Transylvania), Ukraine & the Crimea, Aleppo, Damascus, Petra & Aqaba, and even Moscow, Vladivostok, Tokyo & Nagasaki via the Trans-Siberian Railway. Just don't book seat 61 when I need it!

I also want to thank my wife, Constance Fogler, who, except for some of the early trips mentioned here, saw me to the train station or airport for each of these journeys. Although in recent years she has preferred to tend the home fires more than those of engine boilers, we did have our 1984 honeymoon aboard the *Blue Train* (Johannesburg to Cape Town). Since then, never once—when at dinner I announced a plan to ride trains in Romania or Russia—did she express anything other than complete enthusiasm for the journey. What more could a railroad man wish for in a life companion?

I want to end with a shout out to our four children—Helen, Laura, Henry, and Charles—who spent a considerable part of their early years fighting over who would get to sit next to the window or sleep in the upper berth. Because trains were such a fixture of my own childhood, I wanted them, growing up, also to taste the pleasures of the rails. As a family, we never did make it Club Med or Disney World in Orlando, but we do have the bonds of the night train to Aswan and the sleeper from Ljubljana to Belgrade, on which not even war-hardened Croatian border guards could rouse sleeping teenagers. In this book, only Charles makes an appearance, on the Berlin-to-Baghdad Express that we took across Turkey to Syria. But I never go anywhere without thinking of them all growing up, further proof, if any was needed, that trains offer an uninterrupted service to the past.